D1196453

# A Distinctive Approach
# to Psychological Research

## The Influence of Stanley Schachter

PHOTO BY BILL APPLE

# A Distinctive Approach
# to Psychological Research

## The Influence of Stanley Schachter

edited by

### Neil E. Grunberg
*Uniformed Services University
of the Health Sciences*

### Richard E. Nisbett
*University of Michigan*

### Judith Rodin
*Yale University*

### Jerome E. Singer
*Uniformed Services University
of the Health Sciences*

**LEA** LAWRENCE ERLBAUM ASSOCIATES, PUBLISHERS
1987   Hillsdale, New Jersey                              London

Lawrence Erlbaum Associates, Inc., Publishers
365 Broadway
Hillsdale, New Jersey 07642




**Library of Congress Cataloging-in-Publication Data**

A Distinctive approach to psychological research.

  Bibliography: p.
  Includes index.
  Contents: A personal memory/Leon Festinger—
The role of the mentor Jerome E. Singer—The jury on
trial/Lawrence S. Wrightsman—[etc.]
  1. Psychology—Research. 2. Schachter, Stanley,
1922–    . I. Schachter, Stanley, 1922–
II. Grunberg, Neil E.
BF76.5.D56  1987      150      86-29343
ISBN 0-89859-910-5


Printed in the United States of America
10  9  8  7  6  5  4  3  2  1

# Contents

v

# Preface

The contributions of any individual can be direct or indirect. For a scientist or scholar, direct contributions are made through research and teaching. Indirect contributions are made through the contributions of those individuals whom we teach. The influence of an individual depends on both types of contributions. To succeed at either type is notable; to succeed at both types is extraordinary.

Stanley Schachter's direct contributions are well-known and are widely cited in original investigations, scholarly reviews, and textbooks and courses in general psychology, social psychology, and health psychology. Schachter's distinctive approach to psychological research has broken new ground in the study of deviance, affiliation, emotions, obesity, cigarette smoking, and the psychology of money; has delighted and interested uncountable numbers of undergraduates; has impressed or infuriated uncountable numbers of colleagues; and has indelibly influenced the style and thinking of his graduate students.

In addition to the direct contribution of the particular content areas of his research, Schachter has made major contributions in unfolding and enlightening domains of psychology in which he is not usually associated. The growth of interest in social cognition and its basis in attribution theory are developments foreshadowed by Schachter's work in cognitive attributions as factors in emotional behavior. Indeed, much of the health-psychology attribution research has clear roots in Schachter's work. In an era when social psychology was an almost self-contained entity, divorced even from many aspects of general experimental psychology, Schachter has always considered the broader context in which social behavior was embedded. This is most apparent in his appreciation and consideration of biological processes in the understanding of seemingly social phenomena, for example, his consideration of the role of urinary pH in cigarette smoking at parties or under stress. His delight in embracing appropriate disciplines and weaving their contributions into social psychology has produced a general eclecticism that has influenced for the better the willingness of other psychologists to broaden the disciplinary foundations of their work.

This volume reflects the influence of Stanley Schachter beyond his research. In particular, this volume presents the influence of Schachter on his students, even when their work may, on the surface, appear to bear little resemblance to Schachter's interests. It was created to honor his 65th birthday (April 15, 1987) in the most appropriate manner that we could imagine and produce. Unlike many festschrifts, this volume does not include a direct contribution by the honoree. That is no accident or oversight. Nor does this obvious omission reflect an inability of the honoree to make outstanding direct contributions. Stanley Schachter continues to be a productive and influential scholar and we expect that situation to continue for a long time to come. There are two reasons for compiling this volume without a direct contribution by the honoree: (1) the volume is meant to convey that aspect of Schachter's influence that extends beyond his own publications; and (2) it is unlikely that we would have been able to prepare this volume if Schachter had known of its existence. This second point is discussed in some detail in the Afterword.

The contributors to this volume are Stan's Ph.D. dissertation advisor and close friend, Leon Festinger, and ten of Stan's former graduate students. Schachter has produced more than forty Ph.D.s and many other graduate students assisted Stan on one or several studies. To include all of Schachter's productive students would have required a volume at least three times the length of this one. Therefore, we decided to limit the number of authors. The contributors to this volume were invited by the editors based on our attempt to provide the reader with some sense of Schachter's influence over the last thirty years. We purposely invited authors who worked for Stan during his study of each of his major research areas. All of Stan's students worked on several questions, but in terms of the major thrust of the Schachter lab during graduate student days: Wrightsman (Ph.D., 1959) worked on affiliation; Singer (Ph.D., 1961), Wheeler (Ph.D., 1962), and Latané (Ph.D., 1963) studied emotions; Nisbett (Ph.D., 1966), Ross (Ph.D., 1970), and Rodin (Ph.D., 1971) investigated obesity; Herman (Ph.D., 1972) studied obesity and then, with Kozlowski (Ph.D., 1975), studied cigarette smoking; Grunberg (Ph.D., 1980) studied cigarette smoking and the psychology of money.

The contributors were asked to write chapters that reflected the influence of Schachter on them. The standing instruction was to indicate Stan's influence without discussing aspects of his work available in his own publications. In this way, this volume would provide additional, complementary information reflecting the professional Schachter otherwise unavailable to a wide audience. Everyone readily agreed to contribute; everyone had great difficulty preparing his or her chapter. We each rediscovered that Stan's influence was deep and had become virtually indistinguishable from our own values and approach. Each author chose different ways to convey Stan's influence. We encouraged authors to try to reveal their Schachter through their own work and experiences. We purposely avoided efforts at uniformity among the chapters. Some authors used their own research as the major vehicle for this task. Some took a more anecdotal approach. We believe that together they reflect some significant commonalities, while also revealing the diversity that represents Schachter himself. The order of the chapters is roughly chronological. We decided to reverse the chapters by Singer (Ph.D., 1961) and Wrightsman (Ph.D., 1959) because Singer's chapter provides a general introduction and overview while Wrightsman's chapter picks up with research details. All of the other chapters are in chronological order.

As a final note of introduction, we believe that this festschrift is distinctive in that it covers a rather wide range of substantive topics. That breadth is characteristic of Stanley Schachter. However, the approach to each area of study is remarkably similar. We believe that this collection of chapters accurately reflects the teachings of our mentor.

## ACKNOWLEDGMENTS

No book is written exclusively by the authors and editors. It would have been impossible to assemble this volume without the assistance of many people.

Lee Ross participated as one of the original members of the editorial group. When the working arrangements became cumbersome and five-person conference calls next to impossible, he graciously removed himself from the editorial stream; fortunately his contributions remain.

Diana Lord served unstintingly as editorial assistant, keeping drafts, revisions, and correspondence in order and on time.

Larry Erlbaum was more than a publisher. He helped, advised, and kept the book on a more permissive publication schedule than we had thought possible.

Sophia Schachter was an unfailing source of information in supplying facts, confirming dates, and keeping discussion of Stan Schachter's professional life from intruding on his personal one.

# Stanley Schachter:
# A Biographical Sketch

Stanley Schachter was born on April 15, 1922, in Flushing, New York to Nathan and Anna (Fruchter) Schachter. He attended elementary and secondary schools in the Bronx and, in 1939, attended Yale as an undergraduate. At Yale, Schachter became a protégé of Don Marquis in the Institute for Human Relations. In addition, Schachter was greatly influenced by Clark Hull and his Socratic teaching style.

In 1942, Schachter began graduate school in psychology at Yale. He worked for Walter Miles, doing research on night vision, until Schachter was drafted and served in the United States Army Air Force for the duration of World War II.

In 1946, Schachter decided to continue his graduate education at MIT because he had heard about Kurt Lewin's Research Center for Group Dynamics and the attempt to use psychology to study social problems. The Center's faculty included Dorwin Cartwright, Leon Festinger, Ronald Lippitt, Marian Radke, and (later) Jack French. The graduate students included Kurt Back, Morton Deutsch, David Emery, Gordon Hearn, Murray Horowitz, David Jenkins, Harold Kelley, Al Pepitone, John Thibaut, and Ben Willerman.

Schachter spent most of his time at MIT working on research with Leon Festinger. Most notable among Schachter's efforts in graduate school was his work with Festinger and Back studying social influence and communication in the Westgate student housing project. This study was central to Festinger's theories of informal social communication and social comparison.

In 1947, Kurt Lewin died and in 1948 the Research Center for Group Dynamics, including most of its faculty and students, moved to the

University of Michigan, Ann Arbor. Schachter did his Ph.D. thesis work at Michigan and received his degree in 1949.

In the Fall of 1949, Schachter became an assistant professor at the University of Minnesota in the Department of Psychology and the Laboratory for Research in Social Relations. The Laboratory was under the direction of Jack Darley and it was designed to integrate the activities of psychologists, sociologists, economists, political scientists, educators, and philosophers. At Minnesota, Schachter extended his dissertation research on deviance and began studies of social isolation that led to his classic work on affiliation. By this time (c. 1953), Festinger had joined Schachter at Minnesota and, with Henry Riecken, they conducted their well-known field study of cognitive dissonance that was published as a book, *When Prophecy Fails* (1956). Schachter's studies of affiliation and birth order were published in the monograph, *The Psychology of Affiliation* (1959). This book won the AAAS Social Psychological Prize in 1959 and the research described in the book led Schachter to his work on emotions. This line of research eventually led him to work on obesity and cigarette smoking.

In 1961, Schachter moved to Columbia University in the new Department of Social Psychology. The faculty at that time included Otto Klineberg and Richard Christie. The next year, Klineberg left and William McGuire and Bibb Latané joined Schachter and Christie. Schachter and Latané extended their work on emotions to the study of sociopathy, but that work ended because of logistical problems accessing prisoners as subjects.

Schachter decided to attempt to determine whether his findings on emotions (basically, that physiological states were subject to situational and cognitive labeling) would generalize to the state of hunger. This idea led to Schachter's work on obesity and his internality-externality theory.

In the late 1960s, the Social Psychology and Experimental Psychology departments at Columbia merged and Schachter moved into new quarters better suited for his work on eating and smoking. In addition, he married Sophia Duckworth (June 2, 1967). In 1969, Elijah Schachter was born to Stanley and Sophia Schachter.

In the early 1970s, largely because of Peter Herman's dissertation research, Schachter became interested in the role of nicotine regulation in cigarette smoking in different situations (e.g., at parties, under stress). Schachter's research on smoking became his most reductionistic approach to the explanation of any behavior that he had studied.

In 1976, Schachter became interested in the psychology of money and his research focus shifted away from the study of appetitive and addictive behaviors. However, in 1982 Schachter published an influential article in the *American Psychologist* on relapse among ex-smokers and former obese. Recently, his research interests have returned to this topic.

Among Stanley Schachter's honors are: Fulbright Fellowship (1952–53); Guggenheim Fellowship (1967–68); APA Distinguished Scientific Contribution Award (1969); Cattell Fellowship (1974–75); Robert Johnston Niven Professor of Social Psychology at Columbia. Schachter has authored or co-authored *Social Pressures in Informal Groups* (1950), *When Prophecy Fails* (1956), *The Psychology of Affiliation* (1959), *Emotion, Obesity, and Crime* (1971), *Obese Humans and Rats* (1974). He has written more than 60 journal articles. Stanley Schachter currently resides in New York City and East Hampton, Long Island.

# 1

# A Personal Memory

Leon Festinger
*New School for Social Research*

I do not know what is the proper kind of thing to write for a volume that is intended as a tribute to a man's distinguished professional career. I'm sure other contributions to this volume reflect that career better than I can. Hence, arbitrarily, I have decided to relate the most vivid (to me) instances of the long association between Stanley Schachter and myself, keeping within the professional context. I write this entirely from memory, without reference to any letters, notes or records of any kind. If someone cares to examine the correspondence between what I write here and verifiable facts, discrepancies will undoubtedly be uncovered. Human memory is fallible; being a psychologist I know this from many studies in the literature that have demonstrated that fact. I am also aware of the convincing data that indicate a lack of relationship between confidence in a particular memory and the likelihood that it is accurate. Nevertheless, I prefer to rely on my memory. I have lived with that memory a long time, I am used to it, and if I have rearranged or distorted anything, surely that was done for my own benefit.

In 1944 Kurt Lewin, with whom I had studied at the University of Iowa, moved to the Massachussetts Institute of Technology where he established the Research Center for Group Dynamics. He had wanted to establish an institute but how can you have an institute within an institute? So it became a Center. Soon after the conclusion of the second World War, I joined Kurt Lewin, Marian Radke, Dorwin (Doc) Cartwright and Ronald Lippitt at M.I.T. as an Assistant Professor. One aspect of my situation there was highly peculiar. I had remained a civilian throughout the war and had completed my Ph.D., thereby becoming a member of the faculty. The vast majority of the students who came there had served with the military for some number of years, interrupting their graduate work, and were mostly my own age, some a little younger, others a little older. This was the context in which I first met Stanley Schachter; I a faculty member, he a student.

One of the things that made Stanley stand out amid that group of highly talented students was that he always walked around carrying books and papers in a murky-green cloth bag. If I had been more knowledgeable about the world I would have known, as I was later told, that it was a Yale Book Bag from the place he had gone to school before the war. In the first conversation I ever had with Stanley he told me in detail about research he had done at Yale that had something to do with hangnails—yes, I remember that distinctly, hangnails. I remember very little else about that conversation, perhaps because after hearing "hangnails" I stopped listening.

M.I.T. had built two housing projects for married students, one of which was innovatively designed, according to the people in the Architecture and City Planning Department. They approached Kurt Lewin to explore his interest in doing a study of those living in the projects to assess the effects of the innovative design. There was money available for the study and Kurt passed the buck to me. I then asked Stanley and Kurt Back if they would like to work with me on the study. Kurt Back immediately said "yes," Stanley was rather unenthusiastic and went off to think about it. He finally agreed but remained unenthusiastic, which was not surprising—who could be really enthusiastic about a study that was so vaguely formulated.

We interviewed the project residents about their satisfactions and dissatisfactions with their apartments, with school, with their social life and with every other thing we could think of. Because asking people who their friends were was one of the latest revolutionary methodological breakthroughs, we also asked about that. We then sat down, sometimes separately, sometimes together, to try to find some order in the mass of data we had collected. To fully appreciate the situation one should point out that not one of us had ever taken a course in Social Psychology, nor had we any previous experience doing such research.

That was when Stanley and I started playing cribbage together. No one ever said anything openly to us about it but I imagine there must have been some who wondered about such an activity when we were supposed to be doing research. I don't think people really understood that only with the assistance of cribbage were we able to begin to put order into the chaos of the data. Stanley had a special talent, one that I have rarely seen in such a highly developed state. Give Stanley a set of data to pore over and he will invariably emerge with interesting ideas which, furthermore, have a fair chance of being correct. You couldn't have asked for a study or a set of data more in need of Stanley's talent.

Without going into great detail, the write-up of the study, authored by the three of us, didn't look too bad; actually parts of it looked good. I don't think we could have done it without the assistance of cribbage.

Kurt Lewin died suddenly in 1947 and we discovered that without him M.I.T. was quite disinterested in this little group that was truly peripheral to the main concerns of that institution. Without his prestige and the glue he provided for the group the normal course of events would have been for it to break up, each one going his separate way. This didn't happen, however, for we were, faculty and students alike, determined to preserve the Center that Kurt had created. We elected Doc Cartwright as substitute glue provider and, after considerable shopping around, moved the whole thing, faculty and students together, to the University of Michigan.

Stanley still had to produce a dissertation for his degree and the only things that either of us could think to do at that time were laboratory experiments on whether or not the things we had observed (or imagined) in the housing project would show themselves under controlled conditions. So Stanley designed an experiment to see whether people rejected others who disagreed with them on some issue simply and solely because of the disagreement. It was a difficult experiment to do; he had to produce in each group within any condition the identical disagreement and hold constant such factors as the personality of the one who uttered the deviant opinion. It was also very time consuming, but it was neither the difficulty of the task nor the time involved that created a major problem between Stanley and myself.

By the time Stanley was finished with some pilot runs to iron out whatever methodological bugs existed, he knew how the data would come out and he knew this with an intensity backed by his firmest intuitions. He had convinced himself that the results we expected would not appear and, hence, the rational thing for him to do was to abandon this experiment and find some other topic that would make an acceptable Ph.D. thesis. Our arguments about this never seemed to cease; after each experimental group he finished I was informed that the data from that group showed the same absence of anything, and the argument continued. This problem was never solved; it was dealt with at a practical level by simply increasing the number of hours a day that we played cribbage. It has always been a puzzle for me to understand how people cope with all the problems of doing research if they do not employ interesting ways of doing nothing when they should be working. Ultimately, all the groups were run, the data analyzed, and the results proved to be far from trivial. The outcome of all this was that he wrote the dissertation, received his degree, wrote an article for publication, and accepted a position as Assistant Professor at the University of Minnesota.

Those years at the University of Michigan coincided with the time when money to support research started to flow more freely from the Federal Government. It was not yet much more than a heavy trickle but, because the Research Center for Group Dynamics had to live primarily from the income of research grants, we all spent lots of time writing proposals. The fact that many of these proposals were approved and funded had good and bad aspects to it. The good ones are easy to identify: we could pay our own salaries, pay student assistants and were able to do our research. The bad aspects are more delicate. To increase the likelihood that one would have enough money for oneself and the people to whom there were commitments and obligations, it seemed reasonable to apply, every year, for more money than was needed or wanted. After all, some of the proposals might not be funded. When I found myself with more funds than I wanted I had to hire more people and then, of necessity, apply for even more money. At a time when money was becoming more and more available one could readily become a research administrator rather than remain a researcher.

I had become very restive in this situation when, two years after Stanley went to Minnesota, that University offered me a position of Research Professor with minimal teaching duties and an internally provided, guaranteed, modest research budget. Why they made such an attractive offer to me I do not know. I have never asked people about it. I simply assumed at the time, and I still believe, that Stanley had been unable to find an adequate cribbage partner. The prospect of not having to write more grant proposals, of being able to do my own research without responsibilities for the livelihood of others, was so attractive to me that I jumped at the chance. And so Stanley and I resumed our near daily cribbage competition.

The situation at Minnesota was nearly ideal for me and, I believe, also for Stanley. Our years there were very productive, for me perhaps the most productive four year period of my life. The person who created this situation was Jack Darley, the Dean of the Graduate School, and one of the most powerful men at the University. Jack wanted to build Social Science, at least behaviorally oriented Social Science, and build it he did. This also meant providing whatever was needed for research and protecting those who were doing it.

Stanley and I, although we saw a great deal of each other at the University, and away from it also, worked independently. On only one study did we actively collaborate, but that was a memorable study indeed. We got wind of a small group of people, in a town not too distant, gathered about a woman who was in direct communication with gods who travelled around in flying saucers. One god, in particular, communicated a great deal and had revealed to her that on a given date the Earth would be totally inundated by flood; all would perish except for those few chosen to be saved. Before the flood a flying saucer would land to evacuate these survivors to be and this woman would in due time be told where to meet the saucer.

Henry Riecken, Stanley, and I discussed the matter and reassured each other that the flood was unlikely to occur. It seemed possibly interesting to find out how this group would react to that nonevent. Despite a relative lack of enthusiasm for the project, Jack Darley somehow came up with money to support it. Henry, who was the one among us most skilled at presenting himself favorably to strangers, made a trip to where the group was gathered to get further information but received a rather cold reception. They weren't interested in revealing things to strangers. It was a rather private group, and they felt no need to spread the news because those who were chosen would be saved willy nilly. Henry was sure that the only way we could study the group was to join them and it wasn't even clear how one could maneuver that. We tried the tactic of frequently dropping in on them and gradually we were treated as any other member of the small assemblage.

On the first visit that all three of us made to the group an event occurred that was to make a difficult study much more so. Stanley, with his own characteristic style of humor, introduced himself as Leon Festinger and there I was left to be Stanley Schachter. Once done it could not be undone but had to be maintained throughout—I've wondered if they even noticed the inevitable small lapses that occurred. At times it seemed they must have noticed and we worried but had no idea what they thought about it. Four days before the promised event was due, the three of us began a 24 hour a day continuous presence in the home of the leader of the group together with most of the other believers. In preparation we had rented a room in a nearby hotel where we left recording equipment so that we could periodically dictate what had occurred from notes.

The following days were hectic. The talents of the three of us complemented each other very well. Henry, with his easy social presence and smooth manner of ready interaction started to be seen as almost a minor leader, others confiding in him and informing him of everything. We were, hence, not often caught by surprise but were on hand, as alert as we could manage, to observe and record. Stanley revelled in exercising his intuitive talents. His characteristic position was at the edge of any group, observing relentlessly, and perceiving things that no one else would have detected. Some new person might put in an appearance and Stanley would know their occupation without being told; some occurrence would puzzle us until Stanley explained that a liaison had been building since the previous day; a minor struggle for power in the group by one of the members was predicted ahead of time in Stanley's uncanny way. I was neither socially easy or very intuitive and insightful in my observations. My characteristic position was not at the edge of a group but in the back of the room, looking, listening and remembering. I had an excellent memory and used it to the utmost.

We got very little sleep or rest and had some prescription from a doctor to keep us going. At intervals infrequent enough not to arouse comment each of us would go to the toilet to make notes in private—that was the only place in that house where there was any privacy. Periodically, one or two of us together would announce we were taking a short walk to get some fresh air. We would then dash madly to the hotel room to dictate from our notes, perhaps grab a hamburger quickly (they were all vegetarians), and rush back so that our absence would not have been implausibly long. By the time the study was terminated we all literally collapsed from fatigue.

The last day before the flood was full of activity. Messages kept coming in from her favorite god containing information about procedures to be followed in boarding the saucer, procedures that we then had to practice because errors could be catastrophic. Then information came about the importance of having no metal on anyone because the force fields that drove the saucer wouldn't operate effectively in the presence of metal; I've always been annoyed that I had to cut out the zipper on my trousers while Henry and Stanley simply maintained they had already done so; especially annoyed because later I was refused reimbursement for the cost of the ruined pants. Anyhow, the flying saucer didn't come and the world was not flooded. My last treasured memory of that experience concerns the following day when everyone was calling newspapers and offering interviews. There was Stanley sitting in a comfortable chair, observing everything, and softly whistling Mein Yidishe Mama.

We spent the next summer together in Palo Alto organizing the material and writing a book. To explain how we got there requires a little bit of backtracking. In spite of nearly ideal professional circumstances and a social community that was very congenial, there were some problems with Minnesota. The winters were very cold and I could not overcome my absolute aversion to wearing a hat. But even more than this, the winters were long. I was accustomed to begin expecting spring when the month of March rolled around but that did not fit reality in Minnesota. This made March a dismal time. I am convinced that if one wants to steal someone away from the University of Minnesota, the best time to make the job offer is during the first two weeks in March. Consequently, when I was offered a job at Stanford University, I was dazzled with images of warmth and sunshine. That may have been my only consideration because I seem to have leapt at the opportunity. So we wrote the book that summer at Stanford.

With me in California and Stanley in Minnesota we didn't see too much of each other. I know how I dealt with the problem of not having anyone with whom to play cribbage; I started playing GO regularly with Doug Lawrence. The two games are radically different and I would not assert that one can freely substitute one for the other but it was the best I could manage and it had to do. How Stanley solved the problem I do not know but after a few years he left Minnesota for Columbia where, as I later discovered, he found a more adequate substitute, namely, backgammon.

The most frequent professional occasions for getting together with Stanley during the years I was at Stanford were periodic meetings of a marvelous committee that I chaired for the Social Science Research Council. Social Psychology at the time was almost exclusively an American (more properly, United States) enterprise. There were very few persons anywhere else in the world that thought of themselves as Social Psychologists and even fewer who did research in the area. Under these circumstances how could we know whether or not the body of knowledge we were developing was entirely, or partially, a United States culture bound body of knowledge. The Committee on Transnational Social Psychology was established to encourage the development of active researchers in Social Psychology in other parts of the world. Stanley, who had spent about a year in Amsterdam coordinating a joint research project by persons in England, Holland, France and Norway, was indispensable to the committee.

To be credible and maximally effective the committee itself had to have an international membership and, fortunately, could not meet solely at the quarters of the Social Science Research Council in New York. Some of the meetings were, of course, held in New York but Stanley and I also were forced to go to places like Italy, Spain, Holland, France and Austria to attend meetings. It was through this committee that Stanley and I first met people such as Henri Tajfel, Serge Moscovici, and Martin Irle. In the course of these meetings we learned such things as how good the seafood was in Barcelona, how uninteresting some Italian wines can be and, outside of music, how dull Vienna is. In that city we made the mistake of holding the meeting at a new, modern hotel where everything went wrong. Stanley described the hotel management as showing a startling combination of Viennese efficiency and American charm.

We did, however, also work hard on that committee, locating interested Europeans, bringing them together at meetings and encouraging research activities. I think the committee performed an invaluable service to the field of Social Psychology and, although I am philosophically aghast at the notion, I am also gratified that there are now many Europeans who are intent on developing a European Social Psychology.

Occasionally, when I was in the New York area, I visited Stanley at his summer place in Amagansett. It was there that he introduced me to backgammon. On the surface it appears to be a rather dull and simple, almost trivial game. Below the surface there are vital tactical issues, strategic considerations and psychological subtleties. Without explicit tutelage it takes considerable experience before one begins to grasp some of these things. Stanley taught me the game and under his quite inexplicit tutelage it did take me a long time. Whenever we played Stanley won. Our reactions to this were quite different; I was perplexed and mildly frustrated while Stanley seemed to enjoy it. On one or two occasions when I expressed my feelings about the unfairness of the apparent inequality, Stanley gently reminisced about the past and how that had been the exact situation, with roles reversed, when I was teaching him to play cribbage.

After thirteen years in the clean sunshine and easy living of California, I left to return to New York where the New School for Social Research had offered me a very nice job. I was sorry to leave Stanford but I had developed an ununderstandable hunger for the noise, dirt and inconvenience of living in New York City. Irrationally, I am contented and happy to be here. I am convinced that humans, genetically, have homing urges as strong or stronger than pigeons.

Stanley and I see each other now with moderate frequency—not as much as one might expect of two persons living in the same city who have been friends for about forty years. The problem lies in the nature of New York City. Contrary to the impression of most people who have never lived here, New York is not a large city. It is really a collection of moderate size villages and the residents of each village rarely visit other villages. I live on Twelfth Street while Stanley lives on 90th Street. That distance is not great, it is approximately four miles but in New York that is a problem. The major means of going from one place to another is to find a Taxi, but finding one is a process filled with uncertainty. Sometimes you simply do not see any, at other times you see them but for some reason the drivers do not seem to see you. There is an alternative, the subway, but it requires the sensibilities of a hardened crowd lover to use it. We do, however, get together and, in addition to playing backgammon, each of us periodically tries to get the other interested in what he is currently doing. We each succeed partially.

I have lightly sketched some events from the time when I first met Stanley until the present but I fear that I have not done justice to the quality or tone of our interactions. I have two excuses to offer—to the reader and to Stanley. If I think about it at all, which mostly I do not, I prefer to imagine that Stanley and I are both in our mid-thirties, which makes me feel awkward writing a contribution for a Festschrift for him. There is a second and more important difficulty, a final irony. I am in the habit of getting criticisms of anything I write before completing a final draft. Good, detailed, constructive criticism is very hard to come by; most colleagues aren't interested enough to devote the necessary time. It is much easier to make a few general comments ending with effusive praise. I have always been able to get good, useful criticism from Stanley and, over the years, I have come increasingly to rely on him. Yet, because this volume is supposed to have been a secret from Stanley, I have had to forego this vitally important step in producing this piece. Hence, I ask tolerance from the readers and especially from Stanley.

# 2

## The Role of the Mentor[1]

Jerome E. Singer
*Uniformed Services University of the Health Sciences*

My undergraduate education was a mixture of chemical engineering and social anthropology. When I started graduate school at the University of Minnesota in an interdisciplinary training program in the behavioral sciences, I had never taken a course in psychology and my transcript attested that I was certifiably ignorant of the field. Several years later, I held a Ph.D. in Psychology, and my curriculum vitae proclaimed that I was a psychologist by profession. Somewhere and somehow, while at Minnesota and since, I have learned something about psychology. When I ruminate about how that part of my education transpired, I always return to one striking fact: the truly important part of my education came from my mentor, Stanley Schachter.

    I was fortunate enough to have had several vital and gifted teachers— Harold Kelley, Henry Riecken, Ben Willerman—to name but a few. As much as I learned from them, my real education was the realization, after I went off to my first job, that I had to apply not just psychological knowledge to my teaching and research, but also a way of thinking about the problems that made up the field and a set of standards and values about the work of my colleagues and peers. These beliefs constituted for me the real legacy of a superior education. They are the least changing aspect of my professional demeanor; they are a branch of my apprenticeship for which I remain most grateful; they are the essence of what I hope to pass along to my own students. Nevertheless, I have rarely reflected on how people are socialized into being psychologists, as opposed to being trained in psychology. Now, as I renew the acknowl-

[1]The opinions or assertions contained herein are the private ones of the author and are not to be construed as official or reflecting the views of the Department of Defense or the Uniformed Services University of the Health Sciences.

edgment of my debt to Stan Schachter, is an opportunity to consider several aspects of what a mentor should do.

## LEARNING WHAT IS NOT TAUGHT

As with most other fields, much of what we learn in psychology is not actually taught. There is a wide variety of books on the spectrum of content areas, theories, and research methods that students sample and master. These do not equip someone to become a research psychologist.

The first time an aspiring researcher attempts to run a study, the size of the gap between formal instruction and the knowledge really needed for day to day use becomes apparent quickly. I remember the first time I tried to run a rat experiment as a graduate student project. I came prepared with all sorts of Hullian derivations, distinctions between types of measures, empirical relationships between various methods, and the usual supporting cast of null hypotheses, critical regions, and alpha levels. None of this was any help as I faced the most important question, "Where do I start?"

What every worker knows, and what we and our bright successful students find out the hard way, is that the body of knowledge that provides the routine procedures and the basis for practical judgments simply does not exist in textbooks or manuals.

The problems I faced in my rat study were not weighty ones; no great issue hinged upon them. But they had to be solved. How old should the rats I ordered be? How should I house them? How do I gentle them? There were some books that attempted to provide answers to these questions, but somehow they were always slightly off base. They never gave me exactly the information I needed. For example, my reference sources had told me that for operant work, my rats should be kept at 85% of their normal body weight. It seemed simple enough. Weigh the rats to get their starting weight, then cut back on their food until their weight dropped 15%. It was simple enough if I were dealing with adult rats who were at a stable weight. But I had a group of adolescent rats. They were still growing. I had no idea what 85% of body weight meant for such a group. Eighty-five percent of their current nonmature weight? Eighty-five percent of their estimated adult weight? Should I feed them enough to keep their current weight constant until they reached adulthood? I didn't know and my fancy textbooks were not much help either.

My ignorance in the face of genuine research decisions was not because I was dealing with a strange (at least to me) species of subjects. Every time I did an initial study in a new area involving humans, similar perplexing problems arose. The issues were simple, but the answers hinged on informed judgment in areas where I did not have the experience to make such judgments. The problems arose in social psychology, an area in which I had many instructors and colleagues. There was no source that described how to create a cover story or how to run a debriefing, or as we called it then, a catharsis session, with the subject. The issue is not one of deception as has been sometimes claimed. Rather, in many areas of psychology, the subject is not informed of the true purpose of the study in order to protect the integrity of the data at no cost to the subject. If a cognitive psychologist wishes to see how subjects cluster words in free recall, the experimenter cannot very well say, "We are going to ask you to learn a list of words and then at a later time ask you to recall them so we can see what order you place them in." To do so, of course, would reduce the experiment to a public opinion poll of the subjects on the hypotheses. Yet some rationale must be given to the subject to make the task plausible. The construction of such explanatory cover stories is still not discussed well in the research methods literature; it remains almost an art form.

Even more delicate is the debriefing of subjects. Often our experiments create situations in which subjects behave in ways of which they are not particularly proud. At the conclusion of the study the experimenter has both a moral and a pedagogical obligation to explain to the subject what has happened, why it was necessary to conduct the study in that fashion, and what the possible implications of the study are. Even more, the subject must be assured that no one is making a moral judgment about the behavior exhibited in the experiment. We, as researchers, are interested in behavior in general and not the responses of identifiable individuals. The function and goals of a debriefing are clear. How to devise and conduct a session in a manner that is informative but does not degrade or humiliate the subject is not clear. Once again, these sessions represent an aspect of being a psychologist that must be learned but cannot be readily taught.

## INFORMAL LEARNING

Why do we have to go to school to learn psychology? Most textbooks are quite comprehensive and, in areas where they scrimp over details, they usually provide enough bibliography and references so that conscientious readers can become as informed on the topic as they wish. That's the way in which we all now learn new substantive areas as our interests are piqued. It is true that good teachers can serve in a number of useful ways to make formal learning easier. They can highlight the underlying issues, they can organize the masses of material, they can point out inconsistencies, they can take sides in a debate, they can tell us when we are straying from relevance, they can guide us toward interconnections, and do a host of other pedagogical tasks to make learning easier, more productive, or deeper.

Ultimately, however, people can learn formal material without formal instruction. Reporters who cover psychology as a beat often acquire a good working knowledge of the field on their own. This process is mirrored by reporters of business, health, science, and many similar technical fields. Publishers who specialize in our texts and monographs learn much of what we teach without taking our courses.

The point, of course, is that knowing psychology is not the same as doing psychology. It is a much different task to master a body of published material, even to the point of becoming an informed critic, than to conduct original investigations. A person can become a master of printed material by diligent self-study; it is nearly impossible to learn research from books alone. There is no shortage of books on research methods or how to do research, but as I have already elaborated, these do not answer the real questions about practical choices in the conduct of research.

If research can not be learned by just the aid of books, it certainly can't be mastered by a lone would-be scholar without the aid of books. The key is a research mentor. There is just no substitute for informed experience and judicious counsel, a fact not appreciated by those most in need of informed experience and judicious counsel. Each year, in our graduate program, and I'm sure in most others, a student will present a thesis or dissertation proposal in a novel area of research. The idea may or may not be novel, but the proposed field of study will be one not represented in the experience of anyone on the current faculty. When I try to explain to the student the risks involved in such a choice of topic, for example, that there is no one around who has any hands-on experience in the area, the usual first reaction is of incomprehension. The second reaction, once understanding has set in, is to minimize the importance of direct background and to believe that research in a new area can be mastered in as unaccompanied a manner as the content. After several years of disasters precipitated by just such mistaken beliefs, most graduate advisors simply refuse to supervise (or more accurately, take academic responsibility) for studies outside their field of research competence.

Academic psychology is a bookish sort of enterprise. We frequently mistake a written description of an event for the event itself. It is not uncommon for students early in their graduate careers to design a study, complete with staging, scripts, cover stories, and debriefings, and then to assume that except for the donkey work of actually running the subjects, the task is complete. Only an effective mentor can walk the student through the necessary steps that transform a design on paper to a real experiment.

Given that the research background of the mentor is a necessary condition for a neophyte researcher to design and conduct a successful inquiry, what are the characteristics of the mentor that make that role effective? A mentor can provide general emotional support and encouragement but, valuable as that is, equivalent support can be gotten from one's colleagues, one's parents, or one's dog. In order for a mentor to teach a graduate student, not research methods, but how to actually do research, the mentor must have skill and accomplishment in his or her own research. If the specific details and experience needed to make informed judgments at each choice point in a research project are only passed along by word of mouth, then it is obvious that the mentor must have received this knowledge and possess it in order to transmit it. Clearly, however, there is much more to being an effective mentor than just being a guru about the caging of rats, the writing of an effective script, the conducting of a humane catharsis, or the construction of ad hoc questionnaires. If the transmission of specific technical skills and disciplinary folklore were all that were necessary for someone to be a mentor, there would be as many mentors as there are senior authors of articles in, for example, the *Journal of Personality and Social Psychology*, *Health Psychology*, or *Psychological Bulletin*. Obviously something more is being communicated.

## WHAT A MENTOR TEACHES

The major achievement of a good research mentor is to inculcate a set of ineffable beliefs in the students: a strategy of problem selection, a sense of style, and a sense of taste. None of these characteristics are discussed in the standard literature that is the grist for the professional training mill. Sometimes, popularizations of science, such as Watson's *Double Helix* (1968), give inklings of them. In psychology, perhaps some consideration of these traits appears in some of the chapters in the series, *A History of Psychology in Autobiography* (Boring & Lindzey, 1967) or in individual autobiographies. By and large, these kinds of overarching research strategies or philosophies remain unarticulated and undiscussed, even by the mentors doing the inculcating and even at the time of inculcation.

## PROBLEM SELECTION

Of the three characteristics—a sense of style, a sense of taste and values, and problem selection—the last is the easiest to discuss. How does one define a research problem or select a topic for study? The question can be answered at many levels, but for me the level of interest is the very broad quasihistorical one.

The dominant mode of problem generation in contemporary American psychology has been characterized by two features, a positivistic derivation of theoretical propositions and a heavy reliance on empirical, usually experimental, verification.

In the 1950s and early 1960s, the predominant feature of training in American psychology was an emphasis on learning theory. Students were required to master the various "schools" of learning. Familiarity with the systems of Hull, Spence, Tolman, Guthrie, Skinner, and of their colleagues and disciples was a *sine qua non* for passage of departmental prelims. Many departments offered courses based on only one of these figures, such as Psych 503: Hullian Psychology, or Psych 1103: Learning Theory of Tolman.

Students learned a number of things from this general emphasis and these specific courses. They learned a new language—S–R talk—into which all psychological discourse was to be translated. If a problem was to be stated in a way that avoided all the mentalisms and nonpositivistic biases that had compromised psychological research in the immediate past, then the language of learning theory was the only safe way to conceptualize issues. Social psychologists, in particular, as researchers whose theoretical formulations often came from sources other than learning theory, were frequently put to the acid test in presentations and colloquia. At the end of each presentation, a hand would be raised and a familiar voice, polite, but menacing, would ask, "That's all very interesting, but can you put it into S–R terms?" It wasn't until several years postdegree that I learned the ideal answer to the question. Originally attributed to D. B. Broadbent, the effective reply is, "Yes, I can, but it's a little like doing long division with Roman numerals."

Although social psychologists tried to avoid the constrictions of casting all propositions about human behavior in the restrictive Hullian grammar of D and $_sH_R$ and $_sE_R$, we had theories and derivations of our own. The centerpiece of our theoretical training in social psychology at Minnesota was the work of Kurt Lewin, his contemporaries, and his students. Their work, although often included as learning theory by anthologizers (cf. Estes *et al., Modern Learning Theory,* 1954), was not usually considered such by its students. Rather, it was a separate view of a different group of problems. Yet, in many ways, it paralleled the restrictions of the self-avowed learning theories. The basic steps in conducting Lewinian based research were to set up an axiom system from which were derived theorems and correlaries. Each derivation became a statement subject to experimental test. The major strategy was to locate two slightly different axiom systems that pertained to the same phenomena, show that derivations from each produced contradictory predictions about a particular set of circumstances, establish those circumstances in a laboratory analogue, and run the definitive and crucial experiment to establish which of the two originating theories was the correct one.

This strategy was not only scientifically successful, but it also fostered a growth industry. For if I were able to deduce an incipient contradiction in two theories of, say, attitude change and message construction, I could set up a two condition experiment (suitably embellished, of course, with necessary control groups and other technical niceties) with each condition representing a theory. If I could show a different result in these crucial conditions, I had a publishable finding. Hanging over my shoulder was a phalanx of my contemporaries ready to show that in establishing my two conditions, I had inadvertently confounded another important factor that, if studied separately, would also affect attitude change. This contention would lead them to run another experiment, two groups, with and without the confound. Twenty years or so ago, before the bureaucracy of Institutional Human Experimentation Review Boards and when large psychology subject pools were standard, the latency between the appearance of an issue of *The Journal of Personality and Social Psychology* (or *The Journal of Abnormal and Social Psychology* prior to the early 60s) and the appearance of a rebuttal study was remarkably short.

One of the lessons most thoroughly learned from this style of research was the necessity of theory driven research, the rigorous derivation of propositions from a set of axioms. If the axioms came from the mainstream of learning theory and were Hullian or Spencian in nature, so much the better. But, even within social psychology, systematic theory was a strong tradition. Lewin's original contributions were heavily theoretical. *Principles of Topological Psychology* (1936) and *Field Theory in Social Science* (1951) are as theoretically rigorous and dense as any of the then current theories in other areas of psychology. There were even advanced mathematical derivations built on Lewinian axiom systems, such as Bavelas' (1948) mathematical model for communications in group structures. Whatever the original impetus, clearly theory directed research was the superior sort.

The world was full of interesting things, but our eyes were pretty much still on the pages of our journals. Some work was done outside

these strictures, but it was clear to students and beginning profes-
sionals that "systems and theories" were regarded as higher forms of
psychology than those stemming from less lofty a background. The
theoretical orientation kept most studies in the lab. Field research was
done and valued also, as long as the field studies arose from the
hypothetico–deductive system of the implications of theoretical postulates.

This practice of judging the worth of a study by only its overt
theoretical contribution and not by its practical utility and latent theoretical contributions has fortunately faded from preeminence (*vid.* Singer
& Glass, 1975), but traces of it still linger. Recently, I talked with an old
acquaintance, a psychologist who felt most comfortable in the deduc-
tion from theory tradition. He informed me that he had started to do
applied social psychology. When he described his new, applied work,
the studies struck me as rather traditional abstract laboratory ana-
logues of somewhat philosophical positions. When I inquired, somewhat gingerly, how the studies were applied, he replied that they were
obviously applied because they hadn't been derived from a theoretical
stance.

One of Stanley Schachter's contributions to my education was to
make me realize that the problem was the preeminent concern of
research. The role of the investigator is to understand the problem. If
this could be done by the application of a standard theory, so much the
better. But if there were no cut and dried way to explain the phenomena,
the aim of the researcher was to make some general sense out of the
problem. Theory driven researchers were already conducting studies on
real-life problems, but often their emphasis was to find a real situation
that mirrored their theory rather than to jump in and investigate the
problem for its own sake.

One need only to reread Schachter's classic monograph *The Psychology of Affiliation* (1959) to get a feel for his way of tracing a problem to
its roots with a series of coordinated sequential investigations. The
work is certainly not without theory; it proves to be a fascinating
extension of social comparison theory mixed with a dose of pressures to
uniformity and original consideration of ordinal position of birth. But
the studies are not theory driven in the sense in which contemporane-
ous studies of learning were. "Social comparison" is not postulated as
the dominant explanation to begin with and studies directed to show
how affiliation is a special consequence of that general theory. The start
of the research was the question, "Why do people want to be with
others?" and social comparison was engaged to explain the emergent
experimental findings.

The hypothetico–deductive method was the dominant way of reporting
results in psychological journals. One could always question to what

extent the deductions were applied after the fact. Schachter's influence was to stress the importance of real problems and both the practical and theoretical usefulness of unraveling their complexities.

The danger with an uncritical embrace of a problem oriented focus is that the research becomes unfocused and ad hoc. A concern for only a problem and not a larger context is, by itself, neither a good nor a bad thing. Some important problems have been addressed by single-minded research efforts; frequently these have theoretical import despite the determined practical bent of the researchers. The study by Festinger, Schachter, and Back (1950) was designed as the examination of a university student housing project. It led to major advances in social psychology; these are discussed somewhat more fully later on.

At other times a problem-focused orientation has no significance past its immediate problem. In the worst cases, people may select trivial but tractable problems and beat them to death with experimental overkill. This can occur in many ways. A researcher can apply extraordinary, complex, albeit impeccable, methodology and complex experimental design to what is a rather simple problem. It is hard to appreciate either the theoretical or practical importance of the experimental studies done of pursuit rotor skills. The implicit argument is that the importance of the problem is to be judged by the resources committed to studying it.

Just as common, and equally inappropriate, is the investigator who arrives at a way to attack a problem, sets up a procedure, then spends the next 25 years doing parametric variations of the same basic experiment. This is a very effective strategy for getting an extensive vita, but not a way to maximize scientific conclusions. Obviously, some parametric replications are necessary to shape functional relationships and to establish the reliability of a finding, but the image often evoked is of an experiment running machine that chugs through a study on autopilot. At the end of the study, the "experimenter" comes in with a large screwdriver, resets each of the controls on the front panel by a half turn, resets the machine to autopilot, then leaves while the machine chugs through another study. An enlightened mentor would guide students into choosing a problem of import, without worrying over whether it was theory-derived, and yet not sink into the repetitious humdrum of studying a problem because an efficient research paradigm has been developed and a string of publications in professional journals can be cranked out. There must be a better reason for studying a variant of a problem other than we know how to do it and our lab is all set up. Each study in a series must have its own meaning and logic.

## A SENSE OF STYLE

Once an investigator is productively at work on a scientific problem, the methodology texts would have us believe that there is a set of algorithms for proceeding with the study. First, a design is chosen from a book of experimental plans, null and alternative hypotheses are made specific, a statistic and a critical region are designated, and so on. This may be fine fare for an undergraduate course in research methods, but it bears little resemblance to the way research is actually conducted. In practice, there are as many ways to do research as there are investigators. Each investigator, or more likely, each school of investigators has its own signature style. And, to a great extent, this style is inculcated by a common mentor.

There are different traditions in different areas of psychology. Physiological psychologists do things differently from those in developmental psychology and so for every other subdivision. Even within a grouping, say social psychology, there are different approaches to the study of similar phenomena, often ones that are equally valid. To this extent, there is a style that pervades each area of psychology. Over and above this sort of "national character" aspect of style, there are other stylistic elements that characterize a particular investigator and the students with whom he has worked. In some ways this is the most important legacy of the mentor.

Years ago, when psychology, like everything else, was smaller and more manageable, there were many fewer journals to follow and monitor in one's field. Each issue of the *Journal of Abnormal and Social Psychology* was greeted with especial interest as it was scanned for the latest and most exciting entries to the literature. It was a particularly good issue if it contained an article by any of several people whom we regarded as likely to make interesting and valuable contributions. Their articles were always read first and discussed in the graduate student lab. These included, of course, friends and former student colleagues. More importantly, these were articles by people who were especially respected and valued. The main reason for the respect was their record of providing fresh ideas and solid studies, but also they were looked for first because they were interesting and exciting to read—because they had a sense of style.

A sense of style is composed of many things. It requires lucid communication but it consists of more than clear crisp prose. Indeed, for scientific writing, the prose may be so clear and crisp as to be almost unreadable by all except the inner circle of that branch of science. Good writing helps, but it is not the heart of the issue. Style is a shorthand way of describing an approach to a problem or a way of thinking about or studying a research question. It defines an investigatory attitude, and more, it defines a conceptual approach to research. It is less than a philosophy of science but more than just a way of writing up a report of the research.

Perhaps an example will help to clarify the concept. We all learned in introductory statistics about the proper procedure for making a statistical test. One states the null hypothesis, the alternative hypotheses, selects the appropriate statistic, looks at the sampling distribution, selects an alpha level, determines the critical region, and so on. Such behaviors are the stuff of statistics texts, but I have never seen flesh and blood researchers who followed that prescribed protocol in their own research. "I chose 0.01 as my alpha level, but because my result was only significant at the 0.017 level, I guess I'll keep the null hypothesis and discard my alternative" is a remark only likely to be made in an undergraduate statistics course or in the theatre of the absurd.

However unlikely such procedures are in actual practice, they are often written in that fashion for scientific publication. In order to comply with the belief that "scientific research is theory driven," many researchers write the reports of their work as if they really followed such a formalistic procedure. The articles contain no hint of hunch and not a scintilla of post-hoc examination of data. Such reports would have the reader believe that three-way interactions were differentiated and predicted by the investigator and tested with all the accoutrements of Stat 101. This same stylistic formalism, the presentation of the author as a punctilious investigator whose experiments march by the numbers and who has foreseen and anticipated all possible outcomes, results in a number of locutions that are equally improbable. Statements such as, "We used a one-tailed test because we predicted the outcome of the study" are difficult to accept for complex and often obscure studies.

The essence of the style of good investigation is the chase of a problem as it starts with a well-defined, but simple, guess and yields results that are somewhat askew. Internal analyses are used to check out a number of possible processes that make sense of the unexpected data. New experiments are conducted with the investigator frequently completely in the dark as to which way the results will go. Often a possible explanation for a quirk in the original data becomes interesting in its own right and the line of inquiry shifts from the original focus to the problem unearthed along the way.

Does this mean that all problems lead to other developments and are never solved? Not at all. Consider the study of post-World War II student housing at MIT, previously mentioned, by Festinger, Schachter, and Back (*Social Pressures in Informal Groups*, 1950). The authors started out with a somewhat ill-defined survey of the residents of two projects. Their data led them to the finding that the differing architectural arrangements of the projects resulted in different relationships between friendship, cohesion, and opinion formation within each project. The original study with its emphasis on architectural factors in friendship formation dropped by the wayside and subsequent studies refocused on the unexpected finding of the relationship between cohesion in a group and the homogenization of group members' opinions. This resulted in a set of studies that became the basis of pressures to uniformity theory and the basis for social comparison theory. In contrast, a decade later, when Schachter was exploring affiliation, the general question of why and under what circumstances people want the company of other people, an anomolous result brought about the need to examine ordinal position of birth. There was a diversion as birth order studies were conducted. At first, they were internal analyses, then analyses of archival materials, and finally independent studies. Some of the independent studies were even published as separate manuscripts apart from the affiliation work. But in this case the subsidiary problem, birth order, was only a side issue. The main problem, affiliation, was not neglected and remained the primary focus of the research.

Schachter's monograph reporting the affiliation research, *The Psychology of Affiliation* (1959), is a classic example of the style, both in approach and communication, conveyed by Schachter to his students. Take a problem, observe the phenomenon, form a basis for a study, and from there, worry the problem to death until a resolution is arrived at. The affiliation monograph is classy not just because of the way a research problem is framed and solved, but because it tells about the research in a straightforward manner. There is no nonsense about an omniscient investigator with a preformed complex theory testing third order derivations. Rather Schachter writes about the research in the way it happened, with all the difficulties encountered and alternatives to be tested, and distracting possibilities to be eliminated. Ultimately the account is both more satisfying and more believable than would have been a standard "Mr. Science" presentation with all the distortions necessary to make the research look like the answers to the problems at the end of the chapter in the methodology textbook.

Schachter is not the only psychologist, let alone scientist, who is creative in his research, original in his ideas, and able to convey the written record of his work in interesting, nonstilted prose without the veneer of scientism. What is not so clearly recognized is the extent to which as a mentor he has conveyed the value of doing research in this manner. The sense of style that makes his work distinctive is not just a personal flair but a set of values, difficult to codify and illustrate, that he has transmitted to those working with him.

## A SENSE OF TASTE AND VALUES

If someone were given the question, "What makes for good research?", there are many ways that it could be answered. Some would discuss the formal characteristics of the design, others could relate the role of intuition and creativity, others could talk about factors just discussed in this chapter, such as problem selection and style. Fortunately, we are not usually asked such abstract questions by anyone to whom we are obligated to give an answer. Unfortunately, we must often answer the question in the particular in order to do our own day-by-day research.

Consider the investigator who is starting on a new problem or line of research. The literature is searched and a number of relevant articles are uncovered. They are collected, Xeroxed, and read. Then the hard work begins. Some sense must be made of them. If all of science were cumulative, if all studies replicated, or even if all studies were comparable, then the task of bringing order to a diverse set of other people's findings would be easier. But the most likely result is that some of the studies use different populations, some use different methods, the results do not always agree from study to study. Strong findings from one study are weak or nonexistent in the next. And the situation is even more muddled if the previous investigators were putting forward conflicting theories or explanations. Each then has a vested interest in discrediting the other's methods, data, and interpretations. The journals are full of issues so joined with reports, rebuttals, responses, and rejoinders.

How is the bystander, soon to be one of the players, to choose between competing approaches. There is no problem if one of the parties is clearly wrong; this is not often the case. Or, even if it is the case, the errors are not readily apparent from the public record. If the entering investigator must choose sides in order to begin his or her own work, the investigator is making an implicit decision about how to rank or rate quality of the work of his or her predecessors. It is not always obvious to the investigator making the choice, let alone to others, what were the criteria used.

Problem selection is not a useful criterion: Both of the incipient litigants have chosen the same problem. The quality of the communication is not a reliable guide either. Although a better writing style might make one of the disputants more interesting to read, it is not a guarantee that the data are better or the interpretations more in accord with the world. Ultimately, the question boils down to whom do you trust, not in the sense of whether or not the data are fraudulent, or whether the report is a misrepresentation, but rather whose approach and style do you believe will consistently yield the truest and most useful insights.

All of us must make decisions of this type, and we do make them despite whatever reservations we may have. If pressed for the bases of our choices, we could probably concoct reasonable ones after the fact, but that would misrepresent the actual process. A sense of taste and values is often neither discussed nor appreciated, in large measure because it lies below the surface and is not effectively verbalized. The recent burgeoning of research in decision making has convincingly shown that humans make decisions not by weighing probabilities and expectations in a mini cost–benefit analysis, but by using a series of heuristics to simplify the problem and narrow the range of actions. This particular set of decisions—why is one piece of research good and another to be ignored when both have the same external trappings of acceptability—is most likely governed by each investigator's applying his or her own set of heuristic rules and sets of beliefs about what approaches constitute tasteful science, for example, what approaches are matched to the investigator's own, often unverbalized, opinions about the "right" way to attack the problem. Even when these beliefs are not accessible to the decider, they may be potent determinants of how real research choices are made.

It is this set about the worthwhileness of research and of specific investigators that constitutes a sense of taste; this sense of taste is an inheritance from one's mentor. Good taste in research, like good taste in literature, art, music, food, interior design, dress, automobiles, friends, or any other aspect of human life, is diverse and ineffable. Different clusters of people have different standards, different beliefs, and different choices. The Latin expression, *de gustibus non disputandum est,* is properly unbiased. There is no necessary logic as to what styles people like, and arguments about preferences are essentially fruitless. Yet it is clear that a sense of taste of whatever kind is a distinctive mark of identity, in research in social psychology as much as in other fields.

It is possible to have no taste or to suppress one's taste so no one else knows. In research, this is seen in study counting where, when literature is reviewed on a problem, the reviewer reports merely the number of studies in favor of a particular theory and the number of studies against. The presumption is made that the counting of studies somehow leads to the correct resolution of an intellectual issue in the same manner as the counting of the ballots leads inevitably to the winner of an election. This is just not so. Not all studies are created equal. Some evaluation must be made if the reviewer or potential researcher is to take action and get off dead center. More importantly, to only count without judgment is to seriously mislead oneself and others as to the true state of affairs. Some aspects of this issue can be seen in the present use of metaanalysis—the overall evaluation of a set of studies usually by the size of the effect. There is no objection to the use of modern metaanalysis. It is a powerful and useful technique. If, however, all studies in an area are flawed, no cumulation of them, no matter how sophisticated, will result in a useful outcome. It is analogous to doing a fancy statistical analysis on the data of a badly designed experiment. It is impressive, but it doesn't help. Better to have rotten taste (rotten as defined by current contemporary standards) and take a stand than to show no taste at all.

How does one develop a sense of taste? Once again the answer devolves from the mentor. Over and above the technical characteristics of a piece of research, students learn both to internalize their mentor's sense of taste and aesthetic judgments and to acquire a set of standards as part of the process of evaluating people and products. The risks of such a subjective appraisal procedure is that a mentor and his or her coterie may become smug, self-satisfied, and clubby. But there is no assurance that an investigator who acquires a sense of taste without a mentor's guidance, and thus is not part of a coterie, will be any less insufferable or have any better a set of values. Because the acquisition of judgments beyond the formal properties of the research reviewed are an inevitable necessity, the sooner in one's career that they are acquired, the more useful they will be.

Of course, as people mature and gain experience, their tastes also change and become refined. The role of the mentor is to set the course from which the basic judgments will follow. The canons of science would have us believe that all of our work can be judged in an objective manner and that such questions of taste will not enter into the evaluation of a piece of our work or of us and our capabilities. Clearly, this is not the case. Journal editors assign reviewers to manuscripts not only on the basis of their technical competence, but also on the basis of a myriad of other factors, many of which involve a sense of taste. When people judge grant or contract proposals, consider candidates for employment, or do any sort of judgment of professional ability, it is likely that the subjective element of taste also enters into the consideration.

Few of us are the psychologists we were a decade ago. Our specific projects and research studies are different in ways easy to see and document, but there still is a continuity and a sense in which we are the same. That sense is our set of tastes and values and our approaches not just to our own work but to the evaluation, in our own subjective terms, of the work of others. Once, about 20 years ago, I was visiting with Stan Schachter at Columbia when one of his graduate students came in to discuss his first go round at a dissertation proposal. Stan rejected the proposal out of hand. Not for any technical reason, but because he thought it was too pedestrian for the student's potential achievements.

Stan told the student, "That's a [insert the name of a productive, but derivative and journeyman social psychologist] study." He followed this up with some explicatives and comments that more was expected of the student. The lessons were clear. Not just that more than all right was expected of the student, but the calibration of the field in defining pedestrian research as work done by Dr. X. This type of judgment, usually made more implicitly, is the sense of taste that a student gets from the mentor.

## STUDENTS FROM THE SAME MENTOR

In what ways are the students of a given mentor alike? When they finish their degree or post-doc, they will probably be working on problems similar to their mentor's, with comparable methods and procedures. As their careers develop and their research takes them further afield from their training, and as they develop new ideas, the specific features of their research begin to diverge from their mentor's and from each other. Yet despite the superficial branching, in many ways underlying similarities remain. These are similarities about values, standards, and the general style of research thought that for want of a better term has been called a sense of taste. This legacy from the model and instruction of the mentor eventually becomes the hallmark of the mentor's school of research.

Every profession has its process of socialization. In psychology the predominant mode is still the apprenticeship whereby a neophyte learns from a master how to be a journeyman. Much of the instruction involves didactic material and is given in formal coursework. Other aspects, such as the details and considerations of how research is actually conducted and reported are accomplished in tutorial fashion. The apprentice learns by doing under watchful supervision. The mentor also teaches superordinate types of knowledge as well. These relate to the values, standards, and "philosophy" of conducting and appraising research. These have been discussed as problem selection, a sense of style, and a sense of taste.

There are wide individual differences among mentors in both style and quality. The ideal mentor would be one who could help shape the formal coursework, be a skilled praeceptor in conferring research skills, and who has impeccable taste, style, and selection of problems. It would help if the mentor were also brilliant, creative, patient, understanding, and a model for the students. Few such paragons exist. When I look back in my own experiences in graduate school and since, I realize how fortunate I was in having my career sent into its trajectory by a mentor who was strongest in the most important of these characteristics, the ill-defined internal values and standards that guide, if not the quality of the research, at least the honest appreciation of its place within the larger body of knowledge.

All of Stanley Schachter's students share in the legacy of such a mentor. Not all of them do Schachterian research any more. Their interests and careers have diverged from what they did in graduate school and immediately afterward. Many of them are no longer in close touch with their student colleagues or with Schachter. The part of their training that keeps them bound is their common intellectual heritage.

Other groups of psychologists have had similarly effective mentors. The bonding of these groups as for the Schachter students is a mixture of respect, admiration, ambivalence, resentment, affection, sentimentality, and a soup of other feelings. Behind the affective ties, there are important and substantial intellectual ones that are hard to describe, but are no less potent for that. We have had the good fortune to have seen psychology done right, and the opportunity to observe and learn the real way to go about our profession. And that in a nutshell is the role of a mentor.

## REFERENCES

Bavelas, A. (1948). A mathematical model for group structure. *Applied Anthropology, 7*, 16–30.

Boring, E.G. & G. Lindzey (Eds.). (1967). *A History of psychology in autobiography, Vol. V.* New York: Appleton-Century-Crofts.

Estes, W. K., S. Koch, K. MacCorquodale, P. E. Meehl, C. G. Mueller, Jr., W. N. Schoenfeld, & W. S. Verplanck (Eds.). (1954). *Modern learning theory.* New York: Appleton-Century-Crofts.

Festinger, L., Schachter, S., & Back, K. (1950). *Social pressures in informal groups: A study of a housing project.* New York: Harper.

Lewin, K. (1936). *Principles of topological psychology.* New York: McGraw-Hill.

Lewin, K. (1951). *Field theory in social science.* New York: Harper.

Schachter, S. (1959). *The psychology of affiliation.* Stanford: Stanford University Press.

Singer, J. E. & Glass, D. C. (1975). Some reflections upon losing our social psychological purity. In M. Deutsch & H. Hornstein (Eds.), *Applying social psychology.* Hillsdale, N.J.: Lawrence Erlbaum Associates.

Watson, J. D. (1968). *The double helix: A personal account of the discovery of the structure of DNA.* New York: Atheneum.

# 3

# The Jury on Trial: Comparing Legal Assumptions with Psychological Evidence

Lawrence S. Wrightsman
*University of Kansas*

When I began graduate school at the University of Minnesota in 1954, I was incredibly naive and knew very little about the psychological approach to the world. The only reasons for my choice of Minnesota were that my undergraduate adviser had told me, given my purported interest in intelligence testing, that the Universities of Minnesota and Iowa were the places to go, and even I knew that Minnesota was further away from my native state of Texas (that I had grown to despise for its political conservatism and its arrogant "national character").

At the begining of my second year I wandered into Stanley Schachter's seminar on research methodology. (I still have the yellow and red covered Festinger and Katz *Research Methods in the Behavioral Sciences* book that served as a text, and a guide for many of us in those days.) In Stanley Schachter's course I found a multitude of new research methods that expanded my perspective and motivated me to become an empiricist. In Schachter the professor, I discovered a person who had the rare ability to chastize me and communicate his affection for me in the same breath. The essential task of the course—to analyze social phenomena and apply diverse methods to the understanding of them— was my first immersion in a psychological perspective. I transferred my major field to social psychology and—again naively—asked Stanley to serve as my major professor. It was because of his continuing combination of concern and confrontation that I was able to complete my Ph.D. and begin a professional career that has been much more meaningful and satisfying than I had ever imagined.

Since graduation, my research interests have taken different turns, and they manifest little of seeming continuity with the Schachterian program of research. But his viewpoint has formed the foundation for all my work; I hope that will be apparent in the perspective presented in this chapter.

## THE LEGAL SYSTEM'S ASSUMPTIONS ABOUT JURORS

For the last decade I have concerned myself with the legal system's approach to juries and jurors. I propose that the courts make implicit assumptions about the psychological nature and behavior of jurors. I don't mean to imply that judges and trial attorneys necessarily believe these—in fact, many times they don't—but still these assumptions are cornerstones to general orientations about how jurors are supposed to act. Furthermore, the legal system never evaluates them; they are simply "there" and their validity is unquestioned.
I see these assumptions as the following:

1. Jurors can respond free of bias
2. Jurors can separate evidence from nonevidence in forming their verdicts
3. Jurors can remember all the evidence and comprehend the judge's instructions
4. Jurors can suspend judgment until the end of the trial presentation, when they are instructed in the law and told to begin their deliberations.

Thus I will review the empirical evidence relevant to each of these, to see whether jurors and juries really do perform in keeping with legal expectations. In doing so, I manifest a style I learned from Schachter, of asking "What difference does this make? Who cares?"

## THE ASSUMPTION THAT JURORS
## CAN RESPOND FREE OF BIAS

We are all familiar with the term "a jury of one's peers." What does this mean?
The legal system assumes two basic attributes of jurors: (1) They are representative of the community; (2) They are fair, for example, they are free of biases or prejudices in one direction or the other.
There are two procedures the legal system uses to try to ensure each of these: (1) The creation of a jury pool; (2) The selection of actual jurors from the pool.
The first of these is done to achieve the goal of representativeness;

the second, to achieve the goal of fairness. As Schachter would say, "How well do they work?"

With regard to creation of the pool, before 1968, all kinds of variation existed from jurisdiction to jurisdiction, but there usually was a total lack of representativeness. In some counties, juries would be composed of men who habitually lounged around the courthouse all day. Many states routinely excused all women from service; all they had to do was put an X on a questionnaire.

A federal law in 1968 (the Jury Selection and Service Act) hoped to improve this sorry state of affairs; it required that there be a random selection of the pool for federal trials, and that uniform criteria be established for exemptions. But recent studies indicate that there is still lots of exclusion and underrepresentation.

But let's say that a pool of potential jurors has been chosen, that at least to some degree represents the community. For a particular trial, this pool may be 30 or 40 people, or maybe up to 200. How are the actual jurors selected from this pool?

### The Voir Dire Process As A Source Of Bias

The jury selection process is called the *voir dire*. The expressed purpose is to give the opposing attorneys an opportunity to question prospective jurors, in order to detect those who are biased. If the person's responses indicate to the attorney that the person couldn't be fair, the attorney requests the judge to discharge this person. This is called "a challenge for cause" (i.e., for bias) and an unlimited number of prospective jurors may be challenged for cause.

But the attorney for each side also may discharge a certain number of prospective jurors without having to give a reason. These are called "peremptory challenges" and the judge decides prior to the trial how many of these each side will have. Each side may have the same number or in a criminal trial in federal court, the judge may give the defense a greater number of peremptory challenges, in an effort to compensate for some inherent advantages that the prosecution has in a trial.

So the purpose of voir dire is to eliminate jurors who are biased. But can any of us act without bias? Saul Kassin, who was a postdoctoral student with me, and I (Kassin & Wrightsman, 1983) did a study to try to measure bias and see if it affected verdicts. Our assumption was that for most jurors it is hard to avoid some bias, or prejudgment. The world is so complex that we must simplify, and in so doing we make some assumptions. For example, if people see the police chasing a man on foot down a busy street, some observers, will assume that the man has done something wrong. Kassin and I proposed that some people possess a bias to favor the prosecution; they organize their perceptions around a set of assumptions that suspicious-looking people are guilty or that if someone has been arrested, it is likely that he or she committed the crime. These people have a proprosecution bias; they may be contrasted with people who have a prodefense bias, for example, those who give the accused the benefit of a doubt, who distrust the sincerity of authorities, etc.

### Probability Of Commission And Reasonable Doubt

Proprosecution biases vs. prodefense biases can be differentiated on the basis of the person's responses to two variables:

1. Probability of commission—for example, given ambiguous information (such as man running from police), do you conclude that a crime has been committed by the man?
2. Reasonable doubt—for example, how convinced or sure do you have to be to convict or say "guilty"? "Reasonable doubt" is fundamental to disposition of a criminal trial, but no court has ever defined it very clearly.

So, Kassin and I constructed an attitude scale, composed of about 20 statements, measuring these two variables of probability of commission and reasonable doubt. The purpose was to distinguish between those who leaned toward the prosecution and those leaning toward the defense.

We gave this scale to people on jury registration lists to complete. Later we had them watch a videotape or read a transcript of a trial, and give us their individual verdicts. All the cases were criminal trials; one was an assault, one a stolen car, one a conspiracy, and one a rape case.

We found that in three of the four trials, those mock jurors who had a proprosecution bias on their attitude scales were more likely to find the defendant guilty than were those mock jurors who showed prodefense biases on their attitude scales. Remember that everyone was exposed to exactly the same evidence, but their verdicts—their responses to the trial—differed.

The one case where this attitude–behavior relationship did not hold was the rape case. Our guess is that those with a pro-defense bias—those who ordinarily give the defendant more of a benefit of the doubt—did not sympathize with alleged rapists like they did with other types of defendants. While bearing the outcome of this one trial in mind, I still believe that there is sufficient evidence that our biases, our predispositions, intrude into our perceptions of events to a degree that bias is inevitable in jurors' decisions and verdicts.

## THE ASSUMPTION THAT JURORS
## CAN SEPARATE EVIDENCE FROM NONEVIDENCE

Fundamental to the legal system is the assumption that jurors base their verdicts only on the facts plus the judge's instructions about the use of the law. But can jurors really do this? Can they disregard nonevidentiary influences?

From Schachter, I learned to analyze the types of nonevidence. Psychologists have focused on two types of nonevidence: on possibly prejudicial pretrial publicity and on inadmissible evidence, or testimony that is expressed in court but then is ruled not proper. But I have tried to emulate my mentor and concentrate on understudied aspects; thus my work has been on a different aspect of nonevidence, the opening statements by the opposing attorneys.

### The Impact Of Opening Statements

As a part of a trial presentation, the attorneys for the two sides are allowed to make opening statements that function as pledges to show certain facts and conditions. In some courts, the statement must be limited to a general outline, but in others, counsel are permitted to recite in great detail the evidence that will be put forth by each of their witnesses. I am amazed by the broad limits in both the time and content of these opening statements; in the first Juan Corona trial, the opening statement by the prosecution took a day and a half! What impact do these extensive statements have on the jury's eventual verdict?

In a civil trial the person or organization filing charges, the plaintiff, is permitted to make the first opening statement, and in a criminal trial, similarly, the prosecution makes the initial statement. In both types of cases, the defense has the option of either presenting its overview immediately after the opening statement of the other side, or waiting until the other side has presented its evidence. Textbooks on trial advocacy differ as to which of these is the wiser procedure; on the one hand, it is argued that the defense should make its opening statement immediately after the other side's, in order to try to negate any one-sided bias. But others argue that it is better not to "show your hand" to the opposition until the last minute. Regardless of when the defense chooses to make its opening statement, it would seem that the prosecution or plaintiff has a psychological advantage by virtue of getting to present its side first.

Even though these opening statements are not evidence, they have potential for great influence on jurors, coming as they do at the beginning of the trial. As we know, the legal system insists that jurors should not form their decisions on the basis of opening statements. Judges will often instruct the jury, as LaBuy (1963) states, that: "statements and arguments of counsel are not evidence. They are only intended to assist the jury in understanding the evidence and the contentions of the parties" (p. 41).

Is this kind of instruction necessary? Put another way, do counsel's arguments actually represent a source of nonevidentiary influence? Trial lawyers often believe that a case may be won or lost on the basis of their statements and arguments to the jury. Louis Nizer (1961) has written: "By a skillful presentation of what he intends to prove . . . [the attorney] can convert a mere informative exercise into a persuasive plea . . . the opportunity to condition the jury favorably is as limitless as the attorney's art" (p. 42). Our empirical findings give support to these claims—to a disturbing degree.

Prior to the recent studies, the psychological research on this matter was quite sparse, but quite consistent in its findings. An early study (Weld & Danzig, 1940) showed that individual mock jurors' predispositions toward guilt or innocence fluctuated throughout the trial after hearing one or both opening statements. A more recent set of studies by my colleagues and myself (Pyszczynski, Greenberg, Mack, & Wrightsman, 1981; Pyszczynski & Wrightsman, 1981; Wells, Miene, & Wrightsman, 1985) demonstrates that opening statements can even overrule evidence.

In one of our studies, mock jurors from the community watched an hour-long videotape of a case involving a charge of transporting a car across state lines. Both sides presented their opening statements before any evidence was introduced. Some mock jurors were shown brief opening statements by either or both sides; in these, the attorneys only introduced themselves and whatever witnesses they had and then promised that their evidence would be convincing. Other mock jurors heard, from either or both sides, much more extensive opening statements that consisted of a full preview of what the attorney expected the evidence to be and how he believed the evidence should be interpreted. Then all the mock jurors watched the same evidence and closing arguments. Half of the jurors were asked for their individual verdicts at 12 points during the trial presentation, as well as at the end. This device permitted us to understand the process of decision making. In fact, it indicated that mock jurors were predisposed to favor one side or the other very early in the trial, and they maintained this predisposition throughout the course of the trial. Certainly their midcourse verdicts changed some in light of the most recent evidence; they waxed and waned but only within a limited range. Only when both sides' opening statements were brief was there any *substantial* shift in preferences for a verdict over these 12 data points. When jurors did not have extensive opening statements from either side, they seemed to give the defendant the benefit of doubt and hence started out leaning toward a not-guilty verdict. After hearing the prosecution's first witness testify, however, they began to shift toward a guilty verdict, and stayed there until the trial's conclusion.

It was clear that an extensive opening statement had strong impact on verdicts, but it was the first extensive one that really mattered. Most jurors who heard an elaborate statement from the prosecution began by believing the defendant to be guilty and they maintained that verdict throughout the trial presentation. If the defense made an extensive opening statement, the jurors responded with verdicts of not guilty *only* if the prosecution had made only a brief introduction. Nowhere is the power of first impressions more clearly demonstrated than through these differences.

Why does the first strong opening statement carry such impact? Consider the juror's situation. Called in for jury service, the prospective juror is anxious and yet conscientious. Most prospective jurors fear the responsibility; they fully expect they will be serving in some sleazy murder trial, and they abhor the task of deciding another's fate. Some also fear retaliation from disgruntled defendants. Yet they are attracted to the glamour and the mystery and the importance of the jury trial. All these concerns combine to make jurors very eager to get a handle on the case. The judge may have told them a little about the charge; during *voir dire* there may have been hints about relevant evidence and the witnesses. But it is during the opening statements that they usually get their first systematic overview of the nature of the case.

All of us reject ambiguity to one degree or another. We seek explanations for behavior. The opening statements provide these; they create what social psychologists have called thematic frameworks, or schemata (Lingle & Ostrom, 1979) that guide jurors in their processing and interpretation of actual testimony that is presented later in the trial. Jurors apparently use the theories developed by the attorneys who provide extensive opening statements as plausible scenarios of what took place on the day that the crime was perpetrated. These frameworks assist jurors in their attempts to make sense of the rather disjointed array of information that is presented in a typical trial.

### The Use Of Thematic Frameworks

The oft-repeated conclusion that first impressions affect later reactions is a reflection of the operation of thematic frameworks. In a typical study (Langer & Abelson, 1976) subjects listened to a tape of two men interacting. Half of the subjects had been told previously that the tape was of a job interview and the other half that it was a psychiatric interview. Subjects who believed the tape to be of an intake interview reported more pathology in the interviewee's behavior; they distorted background data in a manner consistent with their impressions. It appears, then, that thematic frameworks affect not only the encoding and retrieval of information from memory, but also the interpretation that is placed on that information.

But how far should lawyers go in opening statements? Lawyers are often faced with a situation in which they are not sure exactly what the testimony of a particular witness will be. Might one run the risk of promising more than can be delivered? If so, how might a jury react? Possibly a total loss of credibility would result.

But from an information processing viewpoint, the dangers of making too extensive an opening statement may not be as great as some observers have assumed. Social psychologists using the concept of thematic frameworks argue that, in most situations, people's inferences and verdicts are affected more by their initial judgments in response to an informational set than they are by the set itself. After hearing a persuasive, extensive opening statement, jurors may make tentative decisions about guilt or responsibility and begin to view the evidence in light of these early "hunches." Even if the subsequent evidence is not exactly as promised, these initial impressions may strongly influence their final verdicts.

To test these ideas, Pyszczynski, et al. (1981) compared the effects of three versions of a trial transcript. In one, the defense attorney, in his opening statement, added a claim that:

> we will provide evidence that will show conclusively that Ron Oliver could not possibly have stolen the car. Specifically, we will present testimony proving that he was seen at the Sundown Motel in Murray, Kentucky, at the very time the crime was taking place. Since Ron was seen at the Sundown Motel at the time the theft occurred, there is certainly no way he could have stolen the car. (p. 437)

*No such evidence was presented to any of the jurors.*

In a second version of the transcript, other mock jurors not only were given this claim in the opening statement, but they were also reminded by the prosecution at the end of the trial that the defense had not fulfilled its promise. The prosecutor said:

> Whatever became of the much-touted evidence showing that Mr. Oliver was at a motel at the time of the theft? No such testimony was introduced in this courtroom. I ask you, ladies and gentlemen, what became of this evidence? Clearly the defense never had any such evidence. If such

evidence had existed, surely the defense would have presented it. Ladies and gentlemen of the jury, beware! The defense has tried to pull the wool over your eyes with a cheap ploy. (p. 437).

The remaining third of the mock jurors were exposed to a trial transcript that contained neither a promise from the defense nor a reminder from the prosecution. The actual evidence was the same for all three types of jurors.

Of course, the greatest danger to the attorney who makes a promise that can't be fulfilled is for the opposing counsel to make the jury aware of the discrepancy, as was done here. And it had the expected effect. Jurors exposed to the opposing attorney's rejoinder apparently began to question the other aspects of the overzealous attorney's case. At least, they were more confident that the defendant was guilty than were the subjects who were not exposed to this unfulfilled promise.

But, more importantly, if the jurors were given an unfulfilled promise and were never reminded of it by the opposition, they were more likely to acquit the defendant than if they had not been given such a false promise. A completely unsubstantiated claim worked.

These disturbing results do need to be qualified. First, the respondents were mock jurors—not true ones—and second, they did not engage in any deliberation. The process of deliberating might weaken or eliminate any tendency of individual jurors to give precedence to the opening promise over the actual evidence. And in the real world, any opposing attorney who is at all alert will remind the jurors of his or her adversary's digression.

Even though we doubt that a blatant lie in an opening statement could be an effective strategy, some attorneys may opt to take the risk to make the strongest, most extensive opening statement plausible. By so doing, the attorney may provide a favorable framework that jurors will use to interpret later evidence. Even if this later testimony does not fully substantiate the lawyer's claims, these results suggest that the final verdicts will not be less favorable than if such strong claims had not been made. Indeed, in their closing arguments, clever defense attorneys could even admit that factors such as capricious witnesses may have prevented them from fulfilling their claims, and thereby eliminate the opportunity for prosecutors to discredit such claims.

## The Assumption That Jurors are Accurate and Complete Information Processors

It is an assumption of the legal system that jurors can understand and retain information, even in complex trials that extend for weeks and months. The mass of isolated facts must be assimilated and comprehended. The fact that jurors are prevented from taking notes during the trial presentation (in the vast majority of jurisdictions) is an implicit indication of the court's view of jurors as able to attend, perceive, understand, and remember. Apparently most judges fear that note taking would cause jurors not to pay attention to some of the testimony, and it would give undue advantage during deliberations to those jurors who had chosen to take notes. These concerns could be alleviated if the jury would be given a complete transcript of the trial—or even better, a videotape—just as they began to deliberate.

One of the major obstacles to jurors' being satisfactory information processors is that seemingly relevant information is not provided them. Jurors often express frustration that significant facts about the case were not introduced during the trial. Why did the defendant have some of the marked bills in his possession? Has anyone located his supposed accomplice? A very few judges permit jurors to ask questions during the trial. Usually these are submitted to the judge in writing, at the end of the testimony of a given witness. The judge eliminates those that are inappropriate, gives each attorney a chance to object, and, if there are no objections, the judge asks the question of the witness. Provision for questioning by the jurors increases their satisfaction with the verdict and occasionally unearths significant new evidence.

A helpful reform would be to vary the timing of the judge's instructions about the trial.

Although the judge may instruct the jury at any point in the proceedings, the general charge is typically read at the close of the trial, after the evidence has been presented and shortly before the jury retires to deliberate. In most jurisdictions, the judge's instruction comes at the close of the trial because the courts apparently believe in the "recall readiness" hypothesis (Jones & Goethals, 1971). This hypothesis predicts a recency effect, suggesting that the judge's instructions will have a more powerful impact on a jury's decision when they are given late in the trial, after the presentation of evidence. The reasoning behind the "recall readiness" hypothesis is simply that immediate past events are generally remembered better than more remote ones, especially when the other events have unfolded over a long period of time. In the trial setting, the sequence that presents the evidence prior to the instructions should thus increase the salience of the latter and make the judge's charge more available for recall during the deliberations. Having just heard the judge's charge, deliberating jurors would have it fresh in their minds and be more likely to make references to it, thus multiplying its potential impact.

As logical as the "recall readiness" hypothesis might seem to some, it has been questioned by a number of authorities from the court system. Two lines of reasoning guide such criticisms. First, Roscoe Pound, one time dean of the Harvard Law School, and others have proposed what is essentially a "schema" theory—that jurors should be instructed *prior to* the presentation of testimony because this gives them a set to appreciate the relevance or irrelevance of testimony as all of it unfolds and thus to make selective use of the facts. This line of reasoning gets indirect support from research findings in experimental psychology that show that people learn more effectively when they know in advance what the specific task is and that schematic frameworks facilitate comprehension and recall (Bartlett, 1932; Neisser, 1976).

Second, a number of judges (such as Frank, 1949) have objected to the customary procedure on the grounds that the instructions, by appearing at the end of the trial, are given after the jurors have already made up their minds. This argument is supported by a research finding (Kalven & Zeisel, 1966) that despite cautionary instructions, jurors often form very definite opinions about a defendant's guilt or innocence before the close of the trial. We may call this argument an example of the "primacy" hypothesis, and Judge E. Barrett Prettyman's (1960) position reflects it:

> It makes no sense to have a juror listen to days of testimony only then to be told that he (sic) and his conferees are the sole judges of the facts, that the accused is presumed to be innocent, that the government must prove guilt beyond a reasonable doubt, etc. What manner of mind can go back over a stream of conflicting statements of alleged facts, recall the intonations, the demeanor, or even the existence of the witnesses, and retrospectively fit all these recollections into a pattern of evaluations and judgments given him for the first time after the events; the human mind cannot do so. (p. 1066)

So there is a clearcut contrast between the "recall readiness" hypothesis and the "primacy" hypothesis, between the effects anticipated by each hypothesis if the judge's instructions are delayed to the end of the trial. As I recall Schachter often saying, this is an empirical question: At what point in the trial proceedings should the judge instruct the jury in order to maximize the jurors' adherence to that instruction?

In an attempt to answer this question, Kassin and Wrightsman (1979) varied the timing of the "requirement of proof" instruction. From the perspective of defendants, this directive is perhaps the most crucial of the mandatory instructions. Specifically, all those accused are entitled to a statement to the jury that they are presumed innocent, that the burden of proof is on the prosecution, and that all elements of the crime must be proven to a constitutional standard of "beyond a reasonable doubt." In our experiment, subjects watched a videotape of one hour's length, in which the trial defendant was charged with auto theft. The trial itself consisted of three phases: The attorneys' opening statements; the direct, cross, and redirect examination of witnesses; and the closing arguments by counsel. The judge's instruction was based on those in current use, and represented a fourth aspect whose presence or absence and timing were varied. In one condition, the instructions appeared prior to the introduction of evidence (that is, between phases one and two). In a second condition, they appeared after the closing arguments (that is, after phase three). In a third condition, no instruction was given the jurors. At the conclusion of the trial presentation, the subjects gave their verdicts, were tested for recall of the facts brought out in testimony, and answered a number of other case-related questions. Also, so that the researchers could examine the mock jurors' evaluations of the evidence as it unfolded, half of the subjects in each condition made judgments of guilt or innocence at various points during the trial presentation.

The "primacy" hypothesis espoused by Judge Prettyman and others was clearly supported by the results of this empirical study. Only 37% of the subjects who received the judge's instructions *before* the evidence voted to convict the defendant, compared to 59% in the condition in which the instructions came at the end of the trial. In fact, the conviction rate for this group—59%—was not significantly different from the conviction rate—63%—for mock jurors who did not receive *any* instructions. In other words, *the judge's instructions affected mock jurors' verdicts when they were delivered before the testimony but not when presented afterwards.* Furthermore, the midtrial judgments made by half the subjects indicated that the sequence of the instructions coming before the evidence produced a lowered conviction rate *immediately*— even from the first decision point, assessed after the direct examination of the first witness. Finally, when subjects were instructed after the evidence, they recalled significantly *fewer* case-related facts than when the instructions were delivered before the evidence or not at all. This latter result is particularly impressive when coupled with previous findings (Elwork, Sales,·& Alfini, 1977) that subjects do not even recall the *instruction* better when it is presented at the close of the trial. From these findings we conclude that the mere timing of instructions may influence jurors' mid- and post-trial judgments; they have a dramatic impact when they come before, but when they follow testimony their effect is minimal.

What practical applications may be drawn from these findings? Mandatory code provisions do not forbid or discourage judges from instructing the jury *before* the trial. A number of states give their judges such discretion; in Indiana, for example, a ruling by the state supreme court requires the presentation of a preliminary instruction on the manner of weighing testimony. The jury is then advised that it will receive further instructions at the close of the trial. In Missouri, the state supreme court's committee on jury instructions recommended:

> That the jury be instructed before the trial begins about its duty to determine the facts solely from the evidence, how it shall determine the believability of evidence, and its obligation to give each party fair and impartial consideration without sympathy or prejudice. The committee believes that it is better to draw the jury's attention to these matters before the trial rather than waiting until after the jurors may have reached a decision. (1964)

These examples are, unfortunately, the exception rather than the rule; judicial discretion, even if permitted, is vastly underutilized. In this regard, I would wonder about the feasibility of publishing a portion of the pattern jury instructions in the "juror handbooks" that are distributed in some jurisdictions as part of the orientation to jury service. Also, if the judge's instructions were presented at both the beginning and the end of the proceedings, the major cost would seem to be some slight additional time.

## The Assumption That Jurors Can Suspend Judgment

Jurors are presumed to be able to withhold judgment until all the evidence is presented, or at the very least, the ideal represents the juror as someone who, though swayed by the evidence first in one direction and then the other, treats these facts as separate inputs, not influenced by their order. But certain kinds of courtroom happenings may challenge the validity of this assumption.

For example, I believe it is possible that one piece of evidence early in the trial can so color a juror's view that he or she develops an unalterable verdict early in the trial.

What if jurors are told early in the trial that the defendant earlier confessed to the crime (and that now he says he is not guilty)? There are numerous documented instances of people who, for a variety of reasons, willingly confess to crimes that they did not commit (Reik, 1966). In 20% of criminal cases, disputed confessions occur, and a defendant may make and then withdraw an out-of-court confession (Kalven & Zeisel, 1966).

The legal admissibility of such a confession as evidence is quite controversial. In *Jackson v. Denno* (1964) the U.S. Supreme Court held that a criminal defendant is entitled to a pretrial determination that any confession he or she made to officials was *voluntarily* given, and not the outcome of physical or psychological coercion, which the Constitution forbids. *Only* if the factfinder (usually the presiding judge) at this coercion hearing determines that the confession was, in fact, voluntary may it then be introduced to the jury at the trial. If it is ruled involuntary, the jurors will never even know about it—unless they read it in the papers.

We all recognize that in the real world, confessions differ with respect to how voluntary or involuntary they are. Some may occur spontaneously; others are the result of extreme threats and coercion. So what should be the standard of proof by which the pretrial fact finder evaluates voluntariness; that is, how certain should the judge be that the confession *was* voluntary?

There is some inconsistency here. Some states adopted the stringent criterion that it must be proved "beyond a reasonable doubt" that the confession was, indeed, voluntary. In other states, by contrast, lesser standards were sanctioned, including proof of voluntariness by a mere "preponderance of the evidence." (Simon & Mahan, 1971, found that these translated into 89% and 61% certainty, respectively.)

In *Lego v. Twomy* (1972) the Supreme Court resolved this question and ruled the admissibility of a confession may be determined by the *preponderance of the evidence;* hence, the chances of the accused for an acquittal were hurt by this, as a lesser standard was all that was required. In this decision, the Supreme Court reasoned that the sole aim of the 1964 decision was to exclude any evidence that was illegally obtained, so as to safeguard the individual's Fifth Amendment right to due process.

The probable unreliability of a coerced confession was—surprisingly— not a consideration. The Supreme Court assumed, in fact, that jurors "naturally" can be trusted to use potentially unreliable confessions cautiously. Specifically, the court justified the latter position by stating that:

> Our decision was not based in the slightest on the fear that juries might misjudge the accuracy of confessions and arrive at erroneous determinations of guilt or innocence . . . Nothing in *Jackson* questioned the province or capacity of juries to assess the truthfulness of confessions. (p. 625)

The Supreme Court having failed to question the capacity of jurors, it is left for the psychologists to do so. Note that we are once more faced with an assumption (of faith) by the Court regarding jurors' capacities. Guided by such a faith, the Supreme Court justified a lower standard by which the fact finder may admit (i.e., accept) confession whose voluntariness is in question.

This is basically an attributional problem (Kassin & Wrightsman, 1980, 1981, 1985). If we try to conceptualize how jurors use information about a confession, we see that these jurors are, after all, confronted with a behavior whose cause is ambiguous. If a defendant has confessed while under threat during an interrogation, that confession may be attributed to be reflecting the defendant's true guilt, or as a means of avoiding the negative consequences of silence.

In fact, even though the Supreme Court assumes that jurors would reject an involuntary confession as unreliable and not allow it to guide their decisions, previous research from the attribution theory perspective (Jones & Harris, 1967; Snyder & Jones, 1974) suggests that jurors might not totally reject the confession when considering the actor's true guilt.

To complicate matters further, the legal system defines coercion as either a threat of harm and punishment *or* a promise of leniency and immunity from prosecution. *Both* are viewed to be *equivalent* conditions for the determination of involuntariness. This assumption of equivalence runs head on in conflict against research findings that observers attribute more responsibility (Kelley, 1971) and subjective freedom (Bramel, 1969) to a person for actions taken to gain a positive outcome than for actions taken to avoid punishment.

There seem to be some clear implications of these findings for how jurors might utilize different types of coerced confessions. Specifically, they lead us to hypothesize that a confession that is made under the coercive influence of a promise of leniency will be perceived by jurors as more voluntary and hence as more indicative of guilt than one that resulted from a threat of punishment.

My colleagues and I have completed five studies on this issue, the major results of which are quite consistent. In the first study, 64 students read a 25-page transcript of the Ron Oliver trial. There were four versions, identical except for the inclusion of testimony that indicated that after the highway patrolman informed Ron Oliver that he was under arrest for stealing the car, Ron Oliver confessed. The four conditions were:

1. Confession, with no constraint or inducement
2. Confession based on promise of leniency
3. Confession, based on a threat of harsher sentence if he failed to confess
4. No confession

The other studies included some other manipulations, and in fact Study 4 and 5 used a different trial, but the important point is that the rank order of conditions is consistent.

The subjects discounted the confession offered after a threat of punishment. In effect, they acted as if it were no confession at all. On the other hand, a confession based on a promise of leniency was treated as an unsolicited confession. One of the subsequent studies that replicated this finding did so even when the positively constrained condition was, in fact, perceived by jurors as involuntary.

These very consistent differences in reaction to positively-induced and negatively-induced confessions by mock jurors are quite contradictory to the court's assumption that, in effect, "a confession is a confession is a confession." I suggest that the courts should explicitly distinguish between positive and negative forms of coercion and exercise caution when admitting the former as evidence. A safeguard that adopts a stringent standard of proof regarding the voluntariness and hence admissibility of a prior confession seems best.

## Some Qualifications and Conclusions

What do these studies tell us? Before drawing further conclusions, there are some important questions about the generalizability of our findings to actual juries. Jury researchers are concerned about such problems of ecological validity.

We can quickly list five major differences between jury simulations and procedures for actual juries:

1. First, we have used as subjects either college undergraduates (most of the time) or adults recruited from the community (when we could afford it). These groups are not the same as the constituency of actual juries.
2. Second, the setting for most of our research has been in a psychological laboratory, although we have used courthouse and law school courtrooms on occasion. (We are doing so more often, now.)
3. Third, the materials we have used have been recreations of actual trials or fictitious trials, either videotapes or transcripts. Some jury researchers have used one-page summaries, a very invalid procedure.
4. Fourth, in most of our studies we have collected responses from individual jurors, in contrast to the task of the actual jury of deliberating to a verdict. However, in our last seven studies we

have had jurors deliberate, as well as getting individual verdicts from them. And I expect other researchers are doing this more often.

5. Fifth, and probably most important, our subjects know that their decision does not carry any real consequences for parties involved in the case.

You may at this point feel that these differences are so severe to make our findings without application to the real world. Rather, I would suggest that the applicability is an empirical question. Let us, for example, compare responses to videotape with responses to actual trial presentations. (Gerald Miller and his colleagues, 1975, have, and find no difference.)

Let us compare students' reactions with those of community members. (Bray & Kerr, 1982, have and find some small differences in process but similarity in outcomes.)

Of course, many more comparisons are needed, and we constantly must move closer to ecological validity, but there are empirical data to indicate our results are at least somewhat generalizable.

Bearing these qualifications in mind, these studies indicate that jurors do come to their trial service with preconceptions that influence their reaction to evidence, that opening statements can color the interpretations given to subsequent facts, that instructions from the judge regarding the application of reasonable doubt are often worthless if they come at the end of the trial presentation, and that jurors tend to make influential distinctions between types of confessions that are ignored by the Supreme Court.

There is enough here to lead us to question some of the assumptions and procedures that have evolved for the jury. My own questioning of this social phenomenon would not have occurred if I had not been the fortunate student of Stanley Schachter; his courage in developing understudied topics in psychology has also served as a model to me. But much still remains to be done, especially with respect to resolving the different perspectives of psychologists and legal scholars toward the legal system. With respect to their views of the jury, it does seem that, as James Marshall (1966) wrote twenty years ago, law and psychology remain in conflict.

## ACKNOWLEDGMENTS

Much of the author's research reported in this chapter was funded from three General Research Fund awards from the University of Kansas.

## REFERENCES

Bartlett, F. C. (1932). *Remembering: A study in experimental and social psychology.* New York: Cambridge University Press.

Bramel, D. (1969). Determinants of beliefs about other people. In J. Mills (Ed.), *Experimental social psychology.* New York: Macmillan.

Bray, R. M. & Kerr, N. C. (1982). Methodological considerations in the study of the psychology of the courtroom. In N. C. Kerr & R. M. Bray (Eds.), *The psychology of the courtroom* (pp. 287–323). New York: Academic Press.

Elwork, A., Sales, B. D., & Alfini, J. J. (1977). Juridic decisions: In ignorance of the law or in light of it? *Law and Human Behavior, 1,* 163–189.

Jackson v. Denno. 378 U.S. 368 (1964).

Jones, E. E. & Goethals, G. R. (1971). *Order effects in impression formation: Attribution context and the nature of the entity.* Morristown, NJ: General Learning Press.

Jones, E. E. & Harris, V. A. (1967). The attribution of attitudes. *Journal of Experimental Social Psychology, 3,* 1–24.

Kalven, H. & Zeisel, H. (1966). *The American jury.* Boston: Little, Brown.

Kassin, S. M. & Wrightsman, L. S. (1979). On the requirements of proof: The timing of judicial instructions and mock juror verdicts. *Journal of Personality and Social Psychology, 37,* 1877–1887.

Kassin, S. M. & Wrightsman, L. S. (1980). Prior confessions and mock jury verdicts. *Journal of Applied Social Psychology, 10,* 133–146.

Kassin, S. M. & Wrightsman, L. S. (1981). Coerced confessions, judicial instruction, and mock juror verdicts. *Journal of Applied Social Psychology, 11,* 489–506.

Kassin, S. M. & Wrightsman, L. S. (1983). The construction and validation of a juror bias scale. *Journal of Research in Personality, 17,* 423–441.

Kassin, S. M. & Wrightsman, L. S. (1985). Confession evidence. In S. M. Kassin & L. S. Wrightsman (Eds.), *The psychology of evidence and trial procedure* (pp. 67–94). Beverly Hills, CA: Sage.

Kelly, H. H. (1971). *Attribution in social interaction.* Morristown, NJ: General Learning Press.

LaBuy, W. J. (1963). *Jury instruction in federal criminal cases.* St. Paul, MN: West.

Langer, E. J. & Abelson, R. P. (1976). A patient by any other name . . . : Clinician group differences in labeling bias. *Journal of Consulting and Clinical Psychology, 42,* 4–9.

Lego v. Twomy. 404 U.S. 477 (1972).

Lingle, J. H. & Ostrom, T. M. (1979). Retrieval selectivity in memory-based impression judgments. *Journal of Personality and Social Psychology, 37,* 180–194.

Marshall, J. (1966). *Law and psychology in conflict.* New York: Bobbs-Merrill.

Miller, G. R., Bender, D. C., Boster, F., Florence, B. T., Fontes, N., Hocking, J., & Nicholson, H. (1975). The effects of videotape testimony in jury trials: Studies on juror decision making, information retention, and emotional arousal. *Brigham Young University Law Review, 1975,* 331–373.

Neisser, U. (1976). *Cognition and reality: Principles and implications of cognitive psychology.* San Francisco: Freeman.

Nizer, L. (1961). *My life in court.* New York: Pyramid.

Prettyman, E. B. (1960). Jury instruction—first or last? *American Bar Association Journal, 46,* 1066.

Pyszczynski, T., Greenberg, J., Mack, D., & Wrightsman, L. S. (1981). Opening statements in a jury trial: The effect of promising more than the evidence can show. *Journal of Applied Social Psychology, 11,* 434–444.

Pyszczynski, T. A. & Wrightsman, L. S. (1981). The effects of opening statements on mock jurors' verdicts in a simulated criminal trial. *Journal of Applied Social Psychology, 11,* 301–313.

Reik, T. (1966). *The compulsion to confess.* New York: Wiley.

Simon, R. J. & Mahan, L. (1971). Quantifying burdens of proof: A view from the bench, the jury, and the classroom. *Law and Society Review, 5,* 319–330.

Snyder, M. & Jones, E. E. (1974). Attitude attribution when behavior is constrained. *Journal of Experimental Social Psychology, 10,* 585–600.

Weld, H. P. & Danzig, E. R. (1940). A study of the way in which a verdict is reached by a jury. *American Journal of Psychology, 53,* 518–536.

Wells, G. L., Miene, P. K. & Wrightsman, L. S. (1985). The timing of the defense opening statement: Don't wait until the evidence is in. *Journal of Applied Social Psychology, 15,* 758–772.

# 4

## Social Comparison, Behavioral Contagion, and the Naturalistic Study of Social Interaction

Ladd Wheeler
*University of Rochester*

### ON THE WAY TO MINNESOTA

I arrived at Minnesota in the early summer of 1959 just after having graduated from Stanford.[1] Stanford had been a fortunate accident. I was born and reared in Texas and had intended to go to nearby Texas Christian University to study for the ministry. At the last minute, my high school counselor told me that there was a scholarship to Stanford, established by a local oil man, that I might be able to get. I had never heard of Stanford, but when I was told that it was in California, I applied. The scholarship paid the magnificent amount of $1,500 a year, which, combined with part-time work as a student policeman and summer employment, was enough.

Soon after arriving at Stanford, my interest shifted from religion to psychology, and the department started a two-year honors program at the beginning of my junior year, taught by Elliot Aronson, Dick Alpert (Baba Ram Das, later), Ralph Haber, and Joe DeRivera. One of the requirements of the program was that we choose a faculty member to act as mentor and advisor. I chose Leon Festinger, not because he was a social psychologist, but because he was colorful—reputed to be brilliant, independent, and tough (I was then in my Ayn Rand stage, having more or less successfully resolved my D.H. Lawrence crisis). Elliot Aronson was Leon's senior graduate student, and I was put under his care, though Leon belied his reputation and always had time for me.

The Department was small and flexible, and I was able to take a

---

[1]This chapter may seem a bit too autobiographical in places, and too full of names. It is quite deliberate, as I think we have too little sense of history in social psychology.

number of graduate courses: social from Leon, learning from Doug Lawrence, statistics from Quinn McNemar, among others. Al Hastorf was there my senior year and provided much encouragement. I even shared an office with a first-year grad student, Jane Allyn, now Piliavin.

When the time came to apply to graduate school, Leon gave me two choices: Bob Abelson at Yale, or Stan Schachter at Minnesota. I was accepted at both places and couldn't make up my mind. I decided to accept the place that first offered me money for the first summer, because I was anxious to get started. The day after I accepted Minnesota, Yale also offered the summer money, but the die had been cast and dissonance reduced.

## THE TWO-FACTOR THEORY OF EMOTION

When I got to the Laboratory for Research in Social Relations at Minnesota, Stan had just published the affiliation book and had done the first of the drug-emotion studies on humans with Jerry Singer (Schachter & Singer, 1962). The results of that study were not very convincing, despite Stan's persuasive writing style and some clever internal analyses. Differences between placebo and epinephrine subjects were borderline at best. The problem, as he saw it, was that a placebo does not prevent subjects from becoming physiologically self-aroused in response to environmental cues. Accordingly, we planned and conducted a second study (Schachter & Wheeler, 1962).

We administered either epinephrine, a placebo, or chlorpromazine under the label of a vitamin and had people watch a funny movie. It was an excerpt from the Jack Carson film, "The Good Humor Man," and I must have spent hundreds of hours viewing films to find something that was ambiguously funny. Of course Stan ultimately had to approve the film, and we had to agree, with our vastly different backgrounds, on what would be moderately funny to University of Minnesota undergraduates. We had to have room for students to see it as hilarious or dumb, depending upon the drug treatment. According to Stan's two-factor theory of emotion, one needed the appropriate arousal, produced in this case by epinephrine and inhibited by chlorpromazine. Arousal produced the raw emotion. And one needed an environmental cue in order to label the raw emotion—the film in this case. The straightforward prediction was that the film should be funnier under epinephrine than under placebo than under chlorpromazine.

The results were not as weak as in the previous experiment, but they were confirmatory mostly because of laughs involving bodily movement, which Art Hill recorded during the film. Such laughs were the only evidence of a difference between the placebo and epinephrine conditions and in retrospect that is very bothersome, as epinephrine simply could have been causing more physical movement. However, there was nothing to stop the placebo subjects from producing their own arousal, so the prediction is difficult to test.

We pretested the chlorpromazine dose at 50 mg on ourselves and other graduate students, and Stan had us make notes of our feelings. Chuck Hawkins wrote that he had decided he was definitely going to die, after he clocked his pulse at 32 and falling. Bibb Latané came out of the testing room and promptly fell on his head, knocking over the coffee pot. Stan consulted all sorts of experts and finally decided to halve the dosage, in the face of totally overwhelming ignorance on the part of the experts. Mental hospital patients are given extreme dosages, but no one knew what it might do to an undergraduate. Even then, we had a cot available for the chlorpromazine subjects, and it was used with some frequency after the experimental session. We were very careful about the welfare of the subjects. They were all cleared through the University Health Service, and a physician gave the injections and was in attendance at all times.

One of my major contributions to the study was to insist on a measure that would demonstrate that the chlorpromazine subjects remained mentally alert. We added a questionnaire about facts in the movie, and this proved to be important in showing that the chlorpromazine subjects were attending to the movie as well as the epinephrine people.

Stan and I then began planning a study using epinephrine and norepinephrine, the idea being that they both produced arousal, but that one was reputed to produce an aggressive arousal and the other a flight arousal. Stan's prediction was that regardless of the source of arousal (we could inject either drug), the environmental cues would determine the emotion. For various reasons, including his departure for Columbia University, we never conducted the study, but the many discussions of it were an important part of my education.

## MY RELATIONSHIP WITH STAN

I was too full of hubris to be a good graduate student, and we sometimes fought. On one occasion during the discussion of this study, I think I accused him of not wanting to perform a fair test of the hypothesis. He shouted me out of his office but came to my desk a few minutes later and said we should continue our discussion. On another occasion I threw away some pilot data before Stan had seen them, on the grounds that I could tell that there wasn't anything there. He was probably more gentle about it than I would be in a similar situation today.

When we were pretesting the "Niatpac Levram" experiment ("Captain Marvel" spelled backwards, a running joke in the Jack Carson film), Stan had to teach me to be "warm and cuddly" with the subjects. He felt that I had the demeanor of a cobra and couldn't establish rapport with the subjects. So he had me go around hugging people prior to the first experimental sessions. I sometimes do that with my students today.

I think that Stan's greatest influence on me was a year-long seminar he taught, in which we covered the material from Lewin and his students from the beginning to the present. Stan's great strength in teaching this course was his ability to tie everything together theoretically, to make it clear how one development led to another. Of course he had been part of much of this work, and the ability to carry a theory one step further has been the hallmark of his career, so we students were especially fortunate. It was here that I developed my long interest in social comparison processes.

The ambivalent attitude Stan and I had toward one another at this time was not hidden from the other members of the class. On one occasion, he asked me to go to the blackboard and use Lewinian bathtub diagrams to illustrate sexual seduction. Thinking that he meant to embarrass me, I did as I was told but labeled everything with four-letter words. When I finished, he quickly erased the board, visibly nervous that someone else might see it. I'd call it a draw.

The only other research I was involved in with Stan was the Stillwater Prison study on avoidance learning in sociopaths (Schachter & Latané, 1964). I was not involved in the planning, but Bibb and I ran the subjects together, which helped to cement our great friendship and helped me to appreciate Stan's ingenuity. Stan did give me the duty of doing a rat experiment, but I simply could not handle injecting the rats in the belly when they knew what I was going to do. I offered to pay someone to do it (though I had no money), but he kindly excused me from the responsibility.

## MY DISSERTATION

I did my dissertation in 1961 (defended in 1962) after Stan had left for Columbia. Ben Willerman was my advisor, though Dana Bramel worked closely with me also. It was the influence of Stan's course, however, that provided the subject matter—social comparison processes.

I was bothered by the fact that there was no *direct* evidence for either upward comparison or comparison with a similar other. Previous research seemed very indirect to me. Furthermore, there was a paradox involved in choosing upward if one wanted to perceive oneself as being well off. Choosing upward was just guaranteed to give evidence of inferiority.

It was necessary to create a situation in which people knew what was up and what was down, and in which people knew who was similar to them. To accomplish that, I gave subjects rank-order information about themselves and six other people tested together; and thus the rank-order paradigm for studying comparison came into existence.

Subjects were tested in groups of seven for their ability to profit from a special psychology seminar course, which they would be required to take if they were chosen for it. In a High Motivation condition, the seminar was described as consisting of exciting discussions without homework, grades, or compulsory attendance. In a Low Motivation condition, the seminar involved much homework, tough grading, and compulsory attendance early Saturday mornings. The ability to profit from the seminar was measured by physiological responses to TAT slides.

I spent many hours sawing and hammering to construct the cubicles that would separate the subjects, much to the dismay of my fellow students. Bill Graziano and Tom Brothern said that students in the Lab in the 1970's often wondered what the rickety old things were used for. A huge bundle of cables ran in front of the cubicles, and at each seat a pair of electrodes emerged. The bundle of cables disappeared into a room where the kymograph was allegedly kept. I carefully applied the electrodes to each person exactly as one would do for real measurement. Subjects were then told to just relax and watch the TAT slides; the kymograph would record their emotional responses, and we would thus know who would be best for the seminar. (Students then had a naive and unbounded belief in science.)

After the TAT slides had been shown, I collected the results from the kymograph and gave individual feedback to the subjects, leading each to believe he occupied the middle rank in the group of seven. Each subject was given his own score and knew the approximate scores of those at the top and bottom of the rank order. I then told them that the only immediate feedback I could give them was the score of one other person in the group, and that they should privately indicate their choice of that person by writing down his rank.

The strongest result of the experiment is that subjects did indeed compare upward, and this was somewhat stronger in the High Motivation condition than in the Low Motivation condition. Furthermore, those who compared upward were more likely to believe themselves to be more similar in score to those above them than to those below them. The interpretation was that subjects assumed similarity upward and then tried to confirm it by comparing upward. And finally, comparison tended to be with similar others. In short, all predictions from social comparison theory were confirmed.

Because everyone in the Lab had been in on the design of the study (we were like that), everyone eagerly awaited each group's data, and there was much discussion. By the time the data were all in, Karl Hakmiller had designed his dissertation, an attempt to get people to compare downward. He used the same cubicles and fake physiological measuring equipment and indeed demonstrated downward comparison when subjects were given unexpectedly negative information about the degree of hostility they felt toward their parents. Although his experiment has been cited over the years mostly as a curious exception to the usual finding of upward comparison in the rank-order paradigm, downward comparison is now all the rage since Tom Wills' paper in *Psychological Bulletin* (Wills, 1981), and Karl's experiment is the only direct experimental demonstration of downward comparison.

Both Karl and I had trouble publishing our dissertations because neither of us could write. Our writing styles, as Stan would say, were clumsy and wooden. Moreover, we tried to write shorter versions of the dissertations rather than start from scratch and write an article. It wasn't until the 1966 Supplement of the *Journal of Experimental and Social Psychology*, edited by Bibb, that short readable versions of the two were published (Hakmiller, 1966; Wheeler, 1966).

John Arrowood, although he was Hal Kelley's student, had also done fine work on social comparison theory (stimulated by Stan's seminars), as had Roland Radloff who left shortly after I arrived, and who was the one who discovered the birth order effects in Stan's affiliation work. I later had the privilege of working with Rollie for several years at the Naval Medical Research Institute. All of these people, and Jerry Singer, had articles in the Supplement. Bibb and I published our only article together to date here (Latané & Wheeler, 1966).

## RESEARCH ON AN AIRPLANE CRASH

In late 1963 I was at the Naval Medical Research Institute in Bethesda, Maryland, and Bibb was at Columbia. A Boeing 707 exploded over open country in Maryland and showered the underlying fields with pieces of the plane and of the 82 passengers and crew. Shortly afterward, volunteers from the nearby Bainbridge Naval Base began the grim duties of policing the scene and picking up the pieces. The Commander at Bainbridge called the NMRI group to alert us to the research possibilities, and I called Bibb to ask him to come down and work with me on the project.

The data collection took place a week after the crash, at which time we gave questionnaires to the men who had worked at the crash site and to men who had volunteered but were not needed. Furthermore, the men who worked at the crash site were broken into two groups: those who had merely directed traffic and those who had engaged in body search and collection. Finally, in addition to various questions about behavior after the crash, we administered Lykken's Activity Preference Inventory (Lykken, 1957). This scale measures emotionality and a low score was one of the criteria for choosing sociopaths in the Stillwater Prison study (Schachter & Latané, 1964). Among other things, we asked the men about their communicative behaviors (wanting to talk to people and writing home) in the week after the crash. Attempting to replicate and extend Stan's work on affiliation, we hypothesized that (1) communicative behaviors after the crash would be greater for men who performed the more stressful duties, and (2) particularly for the more emotionally responsive men.

The great joy and beauty (and perhaps truth) of doing naturalistic research is that you can't mess around with the conditions until you get what you want. On both "writing home" and "wanting to talk," we found that the nonemotional men rather than the emotional men increased communicative behavior as a result of being engaged in the body search. In fact, the emotional men decreased communication. Our *post hoc* speculation about these results was that nonemotional men rarely experience emotion, and thus this was a major event, leading to a desire to communicate about it. The emotional men, on the other hand, may have avoided communication because it would have reinstated the original unpleasant emotions too much, or they may simply have felt no uncertainty about the appropriateness of their emotions. These unexpected results don't stand alone. In a literature review a few years later, I concluded that particularly intense emotions are likely to lead to a desire for solitude rather than affiliation because of (1) a desire to avoid embarrassment or a depressive reaction; (2) the absence of any need to reduce uncertainty; or (3) a desire to avoid having the emotional response further stimulated (Wheeler, 1974).

## RECENT RESEARCH ON SOCIAL COMPARISON

My most recent work on social comparison using the rank-order paradigm has been an attempt to include attributes related to the trait to be evaluated, as suggested in Hypothesis VIII of the original theory (Festinger,

1954). Richard Koestner, Robert Driver, and I showed that subjects chose to learn the performance score of others who had the same amount of practice on the performance as the subjects themselves. However, there was still a strong tendency to compare with those adjacent to the subjects in the rank-order regardless of the amount of practice these others had. And, as usual, there was upward comparison (Wheeler, Koestner, & Driver, 1982). Wheeler and Koestner (1984) showed that subjects chose to learn about the related attributes (number of practice items) of others who performed similarly.

We have cast this in an equity-like formula:

$$\frac{P_p}{RA_p} \geq \frac{P_o}{RA_o}$$

where $P_p$ and $P_o$ are the Performance of person and other, and $RA_p$ and $RA_o$ are the Related Attributes of person and other. Person would like his ratio to be equal to or greater than that of other. The Wheeler, Koestner, and Driver study indicated that people want to know the $P_o$ of someone with a similar $RA_o$. The Wheeler and Koestner study showed that people want to know the $RA_o$ of someone with a similar $P_o$. What this somewhat clumsy exposition means is that the trait to be evaluated and attributes thought to be related to that trait are of equal importance: people are interested in learning about whichever one they don't know.

## WORKING FOR THE ARMY AND THEN THE NAVY

Before Stan left Minnesota for Columbia, he asked me what kind of job I wanted. I told him I wanted to do research in a warmer climate, was not particularly interested in teaching, and by all means wanted to stay out of military service. He called Richard Snyder of HumRRO (Human Resources Research Office), a research organization administered by George Washington University and under contract to the Army. As a result, my first job, which I began in late 1961, was at the HumRRO unit in Monterey, California. Not only did it allow me to do research without teaching and provide me with an occupational deferment, it also was located in one of the loveliest spots in the country! I lived on the side of a mountain in Carmel Highlands and drove my Alfa roadster to work along the coast highway. I began my work on behavioral contagion there, but after a year and a half, the mission of the organization became much too applied and constricting, and I decided to leave. Thomas I. Myers had already left HumRRO to join the Naval Medical Research Institute in Bethesda, where a small group headed by W.W.

Haythorn was doing research on groups in isolation and confinement, and I decided to join him. In addition to Rollie Radloff, my colleagues there included Dalmas Taylor, Carl Wagner, Seward Smith, Irv Altman, and Dave Kipnis. John Lanzetta and Ralph Exline were consultants.

## BEHAVIORAL CONTAGION

My years there (1963–67) were fun and productive. Irv, Dalmas, and I published four articles on groups in confinement; Wagner and I did two articles on helping behavior. I collaborated with Hank Davis on three papers dealing with the social behavior of rats; and there were several articles with various co-authors on behavioral contagion. Bibb was visiting frequently, and it was there that we did the previously mentioned study on the plane crash. Rollie Radloff and I did not collaborate on research, but we spent many happy hours talking about social comparison.

My big interest at the time was in behavioral contagion, and that interest had been aroused in Stan's seminar at Minnesota (Grosser, Polansky, & Lippitt, 1951; Polansky, Lippitt, & Redl, 1950; Redl, 1949; Schachter & Hall, 1952). (Here I will mention some things for the history buff.) Fritz Redl was a Viennese psychiatrist associated with Wayne State and Director of the Detroit Group Project and Pioneer House. He specialized in group therapy with adolescents and ran summer camps for adolescents. He was a particularly astute observer of group behavior and was cited by Lewin in his historic article on the quasistationary equilibrium and social change in the first issue of *Human Relations,* published just after Lewin's death (Lewin, 1947). Ron Lippitt was Director of Research for the Research Center for Group Dynamics, and Redl and Lippitt were awarded a grant from the US Health Service to study behavioral contagion. Leon Festinger provided statistical advice.

My work on behavioral contagion, then, was very much in the Lewinian mode. A paper I published in *Psychological Review* (Wheeler, 1966) was also, however, heavily influenced by the work of Bandura and Walters (1963), and we were even able to get Bandura to consult with us at NMRI.

The basic notion of behavioral contagion is that an individual is in a conflict over performing a certain behavior or not—there are both driving and restraining forces. Observation of someone else performing that behavior or a related behavior without suffering negative consequences, imposed by either the self or others, reduces the restraining forces and allows the individual to perform the behavior or some approximation of it. Various predictions were tested in a series of studies, of which I describe those dealing with aggression.

Tony Caggiula and I (Wheeler & Caggiula, 1966) investigated the contagion of aggression in an experiment involving three-man groups communicating over an intercom. The men were to exchange opinions and evaluate one another's opinions on a variety of topics. The opinions of one person (the target) were designed to arouse hostility in the subject in some conditions but not in others. The third person (the model) was verbally aggressive toward the target in some conditions but not in others. And, finally, the target responded to aggression from the model in different ways in different conditions: he either counter-aggressed, said he had no comment to make, or changed and softened his original opinion.

There was substantial aggression by the subject toward the target only in those conditions in which the target's opinions aroused hostility and in which the model was aggressive toward the target. The subject was not aggressive when the target's opinions aroused hostility but the model was not aggressive toward him; nor was the subject aggressive when the target's opinions were not designed to arouse hostility, but the model was aggressive toward him anyway. We argued that this was a clear demonstration of restraint reduction through modeling.

The response of the target to aggression from the model made no difference at all. This manipulation was included in response to a suggestion by deCharms and Wilkins (1963) that if the target of aggression does not respond to a model's aggression, an observer will be vicariously frustrated and further instigated to aggression. This explanation assumes a process similar to Berkowitz' "completion tendency," which states that the goal of aggression is to injure the target or remove the frustration and that unsuccessful attempts to do this instigate further aggression (Berkowitz, 1962). Ruling out such an explanation bolstered our argument for restraint reduction as the mediating process.

In another experiment, Seward Smith and I (Wheeler & Smith, 1967) investigated the effects of censure of an aggressive model. The experimental situation was similar to the one described earlier, but the model was censured for his aggression toward the target prior to the subject's opportunity to aggress. The model was censured by the experimenter, by a peer who was observing, or the model censured himself. There was, of course, a no-censure condition, and there were the necessary conditions to demonstrate restraint reduction again. The results were that restraints against aggression were indeed reduced by an aggressive model, and that only censure by the experimenter reinstated these restraints and prevented subsequent aggression by the subject. Furthermore, experimenter censure produced high scores on a depression scale. Thus, authoritarian censure of aggression can prevent the contagion of aggression within a group, but at the cost of depressive reactions among group members.

In a third study on the contagion of aggression, Lewis Levine and I investigated the importance of similarity between the model and the subject (Wheeler & Levine, 1967). The experimental situation was similar to those previous except that the subject was given information that the model was either similar or dissimilar to himself in terms of age, family size, ordinal position, parents' ages, home state, hobbies, favorite sports, hometown size, marital status, religion, and race. Although we didn't predict it, the dissimilar model proved to be the more effective in reducing restraints against verbal aggression. In explaining these results, we suggested an extension of social comparison theory: While the agreement of similar others may produce somewhat greater confidence, the increment in confidence will be limited because one expects similar others to be agreeable. If individuals of dissimilar background agree with one, however, one's confidence may be greatly enhanced because justification for one's own opinions has come from an unexpected direction. Such support would be highly effective because it would indicate that the belief in question was not dependent upon any particular set of environmental influences or background factors; hence, it would indicate that the belief was "true." Goethals and Darley arrived at the same conclusion in their attribution approach to social comparison (1977), although they were not aware of the Wheeler and Levine article— perhaps because it was published in *Sociometry*. My strategy in those days was to spread the contagion articles over as many journals as possible; it was not, I now think, wise.

The contagion work never really caught on, although it is still trotted out occasionally to explain something. Most people seemed to be doing dissonance and self-perception research, and I had no graduate students at NMRI.

## MOVING TO ACADEMIA

When Ned Jones went to Texas on sabbatical in 1967–68, I took his place at Duke, joining Jack Brehm and Darwyn Linder. Combining UNC and Duke, there was an incredible array of graduate students: Kent Butzine, Joel Cooper, Al-George Goethals, Larry Gruder, Russ Jones, Jim Robinson (now Luginbuhl), Kelley Shaver, Bob Wicklund, Steve Worschel, and Camille Wortman. I haven't seen such a group of students since, but it convinced me to move into the academic world, and I took a job the next year at New York University. The year at Duke was wonderful. I taught a seminar with most of these students in it that resulted in

*Interpersonal Influence* (Wheeler, 1970), an historical approach to the subject. I still have a 1968 letter from Gardner Murphy, written in response to a letter we wrote when we discovered that Sherif, Asch, and Newcomb had been graduate students at Columbia while Murphy was on the faculty there. Murphy claimed not to have contributed much to any of them, giving credit instead to Woodworth for creating an atmosphere that was "remarkably free, open, generous . . . " The seminar also led to a social comparison paper that was the first to demonstrate the strong tendency to determine the range of scores in a group by choosing to learn first the highest and then the lowest score (Wheeler, et al., 1969).

David Glass and I were hired at the same time at the NYU Research Center for Human Relations, and our job was to establish an experimental social psychology program in place of the social problems program the Research Center had long been noted for (Stuart Cook, Isador Chein, and others). My three years there were not terribly pleasant or productive because of continual political skirmishes, a divorce, and the death of my friend and colleague Arne Mordkoff, with whom I was doing hypnosis research. One bright spot was a graduate student I had one year overlap with, who has been my colleague at the University of Rochester since 1974—Harry Reis. Another was many conversations with Dave Glass over martinis at the Jade Cockatoo. Dave had all the original syllabi from Stan's famous seminar, the one I had taken from Stan at Minnesota, and had added more recent material. We taught the course both jointly and individually.

Another bright spot was that I did get to see Stan occasionally, largely at Polly and David Glass's social functions, but also during the summer in Amagansett. He was trying to stop smoking—as usual. He also experimented informally with ways to help other people stop. He once grabbed a pack of cigarettes from my wife, threw them across the room, and announced, "There, you've stopped!"

It was during that period of time, in 1969, that Stan won the APA Distinguished Scientific Contribution award, in the stellar company of Jean Piaget and Herb Simon.

I've seen very little of Stan since I left NYU in 1971. I have talked to him on the telephone several times, usually trying to get him to come to Rochester for a colloquium, but analyses always seem to be in progress. Certainly, I'll keep trying.

## RESEARCH WITH THE
## ROCHESTER INTERACTION RECORD

After moving to the University of Rochester, I began to worry about the fact that we knew very little about the everyday social life of people. Given a relatively free environment such as a university, how often do people interact with how many people in what size groups? To what extent are there sex differences and other individual differences? What effects do different amounts of interaction have on a person's sense of well-being? I tried having students keep diaries of their social interactions, but too many of them used the diary to deliver a therapeutic monologue to me. David Landy and I then began to develop a short fixed-format method for having people (coinvestigators, we called them) keep records of their interactions. The current version of the Rochester Interaction Record (RIR) is shown in Fig. 4.1. We typically have people keep the RIR for ten days to two weeks, recording every interaction of ten minutes or more. I mention only the most notable results. An incredible number of indices can be derived from the RIR for each coinvestigator subject, and space allows me to mention only a few of these.

In the first published article using the RIR (Wheeler & Nezlek, 1977), we investigated sex differences among freshman students early in the first semester and late in the second semester. We reasoned that females and males might use social resources in different ways in adjusting to university life. Indeed they did. In the fall semester, females had markedly more interactions with their same-sex best friend than did males; by the spring semester, this difference had disappeared because females had decreased the number of interactions with their best friend. Over all interactions, females decreased time per day more than males did, and reported decreased satisfaction with and intimacy in these inter-

```
DATE _____ TIME _____ AM___ LENGTH: ____ HRS____ MINS
                                  PM___
INITIALS ___ ___ ___    IF  MORE  THAN  3  OTHERS:
SEX      ___ ___ ___    # OF FEMALES _____ # OF MALES_____
INTIMACY:              SUPERFICIAL  I  2 3 4 5 6 7  MEANINGFUL
I DISCLOSED:           VERY LITTLE  I  2 3 4 5 6 7  A GREAT DEAL
OTHER DISCLOSED:       VERY LITTLE  I  2 3 4 5 6 7  A GREAT DEAL
QUALITY:               UNPLEASANT  I  2 3 4 5 6 7  PLEASANT
SATISFACTION: LESS THAN EXPECTED  I  2 3 4 5 6 7  MORE  THAN EXPECTED
INITIATION:              I INITIATED  I  2 3 4 5 6 7  OTHER INITIATED
INFLUENCE:    I INFLUENCED MORE  I  2 3 4 5 6 7  OTHER INFLUENCED MORE

NATURE:    WORK    TASK    PASTIME    CONVERSATION    DATE
```

FIGURE 4.1

actions. The general conclusion was that females entering college social-
ize more intensely than males, probably because they experience a
greater increase in freedom accompanied by higher levels of anxiety.
This seems very similar to Stan's work on anxiety and affiliation. As the
environment becomes more familiar, reliance on others decreases.
Nevertheless, and this has appeared in all of our studies, females
remain more satisfied with same-sex interactions.

The next research in this series was Nezlek's dissertation. In the
Wheeler and Nezlek study, we had used a life history questionnaire, a
modification of that developed by Radloff and Helmreich (1972), to show
that females who had experienced a high degree of parental control
were those who interacted most intensely during the first semester. For
his dissertation, Nezlek collected RIR data at four points during the
freshman year and attempted to relate changes to life history events
(Nezlek, Wheeler, & Reis, 1983). Just before the final interview with the
subjects, Harry Reis suggested we take photographs of them (to be rated
for attractiveness by students from another university) to see if physical
attractiveness related to the RIR variables. These data were published
by Reis, Nezlek, and Wheeler (1980). The major results were: (1) Physical attractiveness was positively related to the amount of opposite-sex
contact and negatively related to the amount of same-sex contact for
males, but not for females; (2) for both sexes, satisfaction showed an
increasing tendency over time to be positively correlated with attractiveness, particularly in opposite-sex interactions.

The first of these results was particularly surprising because we had
expected that the attractiveness of females would be more important in
everyday social life than would be the attractiveness of males. After the
article had been published, and after we had spent some time reading
Darwin, it occurred to us that our results might be due to males' being in
a more competitive "mating" situation than females. Because the subjects were freshmen, males were generally limited to spending time
with freshmen females; females on the other hand, could go out with
older men. In addition, there was a 60:40 sex ratio, with men being in
the majority. Taking these facts together suggested to us that only the
most attractive of our male subjects could compete successfully in
spending time with females, while all of our female subjects would have
males available. The obvious implication of this was to replicate the
study using senior subjects. Among seniors, females should be in the
more competitive mating situation, and their attractiveness should predict their interactions with males.

We did the study (Reis, et al., 1982) and got the same results as in the
original study: Attractiveness of males predicted positively the quantity
of their opposite-sex interactions and negatively the quantity of their

same-sex interactions; attractiveness of females was not predictive of quantity of interactions. As in the previous study, attractiveness related positively to the affective quality of social experience for both sexes.

Fortunately, we gave these subjects several personality–attitude measures and discovered that attractiveness affected these measures differently for the sexes. The most important difference was that the more attractive males were the more assertive, and the more attractive females were the less assertive. In addition, the more attractive males were lower in fear of rejection by the opposite sex, and the more attractive females were lower in trust of the opposite sex. Attractive males, then, were fearless and assertive in their quest for female companionship, and they were successful. Attractive females were cautious and non-assertive and thus did not spend more time with males than did their less attractive but more assertive and trusting sisters.

Although we have no direct evidence for it, I suspect that another part of the lack of relationship between female attractiveness and the quantity of their opposite-sex interactions is that many males fear rejection by attractive females and simply don't approach them. Because of some media publicity about this research, I was asked to be on a television talk show in New York City dealing with men's reactions to beautiful women. The other six guests on the show were three Miss Universes and three Miss U.S.A.s. They all bemoaned the fact that men were very much afraid to approach them, and so I too was afraid to approach them.

The final RIR study described was an attempt to relate social interaction patterns to loneliness (Wheeler, Reis, & Nezlek, 1983). Subjects were college seniors who kept the RIR for two weeks; loneliness was measured by the UCLA scale. Subjects were also given the Personal Attributes Questionnaire (Spence & Helmreich, 1978).

For both sexes, loneliness was negatively related to the amount of time spent with females and to the meaningfulness (a composite of intimacy, disclosure, quality, and satisfaction from the RIR) of interaction with both males and females. However, meaningfulness with males was more important than meaningfulness with females. Femininity was negatively related to loneliness for both sexes, leaving us with a regression equation predicting loneliness for both males and females from: (1) time spent with females, (2) meaningfulness with males, and (3) femininity.

I find the first two of these predictors particularly interesting. The data indicate that meaningfulness in interactions involving only males was much lower than in interactions involving only females or both males and females. In other words, the presence of a female in general raises the level of meaningfulness. Thus, it makes sense that spending time with females should reduce loneliness for both males and females, if we assume that meaningful interactions reduce loneliness. Entering the meaningfulness of interactions with females into the regression equation adds nothing; all we need to know is the amount of time spent with them. It is as if there were a threshold of meaningfulness required in an interaction, and interactions involving females usually reach that threshold.

Interactions involving only males usually do not reach that threshold, and thus we must use meaningfulness of interactions with males, rather than time with them, to predict loneliness. (Indeed, spending a higher *percentage* of one's time with males should and did lead to greater loneliness, for both males and females!) An intriguing question to me is "Who are these males who have meaningful interactions?" We have some information about this from a semipartial correlation analysis, which allows us to determine the percentage of loneliness variance accounted for by each variable by itself and the percentage of variance shared by two or more variables. This analysis indicated a strong overlap for males between time spent with females and the meaningfulness of interactions with males. To put it another way, those males who had meaningful interactions with other males also spent substantial time with females. There is no such overlap for our female subjects. These data are all correlational, so we want to be careful, but I would wager at least a small amount that men who spend time with women learn a meaningful interaction style from them and transfer that style to their interactions with men.

## STAN'S GREATEST STRENGTHS

I think that Stan's great influence on the field is due to several factors. First, he has been a determined and often brilliant theorist, always looking for the next implication of what he has just done, or for a new problem to which it can be applied. He worries with problems like a dog with a bone and talks to all kinds of people about them. I've often seen him charmingly corner someone at a party if that person worked in an area that might even vaguely have something to do with Stan's current puzzle.

Second, he writes extraordinarily well and colorfully. "I would be the first to concede that this attempt to reconcile these two lines of data has a vapid and vacuous quality. Ad hoc explanations do have the feel of eating Puffed Rice" (Schachter, 1971, pp. 179–180). His writing is at once a detective story and a persuasive communication. He gives one the clues the data provide, leads you through their possible meanings, and absolutely persuades you that he has the answer to it all. On the other hand, he has never been loath to point out some facts that are "utterly" inconsistent with his interpretation. One gets the feeling though that these are relatively minor problems when compared with the elegance of his formulation.

Third, he is unsurpassed at mining data with internal analyses. If there is anything there at all to support his predictions, he will find it. Sometimes, as he himself admits, it has been carried to extremes. In discussing the research on criminality that he eventually had to abandon for logistical reasons, he noted, "The results are also, in many spots, tentative, and the analyses sometimes suffer the imprint of someone convinced that he's right and willing to force his data to prove it" (Schachter, 1971, p. 141).

Finally, his research has always been both ingenious and simple. You will find no factor analyses, path analyses, or manovas. Tables are simple; figures, also simple, are abundant.

Perhaps some of this is no longer true. I have not seen his recent work on the stock market, but it sounds like a radical departure. I think that the last time I saw Stan was at the opening of Elliott Hall at the University of Minnesota in the early 1970s, when we were the two social psychologists from the past to give talks. I discussed the work I was just beginning using the Rochester Interaction Record to study social interaction. His comment after the talk was, "That's fascinating, Ladd, but where are you going to store all the data?" I suspect that he has now learned the advantage of computer storage.

## MEMORIES OF THE LAB

I often wish I were back in The Lab. There would probably be a cribbage game going on, perhaps at Stan's insistence because he needed cigarette money. Ken Ring would be shaving in the control room, functional in my years only to get Muzak from the student union, while singing Italian operas. Or Ken, John Arrowood, Karl Hakmiller, and Jerry Singer might be playing bridge. Bibb and I played as partners, but infrequently, using no known bidding system, but winning. If the Muzak happened to be playing "Never on Sunday," Hiroshi Ono and I would do a Greek dance. Someone always, perhaps Arnie Dahlke or Chuck Hawkins, would be dropping a mechanical calculator on the desk from a height of two feet to unjam it. John and I would be planning to drink beer at the end of the day to settle our fluctuating cribbage debt account. If it were

Friday, we'd be preparing to discuss some new book as a full group of students and faculty.

Presiding over this was Stan, the wonderful gentleman Hal Kelley, and Ben "I've got a million of them" (alternative explanations) Willerman. In the chaos of this big game room, beset at times with rivalry and petty quarrels, there was the most intense intellectual involvement I've experienced. We didn't worry about publications or jobs or grades, but only "truth" and inevitable progress toward it. Later, Ken Ring would assail us (as a field) for a "fun and games" approach (Ring, 1967); others would come out of the closet; and our "crisis" would ensue. Ken later turned to studying life after death.

Of course we had fun, and to paraphrase Mencken, I hope that some group of students and faculty somewhere, somehow, may be having as much.

## ACKNOWLEDGMENTS

Thanks to John Arrowood, Jon Barnard Gilmore, David Glass, Bibb Latané, Rollie Radloff, and Harry Reis for their comments on earlier drafts.

## REFERENCES

Bandura, A. & Walters, R.H. (1963). *Social learning and personality development.* New York: Holt, Rinehart, & Winston.

Berkowitz, L. (1962). *Aggression: A social psychological analysis.* New York: McGraw-Hill.

deCharms, R. & Wilkins, E.J. (1963). Some effects of verbal expression of hostility. *Journal of Abnormal and Social Psychology, 66,* 462–470.

Festinger, L. (1954). A theory of social comparison processes. *Human Relations, 7,* 117–140.

Goethals, G.R. & Darley, J.M. (1977). Social comparison theory: An attributional approach. In Suls, J.M. & Miller, R.L. (Eds.), *Social comparison processes: Theoretical and empirical perspectives.* Washington: Hemisphere Publishing.

Grosser, D., Polansky, N., & Lippitt, R. (1951). A laboratory study of behavioral contagion. *Human Relations, 4,* 115–142.

Hakmiller, K.L. (1966). Threat as a determinant of downward comparison. *Journal of Experimental Social Psychology,* Supplement 1, 32–39.

Latané, B. & Wheeler, L. (1966). Emotionality and reactions to disaster. *Journal of Experimental Social Psychology.* Supplement 1, 95–102.

Lewin, K. (1947). Frontiers in group dynamics. *Human Relations, 1,* 20–38.

Lykken, D.T. (1957). A study of anxiety in the sociopathic personality. *Journal of Abnormal and Social Psychology, 55,* 6–10.

Nezlek, J. B., Wheeler, L., & Reis, H. T. (1983). Studies of social participation. In H. T. Reis (Ed.), *Naturalistic approaches to studying social interaction.* San Francisco: Jossey-Bass.

Polansky, N., Lippitt, R., & Redl, F. (1950). An investigation of behavioral contagion in groups. *Human Relations, 3,* 319–348.

Radloff, R. & Helmreich, R. (1972). The life history questionnaire. *JSAS Catalog of Selected Documents in Psychology, 2,* 13 (Ms. No. 71).

Redl, F. (1949). The phenomenon of contagion and "shock effect" in group therapy. In K.R. Eissler (Ed.), *Searchlights on delinquency* (pp. 315–328). New York: International Universities Press.

Reis, H. T., Nezlek, J., & Wheeler, L. (1980). Physical attractiveness in social interaction. *Journal of Personality and Social Psychology, 38*(4), 605–617.

Reis, H. T., Wheeler, L., Spiegel, N., Kernis, M., Nezlek, J., & Perri, M. (1982). Physical attractiveness in social interaction, II: Why does appearance affect social experience? *Journal of Personality and Social Psychology, 43*(5), 979–996.

Ring, K. (1967). Experimental social psychology: Some sober questions about some frivolous values. *Journal of Experimental Social Psychology, 3,2,* 113–123.

Schachter, S. (1971). *Emotion, obesity, and crime.* New York: Academic Press.

Schachter, S. & Hall, R. (1952). Group-derived restraints and audience persuasion. *Human Relations, 5,* 397–406.

Schachter, S. & Latané, B. (1964). Crime, cognition and the autonomic nervous system. *Nebraska symposium on motivation, 12,* 221–273. Lincoln, NE: University of Nebraska Press.

Schachter, S. & Singer, J.E. (1962). Cognitive, social, and physiological determinants of emotional state. *Psychological Review, 69,* 379–399.

Schachter, S. & Wheeler, L. (1962). Epinephrine, chlorpromazine and amusement. *Journal of Abnormal and Social Psychology, 45,* 121–128.

Spence, J.T. & Helmreich, R.L. (1978). *Masculinity and femininity.* Austin: University of Texas Press.

Wheeler, L. (1966). Toward a theory of behavioral contagion. *Psychological Review, 73,* 179–192.

Wheeler, L. (1966). Motivation as a determinant of upward comparison. *Journal of Experimental Social Psychology,* Supplement 1, 27–31.

Wheeler, L. (1970). *Interpersonal influence.* Boston: Allyn & Bacon, Inc.

Wheeler, L. (1974). Selective affiliation for purposes of social comparison. In T. Huston (Ed.), *Perspectives on interpersonal attraction.* New York: Academic Press.

Wheeler, L. & Caggiula, A. R. (1966). The contagion of aggression. *Journal of Experimental Social Psychology, 2,* 1–10.

Wheeler, L. & Koestner, R. (1984). Performance evaluation: On choosing to know the related attributes of others when we know their performance. *Journal of Experimental Social Psychology, 20,* 3, 263–271.

Wheeler, L., Koestner, R., & Driver, R. (1982). Related attributes in the choice of comparison others. *Journal of Experimental Social Psychology, 18,* 489–500.

Wheeler, L. & Levine, L. (1967). Observer-model similarity in the contagion of aggression. *Sociometry, 30,* 1, 41–49.

Wheeler, L. & Nezlek, J. (1977). Sex differences in social participation. *Journal of Personality and Social Psychology, 35,* 10, 742–754.

Wheeler, L., Reis, H. T., & Nezlek, J. (1983). Loneliness, social interaction, and sex roles. *Journal of Personality and Social Psychology, 45,* 4, 943–953.

Wheeler, L., Shaver, K., Jones, R., Goethals, G. R., Cooper, J., Robinson, J. E., Gruder, C. L., & Butzine, L. (1969). Factors determining choice of a comparison other. *Journal of Experimental Social Psychology, 5,* 115–126.

Wheeler, L. & Smith, S. (1967). Censure of the model in the contagion of aggression. *Journal of Personality and Social Psychology, 6,* 1, 93–98.

Wheeler, L., Smith, S., & Murphy, D. B. (1964). Behavioral contagion. *Psychological Reports, 15,* 159–173.

Wills, T.A. (1981). Downward comparison principles in social psychology. *Psychological Bulletin, 90,* 245–271.

# 5

## From Student to Colleague: Retracing a Decade

Bibb Latané
*Institute for Research in Social Science*
*University of North Carolina*

I first met Stanley Schachter in the spring of 1958 in his coldwater flat on Gay Street in Greenwich Village, where he was spending a sabbatical writing *The Psychology of Affiliation* (Schachter, 1959). I was charmed and fascinated. Trim and youthful though balding at 36, winner of a Guggenheim Fellowship and soon-to-be winner of the AAAS Socio-Psychological Prize, his work was being touted as the most original in social science. I was a Yale senior, planning a career in corporate law, but tempted by the wild idea of taking a year to get an MA in social research.

### CHOOSING A CAREER

As an undergraduate, I had chosen to major in an interdisciplinary honors program called "Culture and Behavior," in part because of genuine interest in a general approach to social science, in part because I thought it would be a good liberal arts background for law, but mainly because my erratic sleeping habits would conflict less with afternoon seminars than morning lectures. In this enriched program, I got to do individual research with Bill McGuire as a junior and with Bob Cohen and Jack Brehm as a senior, and to take wonderful courses from such offbeat but stimulating faculty as Ed Deavy, August B. Hollingshead, Leonard Doob, and Omar Khayam Moore, whose disciplinary backgrounds included biology, sociology, psychology, and anthropology but who provided a potpourri of new ways of thinking about social life. And in those days when the threat of nuclear war was still fresh and unfamiliar, it was a truism that the security of the world depended on advances in social science comparable to the frightening strides being taken by the physical sciences.

While still in high school, I had already been exposed to academic life in social science, for both my parents were graduate students. My father had quit his secure job on Wall Street to return to the south and get a Ph.D. in economics, while my mother was working on a degree in clinical psychology. I had little interest in following in their footsteps, but their example stimulated my conviction that there is more to a career than making money. When testing revealed that my interests most closely matched those of corporate lawyers, I decided that money itself might not be all bad and that law would be a fine way to promote peace and justice.

As a southerner born and schooled through my preteens in the north, as an eighth generation American with the last name of an immigrant and a first name that required repetition and explanation to everyone I met, awkward and ungainly at 6'3", a year younger than my classmates all through school, I had always felt myself distinctly a minority and, if not an outcast, at least somewhat of an outsider. Perhaps for these reasons as much as for the elegance of the research, I was very excited to read, in Bob Cohen's junior seminar, the series of studies on pressures toward uniformity in small groups initiated by Festinger (1950) and his colleagues, and especially by Schachter's (1951) experiment on "Deviation, rejection, and communication." I pored over the mathematical formulas, understanding very little of them, but thought the ideas had major implications for whether there could be cultural diversity without sacrificing intergroup harmony.

As things turned out, my uncertainties about careers resolved themselves into a choice among three alternatives—to dive right into law school; to join a utopian community named Philia and help set up a collective farm in New Zealand; or to follow the urgings of Cohen and Brehm and go to graduate school. In order to keep my options alive as long as possible, I applied to both Harvard and Yale Law Schools and arranged to take the Law School Admission Test (LSAT), requested an appointment to meet with the organizers of Philia, and applied to four graduate social psychology programs. Michigan was Cohen's alma mater and the original site of the group dynamics research, Stanford featured Leon Festinger and a select group of students busily developing dissonance theory, UNC was in my home town and starred John Thibaut, while Minnesota was home to the interdisciplinary Laboratory for Research in Social Relations, with Stanley Schachter and Harold Kelley as well as a supporting cast of sociologists (Arnold Rose), political scientists (Herbert McCloskey), economists (Andreas Papandreou), and philosophers of science (May Brodbeck).

My usual practice when faced with a choice among good alternatives is to try to find some way to have them all—so I came up with the idea of spending one year in graduate school to develop maturity, better study habits, and perhaps some insights into human nature, and then go on to law school, while perhaps spending summers with Philia until my schooling was complete.

Everything seemed to come to a head at once: the directors of Philia scheduled an interview for Saturday, February 15, I received notice that the last LSAT would be nationally administered on Saturday, February 15, and Bob Cohen got me to call Stan Schachter, who agreed to see me, but only if it could be Saturday, February 15. Cancelling my interview with Philia, arranging to take the LSAT in New York rather than New Haven, I managed to make my meeting with Schachter.

Stan asked me about my honors research project (Cohen, Brehm, & Latané, 1959) and another study I had undertaken with Bob Cohen (Cohen & Latané, 1962). I remember getting very animated and involved in the discussion and only realizing later, with shock, that Stan was mainly trying to sound me out and get a feeling for my thought processes.

Within the span of a few days, I received letters accepting me into Harvard Law School and awarding me full four-year fellowships at Michigan and North Carolina. Stan called to say there were no more fellowships at Minnesota, but that he could support me for a year with a research assistantship in the Social Relations Lab. Since I only wanted a year and since I was drawn to the idea of an interdisciplinary research laboratory, I requested that Harvard Law delay my admission by one year and prepared to head west.

## BULLPEN MEMORIES

The Social Relations Lab, located on the fourth floor of Ford Hall across campus from the Psychology Department, consisted of several faculty offices, two laboratory rooms with one-way windows and an elaborate sound system, and a large bullpen housing the graduate fellows and research assistants. I particularly remember:

- Our initial orientation with Jack Darley, Director of the Laboratory (he was to leave in a few weeks for Washington, D.C. to be Executive Secretary for APA), informing us of the status hierarchy— "secretaries are harder to find than graduate students."
- Discovering that at the faculty level, the Lab had become interdisciplinary in name only, with only Schachter and Kelley maintaining

offices and spending any time there while the other affiliated faculty rarely left their own departments.

- Being stimulated, however, by contact with students from other disciplines (Dan McFadden and Bernard Saffran in economics, Frank Caro and Leonard Weller in sociology) that had assistantships in the Lab.
- Being overwhelmed by the wisdom and savoir-faire of the older social psychology students, Jim Banks, Danuta Ehrlich, Rollie Radloff, and Larry Wrightsman.
- Noticing, while reading Festinger, Schachter, & Back (1950), how well the initial assignment of student desks in the bullpen happened to coincide with our developing patterns of liking and interaction.
- Lunchtime bridge games among the other new social psychology students: John Arrowood, Karl Hakmiller, Ken Ring, and Jerry Singer.
- Jerry coming in every morning with a new set of anecdotes and jokes which he would try out on us in preparation for telling to Hal and Stan when they arrived.
- Penny-a-point cribbage games with Stan, during which we worried over details of design and interpretations of data the way a dog worries a bone.
- Realizing that it's better to be lucky than good during one long winning streak.
- Stan cadging just one more cigarette — promising to give back a whole pack.
- Scurrying between throws to grab a cup of coffee from the pot located just under the dartboard; and, later, falling over it after being injected with chlorpromazine during the pretesting for an experiment run by Ladd and Stan.
- Discussion meetings organized by Kelley, Schachter, and Willerman at which attendance was expected. We read new books such as Heider's (1958) *Psychology of Interpersonal Relations*. Although these meetings soon foundered, either for lack of good material to read or from lack of people willing to take the initiative to organize, I felt they were extraordinarily valuable.
- Analyzing data with Stan. First we would copy all the raw data onto 17 × 11″ columnar tabulation pads and then compare columns, using pencilled pluses and minuses as the bases for the sign tests that constituted our workhorse statistical procedure.
- Watching Rollie Radloff discover the wonderful convenience of analyzing his dissertation using the new system of Royal McBee

keypunch cards and Stan play with his new Curta calculator, a compact peppermill-shaped mechanical adding machine.


## FIRST-YEAR JOBS

As a first-year graduate student, I was assigned a number of tasks, of which five stand out in my mind:

1. Copy-editing *The Psychology of Affiliation*. This book, still regarded as one of the best written research monographs in psychology (a field whose authors are not noted for their lucidity) was short. Every night I would go over a chapter and the next afternoon, Stan and I would wrestle together over issues of sentence construction, the proper flow and sequencing of ideas, and punctuation. Commas were a particular problem—someone had once told Stan that he used too many—and he would agonize over each, trying to decide whether it was fully necessary for comprehension or would unduly impede the pace of the sentence. I think I had relatively little impact on the manuscript, but the experience had a large impact on me, making me ever conscious of the importance of careful writing.

2. Translating Marañon from the French. Stan had somehow discovered an obscure paper written in French in 1924 by a Spanish psychiatrist named Marañon, in which patients injected with adrenalin reported feeling "as if" they were experiencing a variety of emotions. Perhaps misled by my last name, Stan asked me to work up a finished translation with his (French) first wife, Marjorie. The fruit of these efforts was, for some years, the object of much study and discussion by our research team.

3. Playing the role of the euphoric stooge in Schachter & Singer (1962). My tasks included making and throwing paper airplanes, building a tower from manila folders, shooting rubber bands at it, and trying (clumsily) to twirl a hula hoop disguised as an electrical induction coil. I don't know whether this experience did anything to help overcome my self-consciousness, but it was good exercise.

4. Designing and running a condensed and simplified replication of Schachter's (1951) experiment on deviation, communication, and rejection, analyzing the results separately for first-born and later-born participants. Ken Ring and I rotated roles as the experimenter and observer, and Pat Burger, one of the Lab secretaries, played the role of the deviate who thought that love had already been shown to fail in setting Johnny Rocco straight. The results provided strong support for the original findings but only mild support for our predictions with respect to birth order. We

spent lots of time analyzing the results in different ways, but it was clear that Stan's heart was not in it, and we soon went on to other things. I was never clear why Stan's enthusiasm toward this project was so low, but I suspect it had to do with his general disdain for mere "gap-filling" research.

5. Planning a research program on animal emotionality. Since, by this time, I had realized that I would need at least another year to finish a masters degree and therefore would need to put off law school a little longer, I suggested to Stan before leaving Minneapolis for the summer that one way to assess the role of cognition and attribution in emotionality might be to see whether the Schachter and Singer results would replicate with lower animals. He seemed intrigued and promised to come up with a few dollars if I could do the research at UNC. We quickly designed a study in which albino rats were to be injected with adrenalin or placebo and placed in a standard shuttlebox in which they could learn to avoid electric shocks by running back and forth between two compartments.

Back home in Chapel Hill that summer, with help from Dick King and Eugene Long and borrowed lab space in New West, I was able to puzzle through such details as what strain, sex, and age of animal to order, how to house and feed them, where to inject them (in the nape of the neck or intraperitoneally), what to use as a vehicle (peanut oil extended the duration of effect), how to hold them so as not to frighten them (or get bitten), and what dosage and shock level to employ. I built a rudimentary shuttlebox and ran enough rats to find that adrenalin caused a significant increase in learning, presumably due to increased emotionality. Jerry Singer later showed the same thing more elegantly by directly measuring urination and defecation (although he no longer smiles when you ask him whether he still has his raw data).

Just before leaving for the summer, Stan had told me about a new student coming in who needed a place to stay. I was sharing the bottom floor of a house in Dinkytown with Frank Caro and Dan McFadden, but since none of us was going to be around for the summer, they had asked me to look out for someone to sublet. That is how I first met Ladd Wheeler. He was wearing high-heeled boots and a cowboy hat and we hit it off from the start.

## SEMINAR

Stan offered two year-long seminars, one on theory and one on methods, in alternate years. If you worked with him, you were expected to take them. They met once a week on Wednesday afternoon at 3 for two hours. Stan passed out dittoed sheets containing the assigned reading, a brief paragraph setting it in context, and a series of questions which one had to be prepared to answer in class.

In class, Stan was frankly evaluative. If he thought an idea was stupid, he said so. He was always asking "so what" but he meant it as a real question: "If what you say is true, what are the implications?" If an idea was good, he said so also. I still feel a residual glow from his interest in my class suggestion that increased other-directedness in societies that had made the demographic transition to low birth- and death-rates, claimed by David Riesman in The Lonely Crowd (1950), could result from their higher proportion of first-born and only children.

The theory seminar traced the development of the idea of social comparison from its origins in Lewinian thought through the group-based "pressures-to-uniformity" formulation and into dissonance theory and the psychology of affiliation. The course emphasized the Lewinian spatio-temporal-mathematical orientation of this line of research. The goal of theory was to develop formal hypotheses and corollaries, to formulate equations and solve them. There was a heavy emphasis on thought problems—"Which Miami Beach hotel will the inventor of Noxema, worth two million, choose: one whose clientele consists only of people also worth two million, another whose customers are worth two and a half million, or a third inhabited by mere millionaires? OK, now suppose he is a Hopi Indian?"

Stan was a master at encouraging us to push ideas always one step further. His metaphor for theory was the "line of thought" which, although it might wander all over the landscape and even double back upon itself, was always connected, cumulating and extending itself.

The methods seminar covered a wide variety of techniques, from participant observation to field and laboratory experiments, mathematical models, and cross-cultural research. I became increasingly amazed that Stan was able to illustrate each with examples drawn from his own research. I still think the major hallmark of Stan's style, and the aspect of his approach that I have most tried to emulate, is the ability to be methodologically and substantively eclectic, while maintaining a strict theoretical continuity.

As one outcome of this course, John Arrowood and I succeeded in replicating in the laboratory Schachter, Willerman, Festinger, and Hyman's (1961) elaborate field experiment in which the work of whole production lines in a General Electric factory was reorganized while being experimentally assigned to different emotional inductions (Latané & Arrowood, 1963). It is interesting that these studies, still among the few successful bridgings of laboratory and field, were done in the reverse of the lab first-field second order that the conventional strategy of science would suggest.

## CRIME, COGNITION, AND
## THE AUTONOMIC NERVOUS SYSTEM

Although the data from Stan's studies with Jerry and Ladd were not always completely supportive, on balance they were sufficiently strong to keep alive our faith in the cognitive-physiological view of emotion. If this line of thought were to be useful, however, it should lead to ever more testable implications. Building on research by Minnesota colleague David Lykken (1957), Stan and I set out to study the primary sociopath, that type of unrepentant criminal who, despite superior intelligence, seemed unable to learn from experience that crime does not pay. Characterized by Hervey Cleckley in his *Mask of Sanity* (1941) as suffering an inability to experience true emotions, sociopaths, we decided, must have a physiological deficit. Perhaps by injecting them with adrenalin, we could cure their antisocial tendencies and make them fit for normal life.

This line of thought led to the development of a program of applied research carried out first at the Stillwater, Minnesota Penitentiary and later at the Bordentown, New Jersey Reformatory. After carefully selecting samples of sociopathic and "normal" prisoners equated for intelligence and talking them into volunteering, we gave them small doses of placebo or adrenalin and the opportunity to master a mental maze by making a sequence of 20 choices among a set of four switches. For each choice, one switch was "correct" and moved you on to the next choice point, while one of the remaining three incorrect switches carried the additional penalty of a startling and unpleasant electric shock.

With this elaborate procedure, it was possible to calculate simple indices of how well individuals learned to avoid shock as well as how well they learned the correct responses. As we had hoped, injections of adrenalin led to great improvements in avoidance learning by our sample of sociopaths, while having no positive effect on learning the primary task, or on the learning ability of "normals." Stan and I were exultant. "Social Psychologists Defeat Crime!" ran the headlines in our heads, and we planned elaborate follow-up studies tracing the exact nature of sociopathic adrenal deficiency.

## LEAVING FOR NEW YORK

Sudden change came to Ford Hall in the spring of 1961. In March, Hal Kelley announced that he had accepted a position at UCLA, no great surprise since he and Dorothy had never made any secret of their desire to return to their native California. In April, Stan called me in, swore me to secrecy, and told me that he had been offered a position in a new department of social psychology to be founded at Columbia University. The department would consist of four faculty, Otto Klineberg and Richard Christie, who had been at Columbia for some years, and Bill McGuire and Stan himself, who would come in new. It was to be an interdisciplinary department, with joint appointments from sociology (Herb Hyman), anthropology (Conrad Arensberg), and political science (David Truman). Finally, it was to be a graduate faculty department, offering a Ph.D. but with no undergraduate responsibilities. Stan asked if I would like to go to New York on a research assistantship while I completed my Minnesota dissertation. Without hesitation, I agreed, deciding law school could wait another year.

I rushed to complete my other requirements and to wrap up my life in Minneapolis. My biggest problem was Minnesota's requirement that one should be proficient in two foreign languages, at least to the extent of being able to sightread from a book of one's choosing in each. I was able to dredge up enough of my college French to pass that exam, but was at a loss for ways to pass the second, for I had never taken any other language courses. Russian was popular at that time, but the course was long, and I found the Cyrillic alphabet a formidable obstacle. Fortunately, Harvey Winston discovered an elementary statistics book in Spanish, and with its similarity to French, two weeks' cramming of a grammar review from Barnes and Noble, and the ease of translating simple sentences about "la mediana" and "el deviatione estandardo," I was able to put that hurdle behind me.

That summer I found an apartment in Greenwich Village, about halfway between Stan's new apartment and the one where I had first met him, and settled in for life in the big city.

## FROM STUDENT TO COLLEAGUE

In my first year, I devoted my time primarily to trying to gain access to a prison population and to establishing a small animal colony, both as ways of coping with the problem of finding research subjects in New York City and as ways of following up my own contributions to Stan's research program, which seemed to follow the theme of fear and avoidance.

Stan and I submitted an article on adrenalin and avoidance learning in rats (Latané & Schachter, 1962), based on the animal research I had successfully initiated at the end of my first year at Minnesota. He invited me to be co-principal investigator on an NSF grant to pursue the prison research and to be co-author of a chapter for the *Nebraska Symposium on Motivation* (Schachter & Latané, 1964). Writing for each was conducted concurrently, for Stan's firm belief with respect to funding was "Do the research first, then get the grant."

For my dissertation, started in the summer of 1962, I wanted to come up with a topic of my own, yet one that would build upon our joint line of research. I chose to tackle the problem of the extinction of fear, and whether it needed to be reexperienced in the absence of punishment to be lost, by measuring the residual fear of rats re-exposed to environments in which they had previously been shocked after injections of adrenalin, placebo, or chlorpromazine. The topic was appealing to me because it built on research in basic learning theory but had strong implications for clinical practice. Dick Nisbett helped me run the rats, and the results (Latané, 1963) were sufficiently convincing for me to defend them successfully back in Minneapolis before a puzzled committee, including Ben Willerman who stood in for Stan as my adviser, of faculty unfamiliar with the development of the project and uncertain why a social psychologist should be doing such a thing. I submitted a manuscript based on my dissertation for journal publication but it was rejected pending extensive revision, which I never got around to completing.

Our grant application was successful, and I planned to delay law school and stay at Columbia for an additional two years with the title of Research Associate. One day, Otto Klineberg caught me in the hall and told me he was retiring and that it had been decided I was to be his replacement. Thus, without ever experiencing the trauma of applying for jobs, giving colloquia, or negotiating terms, I had my first faculty appointment.

## FINDING SOMETHING TO TEACH

Most new Ph.D.s can get by for at least their first few years teaching undergraduate surveys and reteaching their own graduate school courses. Unfortunately, our department had no undergraduates to teach (although later I taught a one-semester Columbia College course from Roger Brown's 1965 text), Stan had no intention of abandoning his carefully developed sequence, and my other colleagues left little to be covered. Dick Christie taught personality and social behavior, Stacy Adams provided as much as one could want on organizational behavior, and Bill McGuire was entirely sufficient with respect to attitudes and experimental design. What was left for me?

My solutions built upon the fact that social psychology at Columbia was a separate department, and that our students were, at least in part, cut off from basic courses in psychology. I developed a course on motivation and emotion, drawing heavily on learning theory, which was intended to complement and provide some background for Stan's seminar, and I initiated a course on animal social psychology that reviewed the eccentric history of this field dating from when eight of the 23 chapters in Murchison's (1935) original *Handbook of Social Psychology* concerned animals or plants, to the emergence of sociobiology.

Both courses fulfilled their purpose, but neither proved popular with Columbia's psychology faculty, still heavily Skinnerian and disposed against either the Hull-Spence orientation of the first course, or the mildly ethological leanings of the second.

## GETTING STARTED IN RESEARCH

A second problem was my need, continuously emphasized by Stan, to develop a distinctive scientific identity if I were to stay at Columbia. I did not think it was to come from pursuing the cognitive-physiological model further into motivation and emotion or crime and punishment, for I had an increasingly depressing sense of slogging along through mires of ignorance—my insufficient knowledge of physiology, biochemistry, clinical psychology, and the criminal justice system. A major blow had been the discovery that psychopaths were actually *more*, not less physiologically responsive than normals. Although we managed to come up with a plausible interpretation of the body of findings, it was clear that there were to be few simple answers in this line of research. I began to worry that studying a regulated process like the autonomic nervous system by measuring the effects of injections of adrenalin was like trying to understand a home heating system by measuring temperatures before and after building a fire. As long as the thermostat is working, you are likely to get no effect or an effect opposite to what you might expect. Further, ethical and legal concerns made us increasingly leery about experimenting with bodily functions.

I ended up developing not one, but two independent lines of research:

**Animal Affiliation.**    The first line of investigation started as a class project for my course in animal social psychology (and was further motivated by the fact that our lack of undergraduates to teach also meant we had no subject pool). The idea was to replicate the basic findings of the *Psychology of Affiliation,* to see whether social comparison processes worked with animals. At first, this seemed like a long shot. Munn's (1950) *Handbook of Psychological Research on the Rat* called the standard albino rat an "asocial animal." However, the few studies that formed the basis for this conclusion did not allow social interaction, asking animals instead to press a bar for an absent partner or stare at one another through a wire mesh screen. We decided to treat the *pair* of animals as the unit of analysis, let them run loose in an open field, and simply measure how much time they spent in contact and whether they stayed closer together than one would expect by chance. Rats turned out to be extremely affiliative, chasing and playing with each other and huddling together at great length (Latané, 1969).

With David Glass, a social psychologist at the Russell Sage Foundation whom I had met at a downtown cocktail party and who was interested in learning how to do small animal research, I started a search for the stimulus characteristics that led rats to approach each other, a search that led to the conclusion that it was not physical appearance or smell, but something less tangible, the possibility of mutually rewarding interaction (Latané & Glass, 1968). With Judy Rodin, a Columbia graduate student, I started a systematic parametric exploration of the effects of social deprivation—rats seem to become lonely in the absence of other rats (Latané, Nesbitt, Eckman, & Rodin, 1972).

These lines of work continued for a number of years even after I left for Ohio State, were conducted in collaboration with 23 different graduate students and post-docs, led to 25 publications, and in many ways were my most satisfying scientific experience. Results were strong and consistent, provided a good ratio of surprises to fulfilled expectations, and supported non-obvious interpretations that I, at least, felt were relevant to understanding human social interaction (see Latané & Hothersall, 1972 and Latané & Werner, 1978 for overviews).

In the end, the research program foundered as much from an inhospitable environment as from lack of new directions. The research was not much cited, either by social psychologists, who had become enamoured with attribution, or by comparative psychologists, who had adopted the ethologists' disdain for "artificial" creatures like the albino rat. I was never successful in establishing an animal colony any closer than three miles from the social psychology offices at Ohio State, I found increasing difficulty in locating graduate students interested in pursuing the research, and I developed an allergy to small animals that persists today. I never did find out whether there is social comparison among laboratory rats.

**Bystander Intervention.**    My second new line of research, on bystander intervention in emergencies, was an indirect result, not of the murder of Catherine Genovese, but of the inordinate attention given to it. One evening after another downtown cocktail party, John Darley, son of the former director of the Social Relations Lab at Minnesota and a new assistant professor at New York University, came back with me to my 12th Street apartment for a drink. Our common complaint was the distressing tendency of acquaintances, on finding that we called our-selves social psychologists, to ask why New Yorkers were so apathetic. While commiserating on their ignorance as to the true nature and higher calling of social psychologists, we came up with the insight that perhaps what made the Genovese case so fascinating was itself what made it happen—namely, that not just one or two, but thirty-eight people had watched and done nothing. We decided then and there to set up a laboratory study to see whether the mere knowledge that others were aware of an emergency would reduce one's likelihood of helping.

I lined up a good recorder and recruited the more theatrically inclined of our graduate students to gather one evening the following week at my apartment to commit our sketchily constructed script to tape. After several beers and many false starts, we discovered that Dick Nisbett stood head and shoulders above the rest of us in his ability to sound as if he were in the throes of an epileptic seizure.

The research plan was simple—NYU undergraduates participating in a two-, three-, or six-person discussion of the personal problems of urban university students, conducted over an intercom to reduce embarrassment, heard Dick, initially calmly but with increasing agita-tion and urgency, tell of his propensity, in times of stress like the present, to fall into uncontrollable fits. We timed how long it took individual bystanders to emerge from their separate cubicles and report the emergency. As we had suspected, those who alone heard Dick's distress were quickest to respond (Darley & Latané, 1968).

John and I planned a follow up study, conducted by Lee Ross, another Columbia graduate student, to see if the effect depended on people's being able to assume that someone else had acted or whether actually seeing that nobody else had reacted would even further reduce inter-vention. As Columbia undergraduates, volunteers for a study of urban life, sat in a small room filling out questionnaires, a trickle of smoke started to come through a vent in the wall. When alone, they did the sensible thing of coming out to report this strange phenomenon. When one to four others were in the room, however, each tended to look to another, decide that inaction was the socially appropriate response, and remain seated, coughing and waving away the smoke (Latané & Darley, 1968).

To determine the role of relationships among bystanders, as well as to replicate the effect in yet another setting, Judy Rodin and I arranged for Columbia undergraduates to hear a female experimenter fall off a chair in an adjoining room. Again, participants tested in pairs were slower to respond than single subjects, but the effect was smaller for pairs of friends than for strangers (Latané & Rodin, 1969).

After each experimental session, we made a point of allowing participants to discuss their feelings and reactions fully. Although, with hindsight, many wished that they had responded, most denied that the presence of others slowed them down in the slightest. Almost all reported feeling that the experience had been meaningful and important, and went away feeling that they had learned something about themselves.

John and I labeled our phenomenon "the social inhibition of bystander intervention in emergencies," and postulated three processes to account for it: audience inhibition, in which the knowledge that others can see you may make you slow to respond until you know the appropriate thing to do; pluralistic ignorance, in which, until someone acts, each person sees inactive others and is led to think that inaction is the appropriate response; and the diffusion of responsibility, in which the simple knowledge that others share your responsibility for acting reduces the onus on you.

These experiments immediately attracted a great deal of attention. After being turned down by a nervous NIMH (concerned about the public furor aroused by Stan Milgram's dramatic demonstrations of people's willingness to engage in destructive obedience), John and I were successful in getting grant support from the National Science Foundation (we did follow Stan Schachter's example in completing much of the work before trying to sell its merits). Both of us were in great demand as convention, conference, and colloquium speakers, and our manuscript describing the whole line of research won both the AAAS Socio-Psychological Prize and the Richard M. Elliot Award (Latané & Darley, 1970).

In 1981, Steve Nida and I published a review and metaanalysis of ten years of research on the social inhibition of bystander action. We were able to find over four dozen studies, involving a total of almost 100 experimental comparisons between people exposed to emergencies alone or with other people actually present or believed to be available to respond. In almost all of these comparisons, the same effect held—people were less likely to act if others were believed to be present. The social inhibition of bystander intervention is perhaps the most well-established empirical phenomenon in social psychology, and since it was unexpected and indeed somewhat counterintuitive (we usually expect people to be on their best behavior in public), it can be considered a true "discovery" (Latané & Nida, 1981).

Research on bystander intervention has been the major impetus for my development of social impact theory (Latané, 1981), a general mathematical model of social force fields and how they channel and direct the ways in which people influence each other. According to social impact theory, when individuals are the target of social forces (such as those produced by persuasive arguments, critical evaluation, etc.) from others, the resultant impact will be a multiplicative function of the strength, immediacy, and number of persons contributing to the impact. When individuals stand together with others, on the other hand, external influences will be diffused and divided according to the strength, immediacy, and number of those who share the impact.

Social impact theory bears a strong and non-accidental resemblance to the Lewinian models we used to diagram on the blackboard in Stan's seminar, and like the mathematical model underlying his predictions in his study of deviation, communication, and rejection, it allows precise predictions of social relationships.

Social impact theory, in turn, has led to new arenas of research: the role of audience size and status and the number of co-performers on evaluation apprehension and stage fright (Latané & Harkins, 1976; Jackson & Latané, 1981), the relative importance of minority and majority influence (Latané & Wolf, 1981), the relationship between population and political participation (Harkins & Latané, 1986), and social loafing, or the tendency of people to exert less effort when they are working with others than when they work alone (Latané, Williams, & Harkins, 1979). The last body of work won my second AAAS Prize in 1980.

Stan always told me he thought my work on social attraction in animals would have more impact than the research on bystander intervention, which he saw as capitalizing on a transitory quirk of public attention. This has to be one of his few great misreadings of the interest value of research, for next to the work of Festinger and Schachter, bystander intervention has been among the most heavily replicated and cited research in both textbooks and the technical literature, while the small animal research has disappeared with hardly a trace.


## NEW YORK WINTERS, AMAGANSETT SUMMERS

The Social Psychology Department at Columbia, located on the third floor of the Mathematics Building across campus from the Psychology

Department, consisted of faculty and student offices surrounding an inner core of laboratory rooms with one-way windows and sound systems. Among the many vivid memories of seven years are:

- The contrasting but lofty visions of the place and function of social psychology described by Otto Klineberg and Bill McGuire at a symposium celebrating the opening of the new department (Klineberg & Christie, 1965).
- Paul Lazarsfeld at the same event distinguishing between research tactics (the design of particular studies), and research strategy (the development of a coherent program of studies), and praising Stan's special mastery of the latter.
- Grabbing a quick supper with Stan at Chez Brigitte, a French lunch counter, after an expedition to Lawner's auction galleries where we competed to see which of us could furnish his Greenwich Village apartment more cheaply.
- Graduate student groupings: the City slickers (mostly the pre-'61 students) vs. the "hick clique" of new students from midwestern state universities.
- A Christmas banquet in the main lab room complete with roast suckling pig; spring lawn parties at Stacy and Tony Adams'.
- Billiards after lunch at the Faculty Club.
- Frequent Friday afternoon colloquia exploiting the steady stream of psychologists passing through New York.
- Going together with Stan to rent a summer house in Amagansett, a small oceanside town on eastern Long Island, so we could finish off a chapter (I continued to spend summers there throughout my years at Columbia).
- Playing backgammon on a beach blanket between bouts of rewriting.
- Spending a half-hour perfecting the pace and cadence of a single sentence, handwritten in #2 pencil on a yellow legal pad.
- Stan cadging just one more cigarette—promising to give back a whole pack.
- His sheer delight over winning a set at the Amagansett town courts and his pride in his original two-seat classic Thunderbird.
- Watching Stan, convinced there was a link, ask everyone he met about their ordinal position and their marital history.
- Stan, always fascinated by my father's background on Wall Street, wanting to know how he went about selecting stocks.
- After learning about pheochromocytoma, a form of adrenal tumor, from my college classmate Al Davidson, going with Stan to interview two of his patients about their emotional outbursts.
- Stan, at 5'9", walking down the cell block at Riker's Island where

we had hoped to be able to continue our research on sociopathic criminals, flanked by Stu Valins and me, both at better than 6'3".

- His gropings toward technological solutions: seat cushion thermisters (for measuring sexual arousal), finger plethysmographs, denicotinized cigarettes, doctored clocks.
- Having to shave my moustache to look more like an undergraduate as I played the deviate in a segment of the APA–NSF film "The Social Animal" based on Stan's original dissertation study.
- Stan's strong advice to avoid romantic entanglements with graduate students, and his friendly approval of my marriage to the department administrative assistant.
- His disinterest in organizations like APA and SESP, but his willingness to put in long hours on NIMH and SSRC committees.
- Carefully arranging to meet Stan at the corner bar of the Biltmore, knowing he wouldn't come to the EPA meetings otherwise.
- Organizing my first summer conference, a meeting of former Minnesota graduate students and others interested in social comparison processes held at a tiny cottage in the Springs, near Amagansett.
- On a visit back to Chapel Hill, selling John Thibaut, founding editor of *JESP*, on the desirability of publishing a special social comparison issue (Latané, 1966). I now regard this experiment in new forms of publication as a failure, since the issue received neither the wide distribution and easy referencing of a journal nor the publicity and advertising of a book.
- Maintaining lines of contact through sympathetic graduate students with the undergraduate occupiers of our offices during the 1968 SDS sit-ins.

## LEAVING: THE END OF A DECADE

I had never worried too much about my career, because I always felt I had the respect and support of Stan, Bill, and Dick and had been a good colleague and teacher as well as developing something of a national reputation for the bystander intervention research. I felt I would be promoted in due course and that, in any event, my future would be determined by those who knew me best. As it happened, however, the situation changed quickly. In short order, Bill McGuire left to go to UCSD, Stacy Adams left for UNC, and Columbia's administration decided to merge social psychology back into the Department of Psychology.

In the spring of 1968, a Psychology Department committee decided that my research, although promising, was not yet sufficient for tenure.

Stan worked hard to have my case reconsidered, and succeeded in arranging for my promotion to Associate Professor, with tenure likely to follow soon. However, I felt that as long as I would have to adapt to a new department and be evaluated by new standards and criteria anyway, it might as well be in a new university. For the first time I started responding seriously to the job feelers I had been getting for the last few years. I visited Bryn Mawr, Princeton, and Rutgers, but did not resonate particularly to any of them. Finally, Jane and I went to visit Ohio State, found a highly congenial group (Tim and Sherry Brock, Tom and Diana Ostrom, Tony and Jean Greenwald, all within a few years of us in age), no undergraduate teaching requirement, and a large and underutilized subject pool.

When I told Stan about my decision to move, he seemed quite put out and strongly urged me to stick it out at Columbia for another year. My failure, for once, to follow his advice brought to an end the most formative decade of my life.

## MY LEGACY FROM STAN

Stan asked a lot from me and the others who worked with him, but he gave back much more. Although I accepted them all eagerly, I now find some of his gifts more valuable than others.

I am no longer as certain as I used to be that Stan's highly individual style of research is the best model for the rest of us to follow. When I knew him (and I suspect still), Stan was an itinerant scholar, who carried most of what he needed in his head and in his green book bag, and who could pick up everything else through intelligence and charm. He did not believe in elaborate laboratories, institutionalized research programs, or projects that transcended the scale of the individual scientist working with a small group of students. I, on the other hand, have gravitated to organizational matters and now direct an interdisciplinary research institute that tries to provide large-scale research resources of the sort no individual scientist or project could afford.

I am no longer as convinced as I once was that Stan had the knack for always coming up with the "right" interpretation, or that his willingness to push the data didn't sometimes lead him out on thin ice. I am no longer even convinced that his cognitive-physiological theory, based on what can now be seen as a dated and overly simplistic conception of human physiology, is the best account of emotion.

Although Stan's research strategy of always preferring leap to plod was personally appropriate and productive, I now fear that others, drawn by his charisma, may have led the field into a hit and run style of research that has impeded the cumulation of knowledge. As each of us aspires to imitate the brilliance with which Stan's theoretical forays established solid empirical outposts, waiting for others to secure the perimeter, assure the lines of communication and supply, pacify the civilian population, and set up daily camp routines, we are left with a multiplicity of intriguing leads but lack a data base of parametric, descriptive, phenomenon-oriented, or replicative research.

What, then, did I gain from my ten years with Stanley Schachter?

He helped me grow up.

He kept me out of law school.

I still think "Deviation, rejection, and communication" is one of the most important single pieces of research in social science. It helped me learn how to accommodate to being different, and I believe it still has the potential to help us all learn how to allow others to be different as well.

I have tried to imitate Stan's approach to interacting with students, his willingness to provide direct help and guidance while encouraging independence.

Most of all, I have tried to follow his eclectic style, his desire to use multiple methods in following singular ideas, his sense of science as a personal quest that leads into an unknown in which one ignores arbitrary boundaries and reorganizes and reinterprets conventional truths.

I like to hope that my own research has had something of the same quality: that one can detect, if dimly, a consistent line tracing the development of a theoretical idea from "diffusion of responsibility," through its elaborations in research on stage fright, majority and minority influence, to its formalization in social impact theory and its application with regard to social loafing and political participation.

I have always viewed my relationship with Stan as among the most important in my life. My belief in the value of his gifts to me is stronger today than ever before.

Thank you, Stan. You gave me back a whole carton.

## REFERENCES

Brown, R. (1965). *Social psychology*. New York: Free Press.

Cleckley, H. (1941). *The mask of sanity*. St. Louis: Mosby.

Cohen, A.R., Brehm, J.W., & Latané, B. (1959). Choice of strategy and voluntary exposure to information under public and private conditions. *Journal of Personality, 27*, 63–73.

Cohen, A.R. & Latané, B. (1962). An experiment on choice in commitment to counter-attitudinal behavior. In J.W. Brehm & A.R. Cohen, *Explorations in cognitive dissonance.* New York: Wiley, 88–91.

Darley, J.M. & Latané, B. (1968). Bystander intervention in emergencies: Diffusion of responsibility. *Journal of Personality and Social Psychology, 8,* 377–383.

Festinger, L. (1950). Informal social communication. *Psychological Review, 57,* 271–282.

Festinger, L., Schachter, S., & Back, K. (1950) *Social pressures in informal groups.* New York: Harper.

Harkins, S. & Latané, B. (1986). Population and political participation.

Heider, F. (1958). *The psychology of interpersonal relations.* New York: Wiley.

Jackson, J. & Latané, B. (1981). All alone in front of all those people: Stage fright as a function of number and type of coperformers and audience. *Journal of Personality and Social Psychology, 40,* 73–85.

Klineberg, O. & Christie, R. (Eds.). (1965). *Perspectives in social psychology.* New York: Holt, Rinehart and Winston.

Latané, B. (1963). *Autonomic arousal and the extinction of fear.* Unpublished doctoral dissertation, University of Minnesota.

Latané, B. (Ed.) (1966). Studies in social comparison. Special supplement to *Journal of Experimental Social Psychology,* 1966.

Latané, B. (1969). Gregariousness and fear in laboratory rats. *Journal of Experimental Social Psychology, 5,* 61–69.

Latané, B. (1981). The psychology of social impact. *American Psychologist, 36,* 343–352.

Latané, B. & Arrowood, J. (1963). Emotional arousal and task performance. *Journal of Applied Psychology, 47,* 324–327.

Latané, B. & Darley, J.M. (1968). Group inhibition of bystander intervention. *Journal of Personality and Social Psychology, 10,* 215–221.

Latané, B. & Darley, J.M. (1970). *The unresponsive bystander: Why doesn't he help?* Appleton-Century-Crofts.

Latané, B. & Glass, D. (1968). Social and nonsocial attraction in rats. *Journal of Personality and Social Psychology, 9,* 142–146.

Latané, B. & Harkins, S. (1976). Cross-modality matches suggest anticipated stage fright a multiplicative power function of audience size and status. *Perception and Psychophysics, 20,* 482–488.

Latané, B. & Hothersall, D. (1972). Social attraction in animals. In Dodson, P.C. (Ed.), *New horizons in psychology II.* Penguin Books.

Latané, B. Nesbitt, P., Eckman, J., & Rodin, J. (1972). Long- and short-term social deprivation and sociability in rats. *Journal of Comparative and Physiological Psychology, 81,* 69–75.

Latané, B. & Nida, S. (1981). Ten years of research on group size and helping. *Psychological Bulletin, 89,* 308–324.

Latané, B. & Rodin, J. (1969). A lady in distress: Inhibiting effects of friends and strangers on bystander intervention. *Journal of Experimental Social Psychology, 5,* 189–202.

Latané, B. & Schachter, S. (1962). Adrenalin and avoidance learning. *Journal of Comparative and Physiological Psychology, 55,* 369–372.

Latané, B. & Werner, C. (1978). The regulation of social contact in laboratory rats: Time, not distance. *Journal of Personality and Social Psychology, 36,* 1128–1137.

Latané, B., Williams, K., & Harkins, S. (1979). Many hands make light the work: Causes and consequences of social loafing. *Journal of Personality and Social Psychology, 37,* 822–832.

Latané, B. & Wolf, S. (1981). The social impact of majorities and minorities. *Psychological Review, 88,* 438–453.

Lykken, D.T. (1957). A study of anxiety in the sociopathic personality. *Journal of Abnormal and Social Psychology, 55,* 6–10.

Marañon, G. (1924). Contribution à l'étude de l'action émotive de l'adrénaline. *Revue francaise d'Endocrinologie, 2,* 301–325.

Munn, N.L. (1950). *Handbook of psychological research on the rat.* Boston: Houghton.

Murchison, C. (1935). *A handbook of social psychology.* Worcester, MA: Clark University Press.

Riesman, D. (1950). *The lonely crowd: A study of the changing American character.* New Haven: Yale.

Schachter, S. (1951). Deviation, rejection, and communication. *Journal of Abnormal and Social Psychology, 46,* 190–207.

Schachter, S. (1959). *The psychology of affiliation.* Stanford: Stanford University Press.

Schachter, S. & Latané, B. (1964). Crime, cognition, and the autonomic nervous system. *Nebraska Symposium on Motivation, 12,* 221–273. Lincoln: University of Nebraska Press.

Schachter, S. & Singer, J. (1962). Cognitive, social and physiological determinants of emotional state. *Psychological Review, 69,* 379–399.

Schachter, S. & Wheeler, L. (1962). Epinephrine, chlorpromazine and amusement. *Journal of Abnormal and Social Psychology, 45,* 121–128.

Schachter, S., Willerman, B., Festinger, L., & Hyman, R. (1961). Emotional disruption and industrial productivity. *Journal of Applied Psychology, 45,* 201–213.

# Lay Personality Theory: Its Nature, Origin, and Utility

Richard E. Nisbett
*University of Michigan*

I never had a course in social psychology as an undergraduate. I had taken many personality and clinical courses and many experimental courses and had a vague idea that social psychology would allow me to study the individual difference content of personality and clinical psychology using the systematic techniques of experimental psychology. Until the time I made the decision to go to Columbia, I had never heard of Stanley Schachter. Thus I could not know that although I was very wrong about the nature of social psychology I had in fact chosen the best possible place to study the content of personality and clinical psychology using the systematic techniques of experimental psychology. Those were the days when Stan was studying birth order, sociopathy, criminality, and obesity—and setting standards for originality and rigor in studying such topics that remain unsurpassed today.

Meeting Stan and his ideas was the most wrenching intellectual experience of my life. I had thoroughly conventional ideas about the nature of individual differences and about the nature of evidence in psychology. I need not identify these ideas in any detail at this point, because they remain standard views in personality and clinical psychology. I simply note that I thought that individual differences were very marked and believed they were essentially those identified by traditional personality theorists and by clinical psychologists of the dynamic persuasion.

I couldn't tell at first exactly what Stan did believe, but two remarkable things were clear from the outset. First, he didn't have much faith in any of the standard notions about individual differences, and second, he was just extraordinarily willing to believe his own data about some matter—even data that *I* had collected—in preference to the received opinion distilled from centuries of Western intellectual activity. Both of these tendencies struck me as outrageous, vulgar even. One thing kept me strung along, however; this was the fact that Stan had more common sense than anybody I had ever met. I had to assume that there just might be a connection between that fact and his iconoclastic stance toward serious psychological matters.

My graduate career centered on a paradox. I worked on individual differences while learning to disbelieve in the reality, or at least the general utility, of traditional individual difference constructs. This process of construction and deconstruction continues today, and this chapter is a progress report on my view of these matters as I see them now.

I will deal with four questions concerning what may be called "lay" personality theory, which is the personality theory I came to Columbia with and that is the personality theory held by most Western psychologists, whether lay or professional. (1) What is lay personality theory? What are its assumptions about the coordinates along which individual differences lie and the power of those differences in predicting behavior? (2) What is the utility of lay personality theory? To what degree is the layperson helped or hurt by virtue of using lay personality theory as a guide to everyday life? (3) What is the origin of lay personality theory? What observations in everyday life give rise to, and support belief in, the theory? (4) In what ways does lay personality theory differ from a scientifically-correct theory of individual differences? What theory would be superior to lay theory—and what are the prospects that the layperson could be persuaded to adopt it?

## THE TRADITIONAL SCIENTIFIC THEORY OF PERSONALITY

### Qualitative Aspects

The traditional, personologist's view of personality is that people differ from one another along certain broad dimensions of social behavior. At the top level of generality, these dimensions are often identified as a broad factor corresponding to extraversion–introversion, another corresponding to agreeableness–disagreeableness, and another to emotional stability–instability (e.g., Eysenck, 1967; Norman, 1963). Other broad factors are sometimes also identified, and these are usually drawn from a list of the following: dominance–submissiveness, conscientiousness–unconscientiousness, cultured–boorish (e.g., Digman & Inouye, 1986; Norman, 1963). At a lower level of generality than the broad factors are found the traditional traits per se. Under the broad rubric of extraversion (vs. introversion) would be found traits of talkativeness (vs. silence), sociability (vs. reclusiveness), adventurousness (vs. cautiousness), and frankness (vs. secretiveness) (Norman, 1963). Under the broad rubric of agreeableness would be found such traits as goodnatured (vs. irritable), cooperative (vs. negativistic) and so on.

The personologist's view of personality is based in part on factor analyses of inventories of descriptive statements. Self-reports and peer reports about behavior tend to be correlated along lines that correspond to the trait labels. In addition, there are innumerable studies that show that when people are given scores on trait scales, these scores predict their actual behavior in both everyday life and laboratory settings.

### Quantitative Aspects

What about the *degree* of predictability attainable from trait scores? How well can one predict behavior along trait lines from knowledge of one other trait-related behavior, or from knowledge of a host of trait-related behaviors?

The facts concerning these matters are rather clear, although their interpretation has been a matter of bitter dispute until recently. As Walter Mischel and Gordon Peterson pointed out in independent reviews in 1968, the predictability of individual behaviors in particular situations is low. Prediction from knowledge of trait scores derived from personality tests is typically in the range .20–.30. Prediction from another individual behavior is typically in the range .10–.15. (For more recent reviews, see Mischel & Peake, 1982; Nisbett, 1980.)

The initial reaction of personologists to assertions about low predictability was to claim that the evidence was badly flawed—that the wrong behaviors or the wrong populations had been studied (e. g., Block, 1977; Olweus, 1977). More recent reactions from personologists have tended to grant the evidence base but to emphasize the predictability that is obtainable over the long haul (Epstein, 1979; 1983). Thus, although the correlation between one behavior and another may be low, the correlation between *many* behaviors and *many* others can be high. Indeed, if a sufficiently large number of behaviors is correlated with a sufficiently large number of other behaviors, the correlation, as we know from the Spearman–Brown formula, approaches unity.

Exactly what these facts mean from the standpoint of the utility of trait constructs for prediction by the scientist must wait until we address the question of their utility for the layperson. First, we will examine the qualitative and quantitative aspects of the lay personality theory.

## LAY PERSONALITY THEORY

### Qualitative Aspects

One of the lines of evidence that personologists draw on to support their view of personality is its congruence with the layperson's view. For example, people's judgments of the similarity of behaviors map quite well onto the patterns of correlation in self-reports or peer reports about these same behaviors. This fact is often used as evidence that the personologist's view is correct: Lay judgments about the similarity of behaviors are assumed to reflect, at least in part, the covariations actually observed by laypeople among behaviors.

Without agreeing that the convergence of similarity judgments with personologists' categories must be taken as strong evidence of the validity of those categories, one can accept the convergence as evidence of the correspondence between lay and professional theorists. The trait categories of the layperson and those of the professional personologist, are indeed, essentially the same. There is very good agreement between the lay and the professional personologist with regard to the qualitative aspects of individual differences.

As professional personologists often note, in support of their view of the importance of trait constructs, trait terms are extremely prevalent in the language. It was found by Allport and Odbert (1936) that there were 4,505 trait terms in *Webster's Unabridged New International Dictionary*. Taxonomic examination of these terms is often presumed by personologists to be a source of data about actual bases of individual differences. It has been noted repeatedly that factor analyses of these terms bear a close resemblance to factor analyses of reports about behavior (Eysenck, 1967; Norman, 1963). Again, without accepting these arguments, one may certainly take the predominance of trait terms as evidence that the layperson does indeed make heavy use of essentially the same constructs that the personologist does.

Another indication of the psychic reality (again, as opposed to any necessary behavioral reality) of trait constructs is that, when people are asked to rate various behaviors with respect to the degree to which they are representative of one or another of the standard trait terms, their ratings show a degree of agreement that is not far different from the degree of agreement that they show for ratings of the representativeness of various physical objects for standard object category terms (Buss & Craik, 1983; Cantor & Mischel, 1979). This means that the prototypicality structure of trait categories is about as well agreed upon by people as the prototypicality structure of object categories.

Still another indication that lay personology is similar to its professional counterpart is that people rely heavily on trait terms when asked to describe other people. Livesley and Bromley (1973) have shown that the use of trait terms increases steadily over the course of development for children in our culture, eventually becoming the most frequent type of descriptor in free-response characterizations of other people.

It is interesting to compare the frequency with which people use trait constructs to explain behavior with the frequency with which they call on aspects of the situation or overall social context. Miller (1984) asked Americans (and also Indians) to "describe something a person you know well did recently that you considered a wrong thing to have done" and also to "describe something a person you know well did recently that you considered good for someone else." Immediately after narrating each behavior, the subject was asked to explain why the behavior occurred. Half of the explanations offered by the American subjects for deviant behaviors invoked general dispositions to explain the behavior, which was three times the rate of offering situational–context explanations. One third of the explanations offered for prosocial behaviors invoked general dispositions, and this was more than 50% higher than the rate for context explanations. The layperson (at least in Western societies—Miller found different patterns for Indians that will be discussed later) thus would appear to favor personological explanations over social psychological ones.

But perhaps the most convincing line of work showing the layperson's reliance on dispositional constructs of a trait type comes from a series of investigations by Winter and Uleman (1984; Winter, Uleman, & Cunniff, 1985). Early students of impression formation believed that trait interpretations are made at the moment of observation of behavior and are actually included in the coding of the behavior. Winter and Uleman (1984) provided an elegant test of that hypothesis:

> If people make trait inferences when they observe behavior and encode the information, those inferred traits should be stored in memory along with the information on which they are based. Therefore, as part of the encoding context of the behavioral information, the attributed trait itself should serve as a self-generated covert input cue and thus as an effective retrieval cue for the behavioral information. It should be possible, then, to show that people make trait inferences at encoding by demonstrating the retrieval effectiveness for the behavioral information of subjects' most likely trait inference. For instance, if reading "The librarian carries the old woman's groceries across the street," subjects infer that the librarian is helpful, then the word *helpful* ought to be a good retrieval cue for the sentence. (p.239)

Winter and Uleman presented their subjects with a number of sentences by flashing them on a screen. After the slide presentation, subjects were presented with a "recall sheet" on which they were to write down as many of the sentences they had just seen as possible. A recall cue was provided for most sentences. In some cases this was the obvious dispositional cue, such as the word "helpful" for the sentence quoted earlier about the librarian who helped the old woman with her groceries. Sometimes this was a word that was a close semantic associate of the noun phrase of the sentence, for example, "books," and sometimes it was a close semantic associate of the predicate phrase of the sentence.

The investigators found that sentences were much more often recalled when cued by the dispositional word than when uncued. In fact, dispositional cueing was more effective than semantic cueing.

Interestingly, subjects did not report having consciously thought of the dispositional concepts at the time of reading the sentence, and in fact did not regard it as plausible that thoughts about dispositions were helpful in recalling sentences. The evidence thus suggests that people automatically and unconsciously provide a dispositional interpretation to behavioral information. And so far, at least, the dispositions they favor would appear suspiciously similar to the trait constructs fabled in song, story and personology texts. The contours of lay personality theory are far from clear at this point, but it does seem to be the case that laypeople often use constructs that are very similar to the personologist's collection of traits.

### Quantitative Aspects

Given that lay theory appears qualitatively similar to professional theory, what quantitative assumptions do laypeople make? How predictable do they think behavior is along trait lines? Ideally, one would simply ask people how consistent they expect behavior to be, using some metric that is both comprehensible to them and that maps onto the metric that psychologists use to measure consistency, namely the correlation coefficient.

Kunda and Nisbett (1986) did just that. They took advantage of the fact that a tau coefficient is a function of the probability of reversal of a pair ordering. Simple probability judgments about the likelihood that two individuals will show the same rank ordering across occasions therefore provide an estimate of a tau coefficient that can in turn be converted into a standard Pearson r.

Kunda and Nisbett asked subjects for their beliefs about the likelihood that a pair of people would maintain their relative ordering either over two situations or over two sets of 20 situations. Subjects were asked questions like this one:

Suppose you observed Jane and Jill in a particular situation and found that Jane was more honest than Jill. What do you suppose is the probability that in the next situation in which you observe them you would also find Jane to be more honest than Jill?

Subjects answered this question on a scale running from 50% to 100%. Other subjects were asked about the probability that a person observed in 20 situations and found to be more honest on average than another person would again be found to be more honest on average over the next 20 situations. Subjects were also asked for their estimates of the consistency of friendliness.

In addition to these questions about social traits, subjects were also asked comparable questions about abilities. They were asked how likely it was that a child who got a higher grade on a spelling test than another child would also do so on another test (or the comparable version for 20 tests) and they were asked how likely it was that a basketball player who made more points in a game than another player would also do so in another game (or the comparable version for 20 games).

Kunda and Nisbett anticipated that, for the latter questions having to do with abilities, subjects would be relatively accurate in their perception of the degree of consistency. Accomplishments in spelling and basketball, as in most ability domains, lend themselves to accurate coding and consequently to accurate perception of covariation. Such events typically can be coded on a uniform scale and often can be given numbers on that scale. In contrast, the investigators reasoned that the relatively low codability of social behaviors allows people to be mistaken about their consistency. Joe's friendliness in class cannot be coded on the same dimensions as his friendliness at a party, let alone coded on the same dimensions as Jane's friendliness at a party. Even the unit to use for social dimensions is problematic. What is the appropriate unit for friendliness? Smiles per minute? Good vibrations per encounter?

The lack of rigorous unitizability and unambiguous codability for social behaviors should make it relatively difficult to perceive the degree of consistency that exists for them and could serve to welcome on board the kinds of perceptual and cognitive biases that are discussed in a later section of this chapter.

For ease of comparison with the actual correlation data that we have been discussing, subjects' probability estimates were converted into $r$s by Kendall's tau procedure. Fig. 6.1 shows the degree of consistency estimated by subjects for both social traits and abilities. Also plotted are the actual correlations (derived from the literature in the case of the social traits and from studies by Kunda and Nisbett in the case of abilities). Subjects' estimates of the consistency of both honesty and friendliness were very similar, at each level of aggregation, and so were the actual correlations. Thus estimates of honesty and friendliness were combined and so were the actual data for the two traits. The same held for estimates and for actual correlations for the two abilities, so these were also combined.

The most dramatic aspect of Fig. 6.1 is the astonishing overestimation of the degree of consistency to be expected at the level of individual social behaviors. Subjects estimated the consistency from one situation to another to be only trivially less than the consistency from 20 situations to another 20 situations! It is worth spelling out the magnitude of subjects' incoherence in terms of the Spearman–Brown requirement that $r$ is a function of the $N$ of observations of pair orderings. Given that subjects estimate the item to item correlation to be .79, they should be estimating the total to total correlation to be .99. Given, on the other hand, that subjects estimate the total to total correlation to be .82, they should estimate the item to item correlation to be .23.

So far, the data might simply reflect the subjects' inability to work sensibly with the metric employed. The data for abilities indicate that this is not the case, however. Subjects were exactly correct, on the average, in their estimate of the degree of consistency of abilities across occasions. And, although they underestimated the degree of consis-

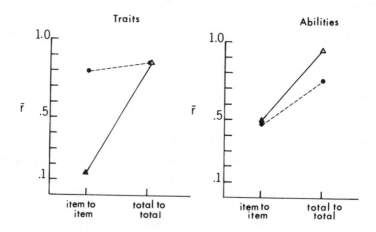

FIGURE 6.1.    Estimated and actual correlation between individual behaviors (item to item) and aggregated behaviors (total to total), for traits and for abilities. (From Kunda & Nisbett, 1986)

tency from 20 occasions to another 20, they recognized that the latter correlation was substantially higher than the former (p < .01). The data thus show that laypeople can be reasonably accurate about covariation between behaviors in the domain of abilities and also that they recognize the force of the aggregation principle for abilities, that is, that correlations based on a large N of observations are higher than correlations based on a small N. Matters seem utterly different for personality traits. Subjects dramatically overestimated the predictability of individual behaviors and they showed no recognition that predictability is dependent on N. The latter point is particularly important because it suggests that laypeople will make confident predictions on a small evidence base and will be unmotivated to increase their evidence base before making predictions.

We have emphasized the similarity of lay and professional views of qualitative aspects of traits. How do professional judgments of the quantitative aspects look? We gave the laboratory version of the experiment to a number of professional psychologists attending a convention symposium on statistical aspects of human judgment. Some of these would be describable as personologists, but most were social psychologists and experimentalists. Our professional sample provided data that were essentially the same as those in Fig. 6.1 — with one exception. The professional psychologists as a group were aware that traits are not very good predictors of behavior. (Perhaps we should say they were *reminded* of that fact. Walter Mischel was seated prominently in the front of the room as they filled out their questionnaires!) The psychologists pulled their *entire curve* down for estimates of social trait consistency, leaving it parallel with that for the lay subjects. They still seriously overestimated the degree of consistency at the level of the situation, whereas, unlike the lay subjects, they also *under* estimated the degree of consistency at the total to total level. This made them no less wrong empirically than lay subjects and even more incoherent!

## THE UTILITY OF LAY PERSONALITY THEORY

Does it matter that people's quantitative judgments of the predictability of behavior are so far off the mark? Do they really make predictions in everyday life as if they believed that behavior is extremely consistent from one situation to another? The next section examines the possibility that people's predictions about behavior are much more sensitive to situational context than the data of Kunda and Nisbett would imply. It then continues to explore in subsequent sections the more general question as to whether people's erroneous beliefs about the predictability of behavior are customarily reflected in their predictions about actual individual behaviors.

## When Trait Ascriptions
## Meet Situational Information

The data just presented could be providing an overestimation of the layperson's beliefs in the power of traits. It is possible that the methodology employed by Kunda and Nisbett encourages people to misspeak, to say that the predictability of behavior from knowledge of one other behavior is higher than they really believe it to be. If people were to be confronted with the actual behavior of a real person in one concrete situation and then asked to predict the person's behavior in another concrete situation, we might find that people gave more consideration to situational factors and less to presumed personality factors.

But we have a great deal of evidence, going back a good many years, suggesting that, on the contrary, people are quite insensitive to situational factors. Indeed, this insensitivity, together with the exaggeration of dispositional factors, is what Ross (1977) labeled the "fundamental attribution error." It is important to review this literature now, including some recent and unpublished data, because it provides us with our largest body of evidence concerning the utility of the trait construct. To the extent that people slight situational information in preference to presumed dispositions when they make predictions about other people's behavior, the utility of lay personality theory is called into question.

The classic study demonstrating that lay perceivers fail to be appropriately sensitive to situational constraints is one by Jones and Harris (1967). They asked their college student subjects to read essays or listen to speeches presumably written by fellow students. Subjects were told that the communicator had been assigned one side of the issue. Despite the fact that subjects clearly perceived the heavy constraints on the communicator in the no choice conditions, their estimates of the true opinions of the communicator were markedly affected by the particular position the communicator had espoused. The study indicates that observers are willing to take behavior more or less at "face value," as reflecting a stable disposition—in this case—an attitudinal disposition, even when it is made clear that the actor's behavior is under severe external constraints.

A study by Taylor and Crocker (1986) provides a nice parallel to the Jones and Harris demonstration for the case of personality traits. To introduce this study, I refer to a result from the trait consistency literature that I did not focus on in my brief review of the topic. This result is that the same data sets that show low consistency *across* behavior types and situational contexts sometimes show rather high stability *within* behavioral types and situational contexts. The average correlation between any two measures of honesty of school children studied by Hartshorne and May (1928) was .23. (Because some of the measures were somewhat aggregated, the individual behavior correlations would have been lower than that.) Yet the reliability of some tests was quite high. For example, the correlation between copying from an answer key on a general information test in March correlated .79 with copying from an answer key on a parallel information test in October. Buss and Craik (1984) present systematic evidence suggesting that within-situation stabilities can often be fairly high even when cross-situational consistency is very low.

Now, it might be argued that observers are sensitive to situational context, and that they simply misspeak themselves when they say that John is talkative, or Jane is honest. What they may really mean is that John is talkative in social contexts, or professional contexts, or just at the lunch table. By this account, people simply neglect to append to every trait utterance a list of the conditions that elicit the disposition in question. It should also be noted that their perception of the degree of consistency might not be all that wrong by this account. If people tacitly mean, by situation-to-situation consistency, consistency within a given context, then their beliefs might be much more nearly correct than, for instance, Kunda and Nisbett (1986) gave them credit for.

As a matter of fact, however, in a secondary study Kunda and Nisbett asked one group of subjects to give their estimates of consistency for behavior of the same kind, in the same context, that is, estimates of stability. They asked another group of subjects to give their estimates of consistency for trait-related behavior of different types, in different contexts, that is, estimates of consistency. Subjects estimated that both stability and consistency were very high, and only very slightly different. Thus, using their methodology, there is no indication that subjects care a great deal about the distinction between stability (that is often high), and consistency (that is almost uniformly low).

Taylor and Crocker (1986) performed an even more direct test of the hypothesis that people are insensitive to situational context when making predictions about consistency. They described targets' behavior along lines of either extraversion or independence in three different situations. For some of the subjects, the behavioral information was drawn from just one setting, namely an academic setting or a social setting. For other subjects, the behavioral information was drawn from both settings, either two academic and one social or two social and one academic. For example, introverted behaviors in academic settings included "Judy was quiet with the professor" or "reserved in class."

Subjects were then asked to predict the target's behavior in an academic setting, a social setting, and an ambiguous setting.

If subjects' dispositional inferences are conditioned at all on setting, then they ought to be more confident that targets would behave in a trait-consistent way in the setting for which they have observations. Thus if the target behaved in an extraverted way in three academic settings, then the subject ought to be more confident that extraverted behavior will occur in an academic setting than in a social setting. In addition, the trait-consistent inferences should be stronger for the ambiguous setting when the behavioral information spanned settings than when it was confined to a single setting. Finally, it would be expected that the overall level of dispositional inferences, across all three settings, should be higher when the behavioral information spanned both academic and social settings than when it spanned only one.

These predictions were not borne out. Subjects were just as likely to say that the target would behave in an extraverted way in academic settings when all three information items concerned extraverted behavior in social settings as when all three items concerned extraverted behavior in academic settings. Similarly, subjects were no more likely to predict trait-consistent behavior in ambiguous settings when observations had been across settings than when they had all been within a setting.

Taylor and Crocker thus found their subjects to be as willing to generalize from one context to another as to generalize within context. This indicates that trait judgments may not reflect a subtle recognition of the situational specificity that can sometimes characterize dispositions.

A study by Nisbett, Caputo, Legant, and Marecek (1973) showed that even such an obvious situational factor as money can be slighted in explanation and prediction if there is a possibility of explaining behavior in dispositional terms.

The investigators allowed observer subjects to watch actor subjects participate in what all were told was a study on decision making. Subjects were all female undergraduates. The experimenter announced, "Before we begin the study, I happen to have sort of a real decision for you to make." He explained that the campus "Human Development Institute" would be sponsoring a weekend for the corporate board and some of their prospective financial backers. The spouses of these people would need entertainment and campus tours for the weekend. If the subject could see her way clear to volunteering, she would be paid by the hour. Some subjects were offered $.50 per hour and some were offered $1.50. (Apply a multiplier of approximately 3 to make the values comprehensible in 1987 terms.) Only 1/5 of the low payment actors volunteered, while 2/3 of the high-payment actors volunteered. Volunteering was thus largely due to the sheer amount of money offered.

Both actors and observers were asked about their perceptions of the actor's reasons for volunteering or not volunteering. The questions included an item designed to tap the extent to which the actor's behavior was considered an expression of a general disposition to volunteer or not volunteer for worthy activities: "How likely do you think it is that you (or the subject) would also volunteer to canvass for the United Fund?" Observers said that volunteering actors would be substantially more likely to volunteer to canvass for the United Fund than nonvolunteering actors, and did so to approximately the same extent regardless of the amount of money offered to the actor. Thus observers were apparently misled by the actor's behavior, assuming it reflected a dispositional tendency to volunteer rather than a response to a contemporary opportunity. (Actors themselves showed no tendency to predict that their behavior in choosing to volunteer for the United Fund would correspond to their compliance in the study.)

If people can fail to perceive the extent to which money rather than personality is determinative of behavior, then it is scarcely surprising to learn that they can also fail to perceive the extent to which roles of various kinds can determine the nature of behavior.

A deceptively simple demonstration of this point was made by Ross, Amabile and Steinmetz (1977). They asked their subjects to play a brief "College Bowl" type game, in which one subject, selected at random, was to ask the questions and the other was to answer them. The questioner's role was to generate ten "challenging but not impossible questions." The contestant was to give his answers out loud. The questioner displayed, again and again, esoteric knowledge in the questions he posed (for example, "What is the sweet-smelling liquid that comes from whales and is used as a base for perfume?") and in the answers he supplied when the contestant failed to answer correctly.

At the end of the session, both of the participants, and, in a subsequent reenactment, observers as well, were required to rate the questioner's and contestant's general knowledge. One might expect that it would have been clear to subjects and observers alike that the questioner's role advantage should have been substantial. The questioner's role guaranteed that he would reveal no area of ignorance. The contestant's role, by contrast, gave no opportunity for such selective, self-serving displays. But the role advantage of the questioner was in fact not sufficiently obvious either to the contestants or to the observers to prevent them from judging the questioner as being unusually knowledgeable. Both contestants and observers rated the questioner as more knowledgeable than the contestant and more knowledgeable than the average student.

Can we generalize from subjects' blindness to the importance of the game-playing "roles" in this study and assume that people will be comparably blind to the importance of social roles as well? No. But fortunately a clever study by Humphrey (1985) allows us to do so.

Humphrey set up a laboratory microcosm of a business office. Subjects were told that he was interested in studying "how people work together in an office setting." Some of the subjects were selected, by an ostentatiously random procedure, to be managers and some were selected to be clerks. Managers were given time to study manuals describing their tasks. While they were studying them, the experimenter showed the clerks the mailboxes, filing system and so on. The newly-constructed office team then went about its business for two hours. The managers, as in a real office, performed high skill-level tasks and directed the activity of the clerks, whereas the clerks were assigned to work on a variety of low skilled, repetitive jobs and were given little autonomy.

At the end of the work period, managers and clerks rated themselves and each other on a variety of role–related traits. These included leadership, intelligence, motivation for hard work, assertiveness, and supportiveness. In addition, they rated the leadership and motivation for hard work they would be likely to display in a future job of a specific type. On all of these traits, managers rated their fellow managers as higher than the clerks. On all but hardworkingness, clerks rated managers as higher than their fellow clerks. (Managers and clerks did not differ in how they rated *themselves* on these attributes, however.)

The parallel of Humphrey's study to the simple Ross et al. (1977) demonstration is therefore complete and the generalizability to real world settings and concerns is enormously greater. People can be surprisingly incapable of penetrating beyond appearances to the role determinants of behavior, even when, unlike real life, the random basis of role occupancy is made abundantly clear.

The final study we have to report is particularly elegant, because it pits a deceptively powerful situational determinant against a deceptively weak dispositional determinant. The study, by Darley and Batson (1973), employed Princeton University theological seminary students as subjects. The subjects were given a questionnaire intended to measure whether the basis for their interest in religion had to do primarily with assuring personal salvation or primarily with their concern for helping others. After filling this out, they were instructed to go to a room in another building across campus where they were to give a sermon. Some of the subjects were told that their audience was already there and that the subject was unfortunately already somewhat late because the experimenter had fallen a bit behind schedule. Other subjects assumed that they had plenty of time. The route subjects were to follow to the other building was clearly marked out for them and they were set upon their way.

The parable of the Darley and Batson experiment is built upon another, quite well-known parable, namely the parable of the Good Samaritan. On the way to the new building, the seminary student was hailed by a man lying in a doorway who asked for help. And did the seminary students offer their help? Did it make a difference what the nature of their religious orientation was? Did it make a difference whether or not they were in a hurry? The answers are, respectively: Some, no, and yes.

Sixty-three percent of subjects who were not in a hurry stopped to offer help to the "victim." Only 10% of subjects who were in a hurry offered help. In contrast, the dispositional measure concerning the nature of religious orientation played no role in determining whether the subject stopped to help. The Darley and Batson experiment thus in a sense reverses the lesson of the parable of the Good Samaritan. Their experiment invites us to surmise that all of the earlier people who passed by on the other side of the road were simply running behind schedule!

How do we know that people aren't properly calibrated for the Darley and Batson study? How do we know they don't think the hurry factor is very important and the religious orientation factor is unimportant? I trust that the reader knows by now that the real reason we know that is that Darley and Batson did the study because they knew they would confound our expectations, because all of us lay personologists, including those who happen to be professional psychologists, had our expectations confounded by the results of the study.

But I speak, as Mark Twain used to say, with the serene confidence of a Christian with four aces. Pietromonaco and Nisbett (1982) described an experiment to subjects that was highly similar to that of Darley and Batson, substituting for the man lying in the doorway a woman who feigns a knee injury and asks the seminary student to call her husband. Subjects thought the great majority of seminary students would help, but that there still would be almost a 20% difference in helping rate in favor of those whose religion was based on a desire to help others. They thought that whether or not the seminary student was in a hurry would make precisely no difference at all.

Pietromonaco and Nisbett conducted their study not just in order to establish the previous facts about people's biases, however, but also to show how very difficult it is to change those biases. They asked some of their subjects to actually read the Darley and Batson study before making their predictions about helping behavior in two different situations. One was the slight variant of the Darley and Batson study just described and one was a situation in which the target was not in an experiment but was on his way to visit a friend in the hospital. The victim was a pregnant woman in obvious need of assistance with her car. Some subjects predicted helping behavior for Princeton seminary student subjects and some predicted helping behavior for a random sample of New Jersey males.

Informing the subjects by having them read about the Darley and Batson study had no significant effect on their predictions about the effect of the dispositional variable of religious orientation. It did have an effect on their estimates of the effect of the situational variable of being in a hurry, but the effect was a mere 18% difference, far less than the 53% difference reported by Darley and Batson.

These results thus cast the most serious doubt on the utility of the layperson's theory of personality. The data are consistent with a very extreme version of the fundamental attribution error view: People readily make trait ascriptions from data that permit only a situational interpretation, or at most the interpretation that the actor behaves in a particular way in a particular type of situation. These trait ascriptions are then used as the basis for yet further predictions that, again, are characterized by little attention to situational factors. People therefore may be expected to pay very dearly in terms of prediction accuracy for their adherence to their strong trait theories. These theories cause them to prefer prediction strategies that are, often, quite suboptimal.

## Situations Versus Persons As
## A Basis For The Layperson's Predictions

The previous hypothesis recently has been given some strong quantitative interpretations—both at the empirical level and at the theoretical level. In two separate series of studies, one from Ross's laboratory and one from Nisbett's, the costs of dispositionally-based predictions have been examined.

In one series of studies, by Dunning, Milojkovic and Ross (1986), a number of situations, either of the laboratory variety or the everyday-life variety, were described to observer subjects. The observers then were asked to make predictions about the behavior of target actors in these situations. For example, subjects were asked to predict (actually to postdict) whether John would have called home last week, and they were asked to predict whether John "will comb his hair when we ask him for a picture" in the context of a laboratory study. In one set of conditions, information available to observers about actors was relatively high: Actors were previously well-known to observers, for example, they were roommates, or observers were allowed to interview actors in preparation for the prediction task. In another set of conditions information was low: Subjects had to make their predictions working only from the actor's name and picture.

The results were quite clear cut. Across several studies and a very large number of predictions, the average accuracy in low information conditions was 57%. In high information conditions, the average accuracy was 60%. And accuracy was not significantly higher for actors who were very well known to observers than for actors whom observers merely met briefly in an interview. This means that whatever information we are able to garner about one another through acquaintance, even very substantial acquaintance, is not of very much use in making predictions about a host of behaviors of some interest.

But perhaps people do not really claim to be accurate about such one-shot predictions of behavior. Fortunately the data of Ross and his colleagues allow us to assess whether or not people think that knowledge about individuals helps them to make predictions. The truth is that subjects actually believed that they could be rather accurate when they had only information about the name and appearance of the actor! In low information conditions, where subjects were right about 57% of the time, their expected accuracy was 72%. In high information conditions, where subjects were right about 60% of the time, their expected accuracy was 77%. Thus subjects were rather confident of their ability to make predictions under both high and low information conditions. In addition, confidence was not closely related to accuracy. Subjects were not much more accurate about predictions that they were more confident about. As a consequence, subjects were rather often wrong but very confident that they were right—a dangerous epistemological stance.

In the studies by Ross and colleagues subjects sometimes made predictions that were consistent with their estimated base rates for the situations in question (or with base rates they were explicitly given by the experimenters) and sometimes not. An important aspect of the data is that subjects typically guessed at chance levels *or below* when their predictions went against the presumed (or known) base rate. Thus, in one study, subjects who predicted with the base rate were right 75% of the time, while subjects who went against the base rate were right only 40% of the time. In this same study, subjects whose predictions were opposed to the base rate were not significantly less confident than those whose predictions were in line with the base rate, despite the fact that their predictions were far less likely to be accurate. The costs of going against the base rate were particularly dramatic when the base rates (that is to say, the situational factors) were extreme. Subjects who went with the base rate when the base rate was 75-25 or even more extreme, were right 85% of the time. Subjects who went against the base rate were right only 23% of the time—but these same subjects showed extreme miscalibration, thinking they were right 72% of the time!

The moral of these studies seems clear. For predictions of the kind studied by Ross and colleagues, the base rate, whether known or presumed, is the best basis for prediction. When the base rate is extreme, one can oppose it in one's predictions only at one's dire peril. *And this is true even if the target is someone who is well known.*

A similar set of studies by A. McGuire (1986) makes a similar set of points. She asked observer subjects to make predictions about target actors in two different helping situations. In one situation the target was asked to volunteer to be a subject in some psychology experiments and in the other the target was placed in a rigged situation in which, as he or she climbed some stairs and began to overtake a woman on crutches, a book bag began to slip off the woman's shoulder. For some observers, the targets were unknown but were described by brief vignettes telling of their year in school, what kind of organizations they belonged to, what kind of day they had been having, and so on. In other conditions, the observers had been identified by targets as people who knew the actors very well.

Predictions in general were only slightly more accurate than would be expected by chance. Subjects believed they were capable of substantial accuracy, however, especially in the conditions where they personally knew the target well. In fact, subjects who knew the targets well were no more accurate than those for whom the subject was described only by the brief vignettes. The results are thus fully congruent with those of Ross and colleagues. Subjects were less accurate than they believed, they did not improve on their accuracy by adding their knowledge about the individual to their presumed base rates for the situation, but they *believed* that they improved their accuracy by drawing on such knowledge. Knowledge can be a particularly dangerous thing when it increases confidence far more than it increases accuracy.

## The Interview Illusion And The Belief In Personal Consistency

The literature reviewed to this point is helpful in understanding what may be called the "interview illusion." This is the assumption that one can learn a great deal of useful information about people's personalities from a brief, get-acquainted interview. This belief may be called an illusion because there are virtually no cross-validated studies of the predictability of unstructured interviews for college or graduate school performance, for blue- or white-collar or executive-level jobs, or for performance as a lawyer, doctor, or research scientist, that exceed the .10–.15 validity coefficient range (Nisbett & Ross, 1980). The majority of studies produce correlations of .10 or less (Hunter & Hunter, 1984).

The research just reviewed helps us to see just how the illusion could be sustained. People are often quite confident that their predictions that are based on limited information about a person are nonetheless accurate. The study by Kunda and Nisbett (1986) helps us to see why this illusory belief can be sustained. The social behavior data in the interview are difficult to unitize and code and the outcome data ("is a helpful co-worker," "is a good leader of the unit") may also be hard to code. In addition, as Einhorn and Hogarth (1978) have pointed out, there is often blurred or even no feedback about job outcome. For example, one usually doesn't know how the people not hired would have fared on the job.

These considerations suggest that it should be possible, using the metric developed by Kunda and Nisbett, to estimate exactly how far off people's estimate of the utility of the interview is, and to compare that estimate with their estimate of the utility of other kinds of information. In order to do this, they asked subjects to estimate the degree to which an interview would predict a trait-related behavior, namely success as a community organizer in the Peace Corps, and the degree to which an interview would predict an ability-related behavior, namely grade point average (GPA) at the University of Michigan. The anticipation was that subjects would overestimate both validity coefficients, but especially the trait-related validity coefficient.

The same sort of probability estimates were requested of subjects that Kunda and Nisbett requested for behavioral consistency judgments. Namely, subjects were asked to indicate what fraction of the time it would be the case that one Peace Corps trainee, rated higher than another in an interview by a psychiatrist, would also perform better as a community organizer. Other subjects were asked to indicate what fraction of the time it would be the case that one prospective college student, rated higher in an interview by an admissions officer than another college student, would also subsequently get a higher GPA.

The actual interview validities are below .10 in each case—.06 for the Peace Corps prediction (Stein, 1966) and probably about the same for predictions of GPA (see, for example, Klitgaard, 1985; Mayfield, 1964; Ulrich & Trumbo, 1965). It may be seen in Fig. 6.2 that subjects overestimated the validity of the interview for predicting GPA. Their probabilities correspond to a validity of .32 ($p$ contrasting actual $r$ with estimated $r < .001$). But their overestimation of the validity of the interview for predicting the Peace Corps outcome borders on the grotesque. Their probabilities correspond to a validity of .59!

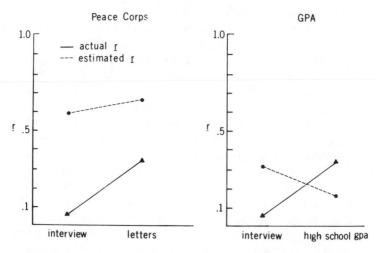

FIGURE 6.2    Estimated and actual predictability of Peace Corps success and of college GPA from interviews and from more highly aggregated predictors. (From Kunda & Nisbett, 1986)

An important question to ask, of course, is whether one might do better than the .00–.10 validity range when making predictions of this kind. The answer is a resounding yes! General ability measures predict job performance in the .40–.60 range when the population examined is not severely truncated (Hunter & Hunter, 1984). General ability measures, and high school grades, predict even undergraduate GPA, where the ability range is truncated, with values in the range .20–.40. (It should be noted in Fig. 6.2 that subjects *underestimate* the validity of high school GPA for prediction of college grades.) Finally, there are some valid predictors even of the trait-related outcome of success as a Peace Corps organizer, including the average rating assigned to letters of recommendation from people who know the candidate well. This validity coefficient was found to be .35 by Stein (1966). It is important to note the difference, from a psychometric standpoint, between an interview and a letter of recommendation. The latter is typically based on many times the amount of information, often many hundreds or thousands of times the amount of information, that an interview is. Thus from a purely psychometric standpoint, the information available to referees would be expected to have much greater utility than that available to the interviewer.

It is possible to assign fairly precise dollar values to the costs of letting low validity interview data enter into judgments such as the decision to hire or not hire particular candidates (Hunter & Hunter, 1984). These costs go up as an inverse function of the size of the interview validity and as a direct function of the size of competing validities. Thus we may say that most institutions that rely on interviews for selection pay for that practice twice—once when they go to the expense of interviewing candidates and, much more dearly, when they actually use the interview data in selection.

### When Are Dispositional Data Useful?

As the previous discussion indicates, sometimes one is better off by virtue of knowing dispositional information about individuals. We may now discuss the cases where the conventional wisdom turns out to be correct, at least in outline.

We hinted earlier at one case where individual difference information can be of value. This is where one has *base rate information for the particular individual for the particular situation.* Thus your belief that Jack talks a lot at the lunch table at work is bankable and your belief that your spouse dislikes parties where people are standing around talking and drinking is equally bankable. It is entirely likely, in fact, that the lay conviction about the utility of traits is in part based on an overgeneralization from successful predictions based on narrow, within-situation stability.

But even the cross-situational predictions can have genuine utility. Ross and Thomas (1986) have worked out a broad range of circumstances where trait-based predictions could in principle have some utility. These turn out to be fully predictable from an old-fashioned psychometric analysis. Where (1) the $N$ of both predictor variable and predicted variable observations is moderately large (that is, predictions are being made from and to an aggregate of events) or (2) where predictor information is extreme, and especially where both are true, individual difference information can be of genuine utility. At least this is true *so long as base rates for behavior in the particular situations to be predicted are not extreme.* Extreme base rates—powerful situations—simply can never be overlooked with impunity. But given that there are actual individual differences in behavior, given that there is substantial variance in other words, trait information can in theory predict even to novel situations in which the observer has never observed the target. But you have to be predicting behavior for an aggregate of events, the person you are making the prediction about has to be extreme on the predictor variable, or you have to know the person fairly well before this has any chance of being true.

This analysis indicates that much of standard personology remains intact. Personologists are in the business of gathering large amounts of information where possible. When the prediction they are making is of one-shot behavior, they are not likely to exceed the .2–.3 range. On the other hand, when the prediction is for an aggregate of events, correlations may exceed that range by a fair margin. And when predictions are about individuals at the extremes of personality dimensions, prediction can also be good. What cannot be done, by psychometricians or anyone else, is to predict to any impressive degree what nonextreme individuals will do in any given novel situation. And unless the information base is very extensive, it cannot be done with much validity at all. Finally, Ross and Thomas call our attention to the fact that, although correlations can be very large for aggregated events, approaching unity when N is sufficiently large even though the correlations between individual behaviors average .10 or less, high correlations are not tantamount to impressive predictability. When individual "item" correlations are low, the separation between "total" scores for individuals separated even by a standard deviation or two will not be very great. Though the rank order prediction may approach perfection, the actual difference between people at very different percentile values may be slight.

How about the layperson? How well can the layperson do at these same prediction tasks? There is every reason to assume that the layperson will rarely approximate the accuracy of the psychometrician, as we see in the next section where we consider the basis for the layperson's belief in the power of traits in the first place.

## THE ORIGINS OF LAY PERSONALITY THEORY

How could people be so wrong in their fundamental construal of the causes of behavior? How could they prefer to base explanations and predictions on trait ascriptions of little or no predictive power for the task at hand while being so insensitive to powerful situational factors and to individual difference data having real predictive utility such as ability data and reputational data?

### Perception and the Dispositional Bias

The explanation I prefer is a fundamentally perceptual one, owing originally to Kurt Lewin but first stated clearly by Fritz Heider (1958): "behavior . . . has such salient properties that it tends to engulf the field rather than be confined to its proper position as a local stimulus whose interpretation requires the additional data of a surrounding field—the situation in social perception" (p.54).

In short, and in the Gestalt terms that would have been congenial to Lewin and Heider, when we observe another person, an actor, it is the actor who is "figure" and the situation that is "ground." People are active, dynamic and interesting and these are the stimulus properties that direct attention. The situation, in contrast, is normally relatively static and often known only hazily. The observer cannot know, and usually does not bother to divine, the "model" of the situation as it is construed by the actor. Nor does the observer normally spend much mental energy trying to figure out what goals the actor might be pursuing, what mood the actor might be in, and so on.

Why does the observer then go on to make a dispositional attribution corresponding to the form of behavior observed? Heider was clear on this:

> Man is not content simply to register the observables that surround him; he needs to refer them as far as possible to the invariances of his environment. Second, the underlying causes of events, especially the motives of other persons, are the invariances of the environment that are relevant to him; they give meaning to what he experiences (p. 81).

We need only add an explanation of why it is the dispositional properties of the person rather than those of the environment that people tend to infer when observing the person in the environment. Well, because what you attend to is what you attribute to. Indeed, there is no generalization coming from the Heider-inspired attribution literature of the 1970s that is better supported than this. For example, McArthur and Post (1977) found that the actor's behavior was attributed less to the situation when the actor was brightly illuminated or moving than it was when the actor was poorly illuminated or stationary. Similarly, Arkin and Duval (1975) showed that an actor's behavior was attributed less to the environment when the environment was stable than it was when it was in motion. Taylor and Fiske (1975) showed that when an observer watches actors A and B interact, but can see A better than B, causal attributions about the outcome of the interaction are made more to A than to B.

The previous analysis implies that the actor and the observer will have very different understandings of the causes of the actor's behavior. The observer will be inclined to invoke dispositions of the actor, whereas the actor will be inclined to invoke situational opportunities and constraints. Jones and Nisbett (1972) argued that this is in fact generally the case. Actors tend not to give the dispositional explanations for their behavior that observers do. For example, in the study noted earlier by Nisbett and his colleagues (1973), observers inferred that actors who volunteered for money were the volunteering type whereas those who didn't volunteer, for much less money, were not the volunteering type. But actors themselves explained their behavior in terms of the amount of money they were offered. In addition, Nisbett and his colleagues found that actors believe that fewer trait terms are applicable to them than to their best friends, a new acquaintance, or the television commentator Walter Cronkite!

## Cognition And The Dispositional Bias

The perceptual factors underlying the dispositional bias are undoubtedly aided and abetted by a variety of cognitive factors. These are noted briefly.

**Linguistic Factors.**   As Walter Mischel was among the first to note, people's dispositional attributions are undoubtedly hastened along by the fact that the same adjective that can be applied to the actor's behavior can usually be applied to the actor. Thus, "hostile" acts are perpetrated by "hostile" people, "dependent" acts by "dependent" people, and so on. The language ordinarily does not allow us to pass so easily from descriptions of acts to descriptions of situations, except in the case of abilities, where we do have a rich set of adjectives for describing the difficulty level of contexts and tasks.

**Impression Perseverance.**   Once one has observed an actor's act and come up with a dispositional attribution, it can be difficult to disprove it, even if disproving their hypotheses were an activity that people frequently engaged in (Ross, Lepper, & Hubbard, 1975). There is evidence for a broad range of mental activities that would conspire to sustain initial impressions. Any subsequent acts are likely to be interpreted in terms that render them consistent with the initial dispositional attribution. Moreover, exceptions can be explained away readily.

**Theory and Ideology.**   One's perceptually-based inclinations are likely to be augmented with theories that capture them and justify them. The Western intellectual and moral tradition gives much support to the habit of dispositional explanations. Much of Western culture, from the Judeo–Christian insistence on individual moral responsibility to the intellectual underpinnings of capitalism and democracy, emphasize the causal role of the actor and attribute actions of different kinds to actors of different kinds. Interestingly, the Marxist tradition is perhaps the major intellectual tradition to focus on situational explanations. Behaviorism, Lewinian field theory, and most sociological frameworks are traditions within the social sciences that take a situational perspective, but the impact of these on the larger society has been relatively slight.

It is usually asserted of Eastern culture that it is far less likely to emphasize individual responsibility and more inclined to explain events in contextual and role-related terms than is Western culture. That this is actually the case, and that the cultural tradition produces different causal attributions for everyday events, is indicated by the study by Miller (1984), mentioned earlier. It will be recalled that she asked subjects to explain prosocial and deviant behavior they had observed. She coded explanations and found that, for her American subjects, dispositional explanations were far more common than situational ones. She also studied Hindu subjects in India, however, and found that these subjects were more inclined to attribute behavior to situational causes than to dispositional ones. This result probably is not due to the Hindu subjects' somehow generating behaviors that, by some objective standards, just *were* more situationally caused. When Miller asked her American subjects to explain the behaviors generated by her Hindu subjects, she found that they explained the behaviors in a much more dispositional, less situational fashion than her Hindu subjects had. Thus Miller's study indicates that the heavy Western reliance on traits is based on nonuniversal theories of human nature.

### Statistics And The Dispositionalist Bias

Finally, it should be noted that many people's statistical failings help to sustain the dispositionalist bias. First, people are rather poor at detecting covariations of the sort that underlie dispositions (Chapman & Chapman, 1967; 1969; Kunda & Nisbett, 1986; Nisbett & Ross, 1980). Secondly, people have little appreciation of the relationship of sample size to evidence quality. In particular, they have little conception of the importance of number of observations to making accurate predictions about trait-related behavior (Kahneman, Slovic, & Tversky, 1982; Kunda & Nisbett, 1986). The statistical problems that people have help to create a vacuum that the perceptual and cognitive biases rush in to fill.

### Role Of Biases In Judgments About Specific Individuals

The very factors that allow or encourage people to hold the personality theory that they do in the abstract, it should be noted, will tend also to lower the utility of the theory in practice, as applied to individual predictions in daily life (Nisbett, 1980). Most importantly, people are likely to inflate the consistency values that they associate with particular traits for particular people. We can safely assume that they habitually will assign trait scores of greater extremity, with greater confidence, than is appropriate. This means that they will make predictions, with assurance, that a sophisticated personologist wouldn't touch with a ten-foot pole. Thus, although the professional personologist can in principle easily avoid the pitfalls of erroneously extreme scores and overconfidence, it is likely that the layperson usually does not.

## TOWARD A CORRECT THEORY
## OF PERSONALITY

How does it happen that the layperson could be so mistaken about the nature and strength of individual differences? What would a more correct theory look like? Would the layperson ever accept such a theory if it were offered?

These questions could be the topic of another entire chapter. And they will be (Ross & Nisbett, in preparation). Here I can only sketch what some plausible answers to such questions might look like.

### How Could We Be So Wrong?

First, the question of how we could make such serious errors about such important matters. The question here is often phrased in the terms of evolutionary theory: Judgments about other people are often important to survival and therefore we could not be expected to be terribly wrong about them. Such evolutionary arguments are extremely dangerous in psychology, as Einhorn and Hogarth (1981) have pointed out. The mere fact that it is manifestly the case that some ability would be of great value to survival does not serve to establish that an organism must have it. The vervet monkey, for example, is constantly imperiled by leopards and pythons, yet ethological work shows that the most seemingly obvious signs indicating the nearness of leopards (such as the presence of a dead gazelle in a tree) do not alarm the vervet monkey. Similarly, the vervet monkey does not recognize the trail of a python, either by its sight or smell (Cheney & Seyfarth, 1985).

There is a serious question as to whether personality judgments of the sort I have been discussing are really all that valuable to humans in the conditions under which they evolved. A critic of the social perception tradition has characterized it as "the social psychology of strangers" and has asserted that the errors that characterize our judgments about strangers may have nothing to do with judgments about intimates. It seems to me that there is a distinct possibility that both the characterization and the assertion are correct, or largely so. The lay personality theory examined, especially its quantitative aspects, may apply mostly to judgments about people we do not know well. Evolutionary pressures are more likely to have been applied to judgments about intimates in the early hominid and human troop than to judgments about strangers. It probably did not become important until at least early agricultural times to be able to make accurate judgments about strangers. (See Festinger, 1983, for a social psychologist's view of early human groups and the social tasks confronting them.)

Of course, many of us today spend most of our time with nonintimates and must constantly make judgments of some importance about them. So the errors of the lay personality theory I have been describing are not mere foibles. In addition, some of the work I have reported (as well as everyday experience) suggests that overconfident judgments even about intimates may be fairly common.

### What Is The Right Personality Theory?

What will a correct personality theory look like when we finally get it? Some elements of it will bear a family resemblance to lay personology. There is some validity to traditional personological factors such as extraversion, agreeableness, and neuroticism as well as more specific traits such as talkativeness, sociability, and cooperativeness.

Many contemporary personality theorists suspect, however, that an accurate theory of personality will be based less on such nomothetic foundations than on more nearly idiographic positions that take into account individual differences in construal of situations. This is the personality theory foreseen by Lewin (1935) and by Kelly (1955). Recently several theorists have pointed to modern cognitive psychology notions that can help us to understand how people can organize their worlds in ways that would produce systematic differences in construal and in consequent social behavior (Cantor & Kihlstrom, 1983, in press; Markus, 1977; Markus & Miller, in preparation; Mischel, 1973). This new tradition invites us to understand individual differences in behavior in terms of differential or even idiosyncratic development of scripts, schemas and heuristics for processing social information and planning social behavior.

### The Selling Of The New Personality Theory

And when psychologists finally make sense of individual differences and offer people a scientifically superior view, will they accept it? Maybe. After all, Easterners and Westerners pretty clearly have different personality theories (Miller, 1984; Shweder & Bourne, 1984), so we won't have to go down to the level of hard wiring. And recent work I have done with my colleagues suggests that general principles often can be taught in such a way that they affect people's understanding of everyday events (for reviews, see Holland, Holyoak, Nisbett, & Thagard 1986; Fong, Krantz, & Nisbett, 1986). Whether human nature is fixed or not, theories about it probably aren't.

Returning to the underlying theme of this book, that of Schachter and his tutelage, what do the concerns of this chapter owe to him? First, the concerns reflect Stan's gift to me of the Lewinian tradition of looking to the situation and to the individual's construal of the situation for an explanation of behavior. Second, it is a direct reflection of Stan's life-long attempt to understand the true coordinates of individual differences in behavior. Third, it owes to him his stance of profound skepticism about received opinions, whether the received opinions of the psychological community or those of the larger human society. Not a "village skeptic's" skepticism—but a balanced and just skepticism.

But a more accurate statement might be simply to say that this chapter, like the rest of what I've done, owes everything to him. I remember Stan telling me of his great sense of satisfaction when he first wrote something in which he legitimately did not have to refer to Festinger. I also remember that happy occasion in my own life when I first published something that most people would have thought was original to me or at least not derived from Stan. But that was accompanied by a deeper, and as it turns out, abiding, knowledge that nothing I would ever do would be unshaped by his concerns, his approaches, and his style.

## ACKNOWLEDGMENT

I am indebted to Ziva Kunda, Lee Ross, and Elissa Wurf for a critical reading of early drafts of this paper.

## REFERENCES

Allport, G. W. & Odbert, H. S. (1936). Trait-names: A psycholexical study. *Psychological Monographs, 47*, Whole No. 211.
Arkin, R. & Duval, S. (1975). Focus of attention and causal attributions of actors and observers. *Journal of Experimental Social Psychology, 11*, 427–438.
Block, J. (1977). Advancing the psychology of personality: Paradigmatic shift or improving the quality of research. In D. Magnusson & N.S. Endler (Eds.), *Personality at the crossroads: Current issues in interactional psychology.* Hillsdale, NJ: Lawrence Erlbaum Associates.
Buss, D. M. & Craik, K. H. (1983). The act frequency approach to personality. *Psychological Review, 90*, 105–126.

Buss, D. M. & Craik, K. H. (1984). Acts, dispositions, and personality. *Progress in Experimental Personality Research, 13,* 241–301.

Cantor, N. & Kihlstrom, J. (1983). Social intelligence: The cognitive basis of personality. *Cognitive Science Program Technical Report,* University of Michigan.

Cantor, N. & Kihlstrom, J. (in press). *Personality and social intelligence.* Englewood Cliffs, NJ: Prentice-Hall.

Cantor, N. & Mischel, W. (1979). Prototypes in person perception. In L. Berkowitz (Ed.), *Advances in experimental social psychology, 12.* New York: Academic Press.

Chapman, L. J. & Chapman, J. P. (1967). Genesis of popular but erroneous diagnostic observations. *Journal of Abnormal Psychology, 72,* 193–204.

Chapman, L. J. & Chapman, J. P. (1969). Illusory correlation as an obstacle to the use of valid psychodiagnostic signs. *Journal of Abnormal Psychology, 74,* 271–280.

Cheney, D. L. & Seyfarth, R. M. (1985). Social and nonsocial knowledge in vervet monkeys. *Philosophical Transactions of the Royal Society of London, 308,* 187–201.

Darley, J. & Batson, C. D. (1973). "From Jerusalem to Jericho": A study of situational and dispositional variables in helping behavior. *Journal of Personality and Social Psychology, 27,* 100–119.

Digman, J. M. & Inouye, J. (1986). Further specification of the five robust factors of personality. *Journal of Personality and Social Psychology, 50,* 116–123.

Dunning, D., Milojkovic, J. H., & Ross, L. (1986). *The overconfidence effect in social prediction.* Unpublished manuscript, Stanford University.

Einhorn, H. J. & Hogarth, R. M. (1978). Confidence in judgment: Persistence of the illusion of validity. *Psychological Review, 85,* 395–416.

Einhorn, H. J. & Hogarth, R. M. (1981). Behavioral decision theory: Processes of judgment and choice. *Annual Review of Psychology, 32,* 53–88.

Epstein, S. (1979). The stability of behavior: I. On predicting most of the people much of the time. *Journal of Personality and Social Psychology, 37,* 1097–1126.

Epstein, S. (1983). Aggregation and beyond: Some basic issues in the prediction of behavior. *Journal of Personality, 51,* 360–391.

Eysenck, H. J. (1967). *The biological basis of personality.* Springfield, IL: Thomas.

Festinger, L. (1983). *The human legacy.* New York: Columbia University Press.

Fong, G. T., Krantz, D. H., & Nisbett, R. E. (1986). The effects of statistical training on reasoning about everyday events. *Cognitive Psychology, 18,* 253–292.

Hartshorne, H. & May, M. A. (1928). *Studies in the nature of character, I: Studies in deceit.* New York: MacMillan.

Heider, F. (1958). *The psychology of interpersonal relations.* New York: Wiley.

Holland, J., Holyoak, K., Nisbett, R. E., & Thagard, P. (1986). *Induction: Processes of inference, learning and discovery.* Cambridge, MA: Bradford Books/The MIT Press.

Humphrey, R. (1985). How work roles influence perception: Structural–cognitive processes and organizational behavior. *American Sociological Review, 50,* 242–252.

Hunter, J. E. & Hunter, R. F. (1984). Validity and utility of alternative predictors of job performance. *Psychological Bulletin, 96,* 72–98.

Jones, E. E. & Harris, V. A. (1967). The attribution of attitudes. *Journal of Experimental Social Psychology, 3,* 1–24.

Jones, E. E. & Nisbett, R. E. (1972). The actor and the observer: Divergent perceptions of the causes of behavior. In E. E. Jones et al. (Eds.), *Attribution: Perceiving the causes of behavior.* Morristown, NJ: General Learning Press.

Kahneman, D., Slovic, P., & Tversky, A. (Eds.). (1982). *Judgment under uncertainty: Heuristics and biases.* New York: Cambridge University Press.

Kelly, G. A. (1955). *A theory of personal constructs.* New York: Norton.

Klitgaard, R. (1985). *Choosing elites.* New York: Basic Books.

Kunda, Z. & Nisbett, R. E. (1986). The psychometrics of everyday life. *Cognitive Psychology, 18,* 195–224.

Lewin, K. (1935). *Dynamic theory of personality.* New York: McGraw–Hill.

Livesley, W. J. & Bromley, D. B. (1973). *Person perception in childhood and adolescence.* London: Wiley.

Markus, H. (1977). Self-schemata and processing information about the self. *Journal of Personality and Social Psychology, 35,* 63–78.

Markus, H. & Miller, D. (in preparation). *The unknown self.*

Mayfield, E. C. (1964). The selection interview: A re-evaluation of published research. *Personnel Psychology, 17,* 239–260.

McArthur, L. Z. & Post, D. (1977). Figural emphasis and person perception. *Journal of Experimental Social Psychology, 13,* 520–535.

McGuire, A. (1986). *The effects of knowledge about the person on predictive accuracy and on confidence.* Unpublished manuscript, University of Michigan.

Miller, J. (1984). Culture and the development of everyday social explanation. *Journal of Personality and Social Psychology, 46,* 961–978.

Mischel, W. (1968). *Personality and assessment.* New York: Wiley.

Mischel, W. (1973). Toward a cognitive social learning reconceptualization of personality. *Psychological Review, 80,* 252–283.

Mischel, W. & Peake, P. K. (1982). Beyond deja vu in the search for cross-situational consistency. *Psychological Review, 89,* 730–755.

Newcomb, T. M. (1929). *The consistency of certain extrovert–introvert behavior patterns in 51 problem boys.* New York: Columbia University, Teachers College, Bureau of Publications.

Nisbett, R. E. (1980). The trait construct in lay and professional psychology. In L. Festinger (Ed.), *Retrospections on social psychology.* New York: Oxford Press.

Nisbett, R. E., Caputo, C., Legant, P., & Maracek, J. (1973). Behavior as seen by the actor and as seen by the observer. *Journal of Personality and Social Psychology, 27,* 154–164.

Nisbett, R. E. & Ross, L. D. (1980). *Human inference: Strategies and shortcomings of social judgment.* Englewood Cliffs, NJ: Prentice–Hall.

Norman, W. T. (1963). Toward an adequate taxonomy of personality attributes:

Replicated factor structure in peer nomination personality ratings. *Journal of Abnormal and Social Psychology, 66,* 574–583.

Olweus, D. (1977). A critical analysis of the "modern" interactionist position. In D. Magnusson & N.S. Endler (Eds.), *Personality at the crossroads: Current issues in interactional psychology.* Hillsdale, NJ: Lawrence Erlbaum Associates.

Peterson, D. R. (1968). *The clinical study of social behavior.* New York: Appleton.

Pietromonaco, P. & Nisbett, R. E. (1982). Swimming upstream against the fundamental attribution error: Subject's weak generalizations from the Darley & Batson study. *Social Behavior and Personality, 10,* 1–4.

Ross, L. (1977). The intuitive psychologist and his shortcomings. In L. Berkowitz (Ed.), *Advances in experimental social psychology. (Vol. 10)* New York: Academic Press.

Ross, L., Amabile, T. M., & Steinmetz, J. L. (1977). Social roles, social control, and biases in social-perception processes. *Journal of Personality and Social Psychology, 35,* 485–494.

Ross, L., Lepper, M. R., & Hubbard, M. (1975). Perseverance in self perception and social perception: Biased attributional processes in the debriefing paradigm. *Journal of Personality and Social Psychology, 32,* 880–892.

Ross, L. & Nisbett, R. E. (in preparation). *The person and the situation: Construing the social world.*

Ross, L. & Thomas, E. (1986). *Notes on regression, aggregation, and the statistics of personal prediction.* Unpublished manuscript, Stanford University.

Shweder, R. A. & Bourne, E. J. (1984). Does the concept of the person vary cross-culturally? In R. A. Shweder & R. A. LeVine (Eds.), *Culture theory: Essays on mind, self, and emotion.* New York: Cambridge University Press.

Stein, M. I. (1966). *Volunteers for peace.* New York: Wiley.

Storms, M. D. (1973). Videotape and the attribution process: Reversing actors' and observers' point of view. *Journal of Personality and Social Psychology, 27,* 165–175.

Taylor, S. E. & Crocker, J. (1986). *Is the social perceiver a behaviorist or a trait theorist?* Unpublished manuscript, University of California, Los Angeles.

Taylor, S. E. & Fiske, S. T. (1975). Point of view and perceptions of causality. *Journal of Personality and Social Psychology, 32,* 439–445.

Ulrich, L. & Trumbo, D. The selection interview since 1949. *Psychological Bulletin, 63,* 100–116.

Winter, L. & Uleman, J. S. (1984). When are social judgments made? Evidence for the spontaneousness of trait inferences. *Journal of Personality and Social Psychology, 47,* 237–252.

Winter, L., Uleman, J. S., & Cunniff, C. (1985). How automatic are social judgments? *Journal of Personality and Social Psychology, 49,* 904–917.

# 7

# The Problem of Construal in Social Inference and Social Psychology

Lee Ross
*Stanford University*

In 1969 I left Columbia, and the watchful eye and inspiration of the mentor whom we honor in this volume, to begin my career at Stanford— where the difficulty of finding enough genuinely fat undergraduates to fill the cells of a single two-by-two experiment in the "Schachter tradition" helped me to decide on a change in research areas. Drawing initially upon Stan's classic work on emotional self-labelling (and some remarkably similar theorizing about the self-labelling of attitudes by an upstart "outsider" named Daryl Bem) I began to study phenomena that seemingly involved *errors* or *biases*, first in specific processes of emotional attribution and, ultimately, in more general processes of personal and social inference.

Since that time, a variety of particular "phenomena" and "effects" have provided focus for my research on the "shortcomings of the intuitive psychologist." These include the "false consensus effect," unwarranted "belief perseverance," perceptions of media bias and hostility, "reactive" evaluations of compromises and concessions in negotiation, overconfidence effects in social and personal prediction, and the lay dispositionalism that manifests itself in the "fundamental attribution error." Increasingly, however, I have come to recognize the extent to which a single problem of human inference unites these seemingly diverse phenomena. The inference problem in question is that of social or situational *construal*. It is, in a sense, the problem that Schachter and Singer's (1962) subjects encountered when they considered the strange happenings around them (and their potential relevance to the strange happenings that were occurring inside them). It is the problem encountered whenever people are obliged to venture beyond the information immediately provided by the direct observation or secondhand report of a stimulus event, in particular whenever they are obliged to infer additional details of content, context, or meaning in the actions and outcomes that unfold around them.

This chapter gives me an opportunity to discuss the relevance of the construal problem to my own research and to broader concerns within our discipline. My basic contention is not simply that the social perceivers are often forced to engage in difficult and complex tasks of situational construal, or even that errors in construal prompt errors in social inference. Rather, it is that social perceivers fail to appreciate, and fail to make *adequate inferential allowance* for the inherent uncertainty of the processes by which they construct social reality. It is that they fail to recognize the full extent, and implications, of their own role in constructing the evidence and information from which they derive social meaning.

## SOME HISTORICAL BACKGROUND

The insight that social perceivers go "beyond the information given" (Bruner, 1957) and, accordingly, that the psychologist must seek to understand the "meaning of the situation" to the actor in the particular context of his or her goals and experiences (Asch, 1954) is hardly a new one. Indeed, the relevance of subjective construal has been acknowledged by researchers and theorists within virtually every subdiscipline in psychology. Lewin (1935, 1936) recognized it in emphasizing that the individual's life space must be characterized in a way that captures its subjective reality and personal significance, and the gestalt psychologists (e.g., Koffka, 1935) and many early "cognitivists" (e.g., Brunswik, 1956) consistently gave heavy emphasis to the same objective–subjective distinction. Indeed, the admonition to focus on subjective representation in understanding the behavior of the individual has been echoed by successive generations dealing with a variety of issues, from Murray's (1938) discussion of "beta press," through Kelly's (1955) account of personal constructs and Merleau-Ponty's (1962) reference to personal situations, to more recent discussions by personality theorists (e.g., Bem & Funder, 1978; Endler, 1983; Magnusson & Endler, 1977; Mischel, 1973; Pervin, 1978) pursuing questions of cross-situational "consistency" and person–situation interaction.

Beyond recognizing that construal occurs, investigators have long pondered the social and cognitive processes that govern its occurrence. The great sociologist W. I. Thomas (1928) talked about the role of the individual's unique life history in defining his or her social reality (see also Ball, 1972; Schutz, 1970). The symbolic interactionists (e.g., Mead,

1934; Goffman, 1959) discussed the processes by which situational definitions are communicated and "negotiated" in a way that permits smooth social interaction. And the possibilities for misunderstanding and miscommunication between actors with divergent cultural (or subcultural, or even gender based) meaning systems have been commented upon frequently (see Triandis, Vassiliou & Nassiakou, 1968; also Abbey, 1982; Forgas, 1976; and Waller, 1961).

Cognitive psychologists perhaps have been most active of all in specifying the processes by which social perceivers go "beyond the information given" on the basis of their prior theories, beliefs and expectations. Perhaps their most consistent and enduring contribution has been to emphasize the role of systematically organized generic knowledge "packages," dynamic "schemas" (Bartlett, 1932; Piaget, 1936; also Rumelhart, 1976), or "scripts" (Abelson, 1976, 1981; Schank & Abelson, 1977) that help perceivers to resolve ambiguity, fill in the gaps, and generally perceive predictability and coherence. (See reviews by Fiske & Taylor, 1984, chapter 6; also Nisbett & Ross, 1980, chapter 2; Taylor & Fiske, 1981). Descriptions of and labels for such knowledge structures have multiplied rapidly over the past decade. So have demonstrations of differences between schematic and nonschematic information processing. What remains elusive, of course, is an adequate theory of schema activation (see De Soto, 1961), a theory that tells us how and why particular schemas are selected (and others rejected or never considered) in the service of particular assessments by particular assessors.

There is no denying the richness and importance of the intellectual legacy that we build upon when we discuss the problem of social construal. Asch's (1952) eloquent text, in particular, anticipates the general thrust of the discussion to follow on the role of construal processes both in social inference phenomena and in the theory and methodology of social psychology. Nevertheless, the immediate impetus for my own preoccupation with social construal came less from any formal literature than from an informal, largely oral, legacy passed on by Leon Festinger, Stanley Schachter and others in the Lewin tradition who brought new standards of care and craftsmanship to the art of social psychology experimentation.

An important part of that legacy was the insistence that the social psychology experiment had to be viewed from the perspective of the subjects—that the experimental manipulations and other events experienced had to "make sense" to the subjects, and permit them to respond naturally, calling upon essentially the same motives and modes of understanding and responding that governed their behavior in the "real world," without concern for the *experimenters'* motives and hypotheses.[1] (Often, of course, this entailed the use of fairly elaborate staging and a good deal of deception, not only about the "real" purpose of the experimental tasks and context, but also deception about when the "real" experiment began or ended.) All Schachter students, I suspect, can share their own recollections about his frank assessment of their first attempts to "script" the manipulations, measures, procedures and "cover story" that would turn an "idea" into a real experiment. When the experimental subjects were obese undergraduates who had to be confronted with a platter of roast beef sandwiches, four pounds of cashew nuts, or some other temptation from Schachter's Delicatessen, the subjects' "construal" of the situation mattered a great deal and received considerable attention in our planning.

Concern with situational "construal," and the impact of social context on such construal, figured heavily not only in our discussion of our own work, but also in our discussion of already classic social influence experiments by Sherif (1937) and Asch (1955, 1956; see Ross, Bierbrauer, & Hoffman, 1976) and of soon-to-be recognized classics by Freedman and Fraser (1966); Latané and Darley (1968, 1970); and, of course, Milgram (1965). The exciting dissonance research by Festinger and his colleagues (like Schachter's work on emotion) focussed our attention on the idea that construal processes were not only important but also subject to experimental manipulation. A concern with construal processes also figured heavily in our misgivings about some contemporary studies that were starting to launch a new, and very different research tradition— that is, the work of Bem, Kelley, and others who were making heavy use of procedures that asked subjects simply to complete questionnaire measures interpreting events that were presented in written descriptions rather than directly observed or experienced.

At that time, I joined my peers at Columbia with the vague feeling that such procedures somehow debased the noble experimental traditions that we were learning at the side of our mentor. We worried about the meaning of the stimuli and experimental tasks to the subjects, without ever dreaming that the processes governing such problems of interpretation (and the practice of using hypothetical vignettes and

---

[1]It is interesting, in this context, to note the controversial discussion of experimental manipulation offered almost two decades ago by two young Festingerians, Elliot Aronson and Merrill Carlsmith (1969); see also Carlsmith, Aronson, & Ellsworth (p. 55, 1976). Observing that the "same" manipulation might have very different meaning for different subjects, Aronson and Co. caution that the traditional strategy of holding all procedures "constant" may be inappropriate and inadequate. Rather, they suggest, it may sometimes be necessary to treat different subjects *differently* if one is to achieve a uniform manipulation.

paper and pencil questionnaires) would soon come to dominate our field. For me personally, the possibilities of variable and/or biased interpretation of "vignettes" emerged as a unifying theme once I succumbed to the temptation to try my own hand at sinfully quick and easy questionnaire-style research. In fact, the possibility of variable or biased "construal" gradually changed from a "problem" to be anticipated, and handled through measurement or experimental control, to a central explanatory mechanism.

## SOCIAL PERCEPTION PHENOMENA
## AND UNDERLYING CONSTRUAL PROCESSES

Before discussing situational and social construal in the context of my own research, it is appropriate to note two much earlier cases in which construal processes were invoked to explain specific phenomena of interest to social psychologists. In each instance, questions about the experimental subjects' interpretation of words and phrases presented to them within relatively impoverished "paper and pencil" methodologies figured in the debate about the correct interpretation of findings. And in each instance it was Solomon Asch—the theorist who most compellingly stated the general proposition that we must attend to the *subjective* meaning of situations, stimuli, or events—who furnished the relevant "construal" interpretations. I refer to Asch's discussion of impression formation, and his analysis of "communicator credibility" effects in persuasion.

### Asch's Construal Interpretations in
### Impression Formation and Attitude Change

In Asch's (1946) impression formation paradigm subjects were given simple lists of personality traits and then asked to make various judgments and inferences about the possessor of the relevant traits. Two of the "phenomena" he demonstrated became very well known. The first was the so-called primacy effect, whereby traits listed earlier in the sequence seemingly exerted more impact on the subjects' overall impressions than traits listed later; the second phenomenon involved the seemingly disproportionate impact of certain key dimensions or evaluations categories such as "warmth" versus "coldness," While both of these phenomena readily can be interpreted in terms of attention, retention, and weighting of individual items of information, Asch's own interpretation was more dynamic and more configural. He argued that the stimulus traits in his list (like virtually all descriptors or other isolated bits of information about an actor) are susceptible to variable interpretation or construal—and that the specific *meaning* attached to particular items of information depended upon the more global impressions or schemas adopted by the subjects. Thus, a seemingly straightforward descriptor like "intelligent" would have very different connotations when construed in light of a global impression that is positive (invoked either by initial positive information, or by an important organizing dimension like overall "warmth") than when it was construed in light of a global impression that is negative.

Asch's controversial construal or "change of meaning" hypothesis similarly invigorated debate about the communicator credibility effect demonstrated by attitude researchers in the Hovland tradition at Yale. Again, it was not difficult for investigators to offer straightforward learning theory interpretations for the "obvious" finding that written arguments produced more attitude change in the undergraduates who read them when they were attributed to positively regarded (i.e., attractive, trustworthy, expert) communication sources than to negatively regarded ones. Conventional interpretations noted that a given message associated with an attractive, high credibility source would be attended to more closely, recalled more successfully, regarded as more accurate and reliable, and deemed more worthy of emulation by the recipient, than the same message associated with an unattractive, low credibility source. Asch, however, offered a less conventional, more controversial, and more "dynamic" hypothesis. He argued and attempted to illustrate (Asch, 1948, 1952) that the very *meaning* of a message (i.e., the "object of judgment," as opposed to the "judgment of the object") can change as a function of the source to which it is attributed. Thus, to cite Asch's classic example, an assertion to the effect that "a little rebellion . . . is a good thing" has a different (and more acceptable) meaning to the recipient when it comes from Thomas Jefferson than it does when it comes from V. I. Lenin.[2]

Asch's controversial claims about "change of meaning" or differing "objects of judgment" are frequently cited in textbooks. Hastorf and Cantril's (1954) constructionist account of the perceptions of opposing partisans watching the film of a particularly rough football game is similarly popular. Nevertheless, I believe the significance of their broader contentions about subjectivity and construal have been insufficiently

[2]Contemporary investigators in the human judgment tradition would likely emphasize that such biased construal is entirely defensible on normative grounds—for example, that it is reasonable (and, in fact, quite likely correct) to assume that the same quoted utterance, especially when offered "out of context," *does* have two different meanings from two different sources (meanings congruent with the sources' presumed values and views).

appreciated by practitioners in the "social cognition" mainstream that came to dominate our field. More specifically, I know that my own appreciation has continued to grow as I have tried to find coherence in my work, and that of my colleagues.

## The False Consensus Effect

In an early paper on attributional shortcomings (Ross, Greene, & House, 1977) my students and I pursued a very simple and, it now appears, a very robust phenomenon involving biased estimates of response consensus. Our first study had subjects read descriptions of a series of hypothetical situations, each of which prompted a choice between two specified response alternatives. For each situation, subjects were asked to indicate what their own response would be, to estimate the commonness of their own and the opposite response alternative, and to assess the degree to which each alternative permitted strong and confident inferences about the actor's distinguishing personal dispositions. Our principal finding, which we termed the false consensus effect, was that actors tended to see whichever response alternative they themselves had selected as relatively more common and relatively less reflective of personal dispositions than the response alternatives they rejected; more specifically, the actors who selected a given alternative saw that alternative as more common and less revealing of personality than did the actors who chose the other alternative.

References to "egocentric attribution" or "attributive projection" and reports of specific findings related to this false consensus effect had appeared sporadically in the social perception and attribution literatures (e.g., Holmes, 1968; Katz & Allport, 1931; and Kelley & Stahelski, 1970). Generally, the interpretations offered for such phenomena had been motivational, centering on the actor's need to feel that his or her behavioral choices are rational and normative. Our own initial interpretation of this bias in consensus estimates was more "informational." We argued that social actors are selectively exposed to (and likely to expose themselves to) other people who share their background, values, priorities and other determinants of response—that is, other people who do, in fact, respond to the majority of situations in the same manner as the actors themselves. We also argued that in trying to imagine how "typical" actors might respond, actors' own responses, the responses of other actors very much like themselves, and the motives prompting such responses, are all likely to be more cognitively salient or "available" than the relevant alternatives. In considering our results, however, we were troubled by a possible alternative explanation that we felt would trivialize our findings, one that arose because of our reliance upon the kind of "hypothetical story and hypothetical response" methodology that had always led our distinguished mentor to mutter about "laziness," "declining standards" and the increasing paucity of "real experiments" in the journals.

This alternative interpretation involved the resolution of uncertainties and ambiguities present in stimulus materials dealt with by our subjects. Our brief verbal descriptions of situation had necessarily left a lot of details and contextual information to the subjects' imagination, and it seemed likely different subjects would resolve ambiguities and fill in details in different ways. Consider, for example, the first of the four brief situational descriptions that had been offered to our subjects.

As you are leaving your neighborhood supermarket a man in a business suit asks whether you like shopping in that store. You reply quite honestly that you do like shopping there and indicate that in addition to being close to your home the supermarket seems to have very good meats and produce at reasonably low prices. The man then reveals that a videotape crew has filmed your comments and asks you to sign a release allowing them to use the unedited film for a TV commercial the supermarket chain is preparing.

Now consider what is not specified in such a description. What exactly does this "man in a business suit" look like, and how exactly does he ask? (Is he a fast-talking huckster wearing a pinky-ring who prompts instant distaste, or a pleasant clean-cut chap whom one would hate to disappoint?) How are you dressed at the time (in sweaty jogging togs, or in a snappy new outfit?). And what exactly did you say in the "interview," and exactly how did you say it? Beyond these details of content and context, there are questions of prior experience that would be highly relevant if the hypothetical dilemma were real. (Had you seen any such commercials in the past and, if so, what had you thought of them?) There would also be additional issues about feelings and ideation. What kind of mood would you be in at the time, and what else would be going on in your life? What specific ideas, schemas or associations would happen to be invoked by the request and the immediate, real, context in which it occurred (fears about "being exploited," norms about "helping out someone just doing their job," joy or dread at the notoriety of "being seen on television," or something quite different)? Obviously, readers would differ in the concreteness and completeness of their construals. But the way in which you, or any other reader of the story resolves these and other ambiguities too numerous to mention would influence not only your own "hypothetical" response but also your estimates of response consensus and your assessment of the meaning of the two response alternatives. Similar uncertainties of construal, moreover, existed with respect to each of the hypothetical situations and other questionnaire items used in our false consensus studies.

The fact that ambiguities exist in written or oral accounts, and the certainty that they will be resolved differently by different individuals, is rich in its implications—especially in a world where so much of the knowledge we have about each other's actions and outcomes does, indeed, come "secondhand," Nevertheless, at that point in our research, construal problems represented a methodological artifact to be "handled" (preferably by eliminating the ambiguities that permitted variable interpretation) rather than a promising vehicle for conceptual integration.

To eliminate the role of "semantic" ambiguity, and perhaps more importantly to show that we remained faithful to the tradition of doing real experiments, we elected to do one final study. In it, we abandoned the use of hypothetical stories and forced our subjects to face a real dilemma, make a real choice, and make consensus estimates and personal attributions about purportedly real peers who had done likewise. Accordingly a sample of eighty Stanford undergraduates were recruited for a study on "communication techniques." After a few preliminary remarks about the general topic, the experimenter abruptly asked them if they would be willing to walk around campus for 30 minutes wearing a large sandwich-board sign bearing a simple message (e.g., EAT AT JOE'S), and record the responses of their peers to this unusual "communication technique." The experimenter made it clear to subjects that they could easily opt out of the sandwich-board study but that he would prefer that they participate and thereby "learn something interesting while helping the research project." Subjects were subsequently asked to decide about their own participation, to estimate the probable decisions of others, and to make trait inferences about particular peers who agreed or refused to participate.

The results using this "real" conflict situation confirmed the findings of our earlier questionnaire studies dealing with hypothetical responses. Overall, subjects who agreed to wear the sandwich-board sign estimated that 62% of their peers would make the same choice. Subjects who refused to wear the sign estimated that only 33% of their peers would comply with the experimenter's request. "Compliant" and "noncompliant" subjects also disagreed about the relative diagnosticity of agreement versus refusal to wear the sandwich board on the part of two specific peers. As predicted, compliant subjects made more confident and more extreme inferences about the personal characteristics of the noncompliant peer, while noncompliant subjects made stronger inferences about the compliant peer.

At first consideration, the success of this demonstration seemed to rule out or at least reduce the plausibility of construal explanations, because all participants had faced the same concrete dilemma. Upon further reflection, however, we realized that it did nothing of the kind. Possibilities for divergent construal can remain even when the situation confronted is concrete and objectively identical for all concerned. Thus subjects who imagine that their sandwich-board adventure will prompt ridicule from the peers they encounter, or imagine that refusal to participate will be accepted with equanimity, or construe the overall situation as a test of their assertiveness, likely will refuse to wear the sign. They will also make "appropriate" predictions and inferences about acquiescence versus refusal by others in that "same situation," By contrast, subjects who imagine that the peers they encounter will applaud their good sportsmanship and recognize that they are contributing to science rather than making fools of themselves, or who imagine that their refusal to participate will meet with incredulity and scorn from the experimenter, or who construe the overall situation as a test of their "uptightness," will agree to wear the sign; and they too will make appropriate predictions and inferences about others who elect to do likewise or otherwise in the "same situation."

Our construal interpretation, it should be emphasized, depends on more than the simple assumption that subjects engage in variable construals of situation and context. It depends on the additional assumption that in doing so they fail to recognize, and/or fail to make adequate inferential allowance for the fact that many if not most of their peers may construe the "same" situation quite differently. In a sense, our contention is that subjects fail to recognize the degree to which their interpretation of the situation is just that—a set of constructions and inferences rather than a direct perception of some objective and invariant reality.

### Biased Processing of Evidence and the Perseverance of Beliefs

In 1975 Mark Lepper and I began to investigate the possibility that erroneous impressions or beliefs induced by experimental deception might survive standard postexperimental "debriefing" procedures (see Ross, Lepper, & Hubbard, 1975; also earlier work by Walster, Berscheid, Abrahams, & Aronson, 1967). Our concern, however, soon shifted from this specific methodological and ethical problem to the more general phenomenon of unwarranted belief perseverance—that is, the capacity of ill-founded theories about oneself, about others, and about functional relationships among signs and symptoms or causes and effects in the world around one, to survive in the face of seemingly decisive logical or empirical challenges. Ultimately, we focussed on two specific cognitive mechanisms that we felt were implicated in instances of normatively suspect belief perseverance. Both of these mechanisms, it will soon become apparent, can be discussed in terms of construal biases.

The first mechanism is simply the *biased assimilation* of evidence relevant to one's theory. If theory holders accept supportive facts and arguments at face value, subject nonsupportive facts and arguments to critical scrutiny and alternative interpretation, and resolve any ambiguities about the meaning of ambiguous evidence in the light of their preexisting theory, such theory holders will generally find support for their views in the face of evidence and analysis that disinterested observers would find neutral or even disconfirming. By way of illustration, we demonstrated (in Lord, Ross, & Lepper, 1979) that partisans holding opposite views about the deterrent efficacy of capital punishment would respond to the same set of mixed empirical evidence by becoming more certain and more polarized in their respective views.

How could partisans find support for opposite views in the same empirical findings (particularly when the findings seemed, on normative grounds, to demand some decrease in certainty and extremity on the part of *both* partisan groups)? The answer was clear in our subjects' assessments of the pertinent deterrence studies. Both groups believed that the methodology that had yielded evidence supportive of their views had clearly been superior, both in its relevance and freedom from artifact, to the methodology that had yielded nonsupportive evidence. In fact, however, the subjects were evaluating exactly the same designs and procedures, with only the purported results varied (for we had employed a counterbalanced design whereby half the partisans in each group were led to believe that a "matched states" design had yielded "supportive" evidence and a "before/after" design had yielded non-supportive evidence, while the other partisans were led to believe exactly the opposite). To put the matter more bluntly, the two opposing groups had each construed the "box-score" vis a vis empirical evidence as "one good study supporting my view, and one lousy study supporting the opposite view"—a state of affairs that seemingly *justified* the maintenance and even the strengthening of their particular viewpoint.

The second belief perseverance mechanism we postulated is a bit less obvious and familiar, but it similarly involves a bias in the process of construing data relevant to a hypothesis. Subjects who come to hold a belief about themselves, their peers, or the social world in general, may do more than engage in the biased assimilation of evidence relevant to that belief; they may also attempt to furnish a *causal explanation* or *scenario* that accounts for the state of affairs they believe to be true. This explanation or scenario, in turn, encourages them to persevere in their belief when its *original* basis is discredited, or when new evidence is introduced that, viewed objectively, offers little support for that belief. Consider, for example, the subjects in the original Ross, Lepper, & Hubbard (1975) "debriefing study" who were initially led, via deceptive outcome feedback, to believe that they had succeeded brilliantly or failed miserably at the assigned task of discriminating authentic suicide notes from fakes. A "successful" subject might reason, "I'm good at the task because I play a lot of poker . . . I know who is bluffing and who is not;" while an unsuccessful subject might reason, "It's not surprising I failed so badly, I'm just too upbeat a person to identify with feelings that could lead someone to commit suicide." The two subjects in question, even after receiving a convincing "debriefing" about the deceptive nature of their original outcome feedback, would thus have a basis for anticipating, respectively, either high ability and success, or low ability and failure—and neither would recognize that an alternative initial outcome would have led both to alternative predebriefing explanations and to alternative postdebriefing expectations.

In a followup study (Ross, Lepper, Strack, & Steinmetz, 1977) we pursued this speculation about the effect of formulating explanations or "causal scenarios" by manipulating the process we had postulated. Subjects were given actual clinical case studies and then explicitly asked to *explain* later events that we purported to have occurred later in the clients' lives. The results were quite dramatic. Once a given outcome had been explained on the basis of available evidence, that outcome seemed highly likely—even after the subject had discovered that no credible evidence really existed about the occurrence or nonoccurrence of that outcome. In fact, even when subjects were aware from the outset that valid outcome information was unavailable, and therefore that their explanation task was merely hypothetical, the task of constructing a causal scenario altered subjects' estimates of likelihood.

An examination of the subjects' written "explanations" attested to the predicted construal biases. Again and again we saw the overall thrust of the case history, and the meaning of specific incidents, construed in the light of the outcomes that had been suggested. For example, in explaining a patient's purported suicide, subjects would note that the patient left home at an early age to join the Navy (i.e., an early instance of "running away" revealing the same disposition that would lead to the patient's suicide!). In explaining a purported decision to seek elective office, the same events in the patient's clinical history are construed quite differently. The early departure from home to join the Navy is construed as an act of independence and confidence—even an early symptom of the dispositions that would lead the patient to seek opportunities for "public service."

The mechanisms of biased assimilation and causal explanation, we believe, play a role not only in unwarranted belief perseverance (see also Anderson, Lepper, & Ross, 1980; Jennings, Lepper, & Ross, 1981; Lepper, Ross, & Lau, 1986) but also a variety of laboratory and real world phenomena, from Asch's classic primacy effects to the provocative hindsight bias described by Baruch Fischhoff (e.g., Fischhoff, 1975; Fischhoff & Beyth, 1975). Lepper and I, however, have recently found the study of these mechanisms, and of construal biases in general, taking us off in a new and unanticipated research direction. Specifically, we found ourselves becoming increasingly concerned with the relevance of these biases to the perceptions and behavior of partisans involved in social conflict.

## Perceptions Of Media Bias And Hostility

Our initial venture into new terrain dealt with the tendency for partisans in social or political conflict to perceive hostility and bias in those who would endeavor to report on (or mediate!) that conflict. Armed with hindsight wisdom, the link between belief perseverance and perception of media hostility becomes fairly simple and obvious. To the extent that partisans really do accept supportive facts and arguments at face value, subject nonsupportive facts and arguments to critical scrutiny and alternative interpretation, and resolve ambiguities in the meaning of ambiguous evidence in a way that favors their preconceptions, such "processing biases" would have obvious consequences for the partisan's perceptions of any other individuals who must evaluate the same body of evidence. Specifically, the partisans would be bound to perceive objective or evenhanded evaluations—and those who offer them—as unfairly biased and hostile. (Conversely, evaluations that are strongly biased in the partisans' favor are apt to be perceived as objective and evenhanded.)

Our research to date (Vallone, 1986; Vallone, Ross, & Lepper, 1985) has documented this "hostile media" phenomenon in examining partisan responses both to mixed media coverage of the 1980 and 1984 presidential elections and to television news coverage of the 1982 massacre of civilians in Lebanese refugee camps. Data from the latter study, which presented Pro-Arab and Pro-Israeli viewers with specific videotapes, were particularly compelling. On measure after measure there was virtually no overlap in the evaluations offered by the two partisan groups. Pro-Arab and Pro-Israeli viewers showed consensus only in their conviction that the other side had been favored by the media, that their side had been treated unfairly, and that these biases reflected the personal interests and ideologies of those responsible for the programs.

Our data, however, also suggested the operation of mechanisms that we had *not* anticipated. Rather than simply disagreeing about whether the facts and arguments presented were valid, or the overall tone and emphasis of the programs was fair, the two partisan groups seemed to disagree about what they actually had seen. Thus both pro-Arab and pro-Israeli viewers of the same 30-minute videotapes reported that the other side had enjoyed a greater proportion of favorable facts and references, and a smaller proportion of negative ones, than their own side. Both groups also believed that the overall tone, emphasis, and message of the videotapes was such that it would lead neutral viewers to change their attitudes in a direction favorable to the other group and hostile to their own. Dissertation research by Robert Vallone (1986) has begun to tease apart mechanisms underlying the hostile media effect using print and television coverage of the 1984 Presidential Election. In particular, his study attempted to determine whether partisans differ in their construal of specific statements, images, and passages—in other words, whether they "sharpen and level" (Bartlett, 1932) or otherwise assimilate the information in a manner that renders it more offensive to them. Such a result, of course, would be a dramatic exception to the standard notion of assimilation biases, whereby information is processed in a way that makes it more *acceptable* and *congruent* with the individual's own views, motives and presuppositions (e.g., Allport, 1954; Bower, Black, & Turner, 1979; Bruner, 1957; Hamilton, 1979; Katz, 1960; Lord, et al., 1979; Ross & Lepper, 1980; Snyder, 1981).

### "Reactive" Perceptions Of Proposals, Concessions, And Compromises

The same conceptual analysis that we have applied to partisan evaluations of media coverage could be applied equally well to partisan evaluation of judgments or proposals arising in the context of third party mediation or arbitration. (Imagine how the partisan spectators recruited for Hastorf and Cantril's (1954) famous study would have evaluated the efforts of a referee who claimed that both sides were equally guilty of infractions, and punished them accordingly!) The same analysis, moreover, permits us to anticipate, and has prompted us to begin investigating, the responses that adversaries make to each other's proposals for conflict resolution. Our working hypothesis is very simple: We assume that the same proposal that seems equitable and forthcoming to the partisan offering it will seem inequitable and unforthcoming to the partisan receiving it. In part, of course, this hypothesis arises from the expectation that the two sides will differ both in what they believe would be "fair" (in the light of their divergent views about past history and present context) and in their construal of the terms and balance of the proposal itself. We believe, however, that there is an additional construal bias that comes into play and constitutes a further barrier to conflict resolution. The very act of offering a proposal, we suspect, *changes* its attractiveness (and very possibly its "meaning") in the eyes of the recipient. As a consequence of having been offered, specific concessions or compromises come to be perceived as "smaller" than they had been perceived (or would have been perceived) prior to the offer. Concessions sought, conversely, come to be perceived as more significant and less appropriate to cede.

In the past year we have begun to test our pessimistic hypothesis, and our more specific ideas about underlying construal biases in a series of pilot studies. Although it is far too early for a comprehensive research report, some initial findings have been encouraging. In one such study Constance Stillinger and I seized the opportunity provided by a Soviet diplomatic initiative to show that the authorship of a proposal can indeed change its attractiveness and apparent balance. Early in 1986, the Soviet leader Mikhail Gorbachev made a dramatic arms reduction proposal; one that might have seemed, at least at first blush, to offer a promising basis for future negotiation. Essentially, the proposal called for a three stage reduction of nuclear weapons: In stage one, to be accomplished within the next three to five years, both the U.S. and the U.S.S.R. would reduce its numbers of weapons capable of reaching each other's territory by 50%. In stage two, to follow, shorter range tactical weapons would be reduced and eliminated. In stage three, to begin in 1995 and end at the turn of the century, the elimination of all nuclear weapons would be completed. Accompanying this proposal was an announcement that the U.S.S.R. would extend, by three months, its unilateral moratorium on nuclear testing (begun six months earlier) and a renewed insistence that the U.S. abandon (or at least severely limit) its attempt to develop the so-called "Star Wars" system of space-based weapons.[3]

Despite the simple, relatively unambiguous, and nontechnical terms of this proposal, its attractiveness seemed to depend largely upon its

[3]It is worth noting, especially in view of our research hypothesis, that President Reagan may have helped to prompt this specific proposal by claiming that the general nuclear disarmament was the ultimate goal of U.S. policy, and that the development of space-based defense weaponry was a means to that end—a claim that seemingly invited the proposal to forfeit such "means" if progress towards the goal in question could be achieved through *other* means.

purported authorship. When we attributed it (correctly) to Mr. Gorbachev, over 60% of subjects surveyed said that its provisions disproportionately favored the interests of the U.S.S.R., and less than 12% thought it disproportionately favored the U.S. By contrast, when the proposal was purported to be Mr. Reagan's, less than 10% thought it favored the U.S.S.R. and over 60% thought it favored the U.S. Fewer than a third of the respondents in these two conditions thought the proposal was "equally favorable to both sides." However, when the same proposal was presented as the product of an unknown group of policy analysts, the most common evaluation (i.e., by almost half the respondents) was that the proposal was equally favorable to both sides, and only a minority thought the proposal disproportionately favored either the Soviets (roughly 30%) or the U.S. (roughly 20%).

In another "opportunistic" venture, Stillinger and I asked Stanford students to evaluate various purported University proposals made in response to widespread demands for immediate and total "divestment" of all holdings in American companies doing business in South Africa. Of particular interest were the student's ratings of two "compromise" proposals—one of which would have seen the University immediately divest itself of stockholdings in companies that had been specifically linked to the South African military, to the police, or to apartheid practices in the work place (i.e., *partial divestment*), and one of which would have seen the University specify a two year *deadline* for major reform of the apartheid system, after which total divestment would follow if such reform had not occurred. When we simply told students that the University was considering both proposals, along with many others, they were rated about equally satisfactory and significant. When we told students that the University was about to offer a specific plan for partial divestment, a clear majority rated this concession to be less satisfactory and significant than the nonoffered alternative of a deadline for total divestment. Conversely, when we told students that the University would propose a deadline, the clear majority rated such a deadline as less satisfactory and significant than a plan for immediate, albeit only partial divestment.

In follow-up research, we are trying to determine whether such biased and "reactive" evaluations really result from differences in construal, or whether they are "knee jerk" responses made in the absence of any interpretation of context (i.e., "if they offered this package proposal, it can't be very good for us" or "if they are willing to make that concession it can't be very significant"). We are also exploring various strategies for overcoming the relevant cognitive barriers to conflict resolution—including the simple strategy of making participants fully aware of the existence and nature of such barriers. In so doing, we hope to honor the conviction of my mentor, and *his* mentors, about the "practicality" of a good theory.

## Overconfidence Effects
## In Personal And Social Prediction

In exploring the shortcomings of lay inference and judgment, psychologists increasingly have focussed on the task of social prediction. There are several reasons for this popularity. First, and most obvious, is the central role that social prediction plays in the phenomena that we academic psychologists seek to understand. Predictions about the future help to determine the actor's behavior in the present. They also tell us something about the way the actor has interpreted the past. Indeed, the goal of making accurate predictions about future actions, outcomes, and events is frequently what prompts the types of inferences and judgments that cognitive and social psychologists have studied so carefully over the past two decades. Predictions also have an important advantage over many other products of human inference—their accuracy and/or their "normativeness" frequently can be assessed in relatively straightforward fashion. Most important of all, perhaps, when we do evaluate their accuracy and normativeness, we generally find a variety of errors and biases that seem worthy of further investigation.

Most recently, my students and I (i.e., Dunning, Milojkovic, & Ross, 1986; Vallone, Lin, & Ross, 1986) have focussed on one particularly pervasive prediction bias, the tendency for laypeople to be "overconfident," that is, to express and exhibit more subjective certainty in their predictions than proves warranted by any assessments of their objective accuracy. A comprehensive review of results and procedures would expand this chapter beyond reasonable limits. For present purposes it should suffice to note the particular findings that I hope to relate to issues of social or situational construal. Our primary finding (Dunning et al., 1986) as noted, is that subjects across several different social prediction tasks and paradigms proved to be highly "overconfident." That is, regardless of the type of prediction item (e.g., responses to hypothetical dilemmas, responses to contrived laboratory situations, habit inventories) and regardless of the amount and source of information available about the target of their prediction (e.g., predictions about roommates, predictions about strangers interviewed by the subject, predictions about anonymous targets shown in photos), achieved levels of accuracy remained far below the levels required to justify the subjects' confidence levels. Further analysis revealed that although relatively higher confidence levels were associated with relatively higher rates of accuracy, the gap between anticipated and achieved accuracy was greatest precisely when subjects were most confident in their success. Relatively high levels of confidence also proved unrealistic to the extent that subjects knowingly or unknowingly went "against" the relevant response base rates—that is, predicted that particular targets would idiosyncratically differ from the consensus of their peers.

In a pair of followup studies, Vallone et al. (1986) extended the domain of inquiry from social prediction to personal prediction. Newly arrived Stanford undergraduates were asked to predict their own future actions and outcomes (as well as those of their roommates) over the weeks and months of their freshman year. For every type of prediction item we studied, from academic choices and outcomes (e.g., where will I study; what major will I choose; what courses will I drop?) to social and leisure activities (e.g., will I end up close friends with my roommate, will I take part in the dorm play, will I go to San Francisco once a week?) we again found marked overconfidence, and again overconfidence was most marked precisely when confidence itself was greatest and/or when subjects' predictions went against the relevant behavioral base rates. Moreover, while subjects were, overall, more accurate in predicting their own actions and outcomes than those of their roommates, the discrepancy between subjective certainty and objective accuracy was virtually identical in both cases. In other words, even in predicting the behavior of the person whose personal attributes and past experience they knew best—that is, *themselves*—subjects were overconfident. Furthermore, the degree of their overconfidence was greatest precisely when they assumed that their self-knowledge justified the prediction that their behavior would differ from that of their peers (and, presumably, from the dictates of the situational pressures and constraints that govern the behavior of people in general).

The overconfidence effect in personal and social prediction obviously cannot be traced to a single cause or underlying mechanism. Like most interesting and robust phenomena it is no doubt multiply determined. In fact, it very probably is "overdetermined," in the sense that it reflects the joint impact of many different processes that may be *sufficient* to produce the phenomena in at least some contexts without being *necessary* to do so in other contexts. Indeed, social prediction and self-prediction errors (and undue optimism on the part of those making such predictions) would seem to be the inevitable byproduct of a whole range of human inferential shortcomings and biases that investigators have documented over the past decade, from incomplete appreciation of abstract statistical and inferential principles (e.g., regression to the mean, the law of large numbers, the importance of sampling bias) to domain-specific misapprehensions about the relative predictive power of situation versus dispositional factors (see Kahneman, Slovic, & Tversky, 1982; Nisbett

& Ross, 1980; Ross, 1977, 1978). Nevertheless, as we have reflected upon the results of these studies, one particular source of overconfidence has increasingly dominated our speculations. That source of error and misplaced confidence, as our readers can by now no doubt anticipate, involves the flexibility or uncertainty of construal processes. More particularly, it involves the failure of subjects to make adequate inferential *allowance* for the uncertainty of the processes by which the "situation" (i.e., whatever features of relevant stimulus objects and/or context prompt and constrain the actor's behavior) is interpreted or construed by the actor.

There are two different aspects to the construal problem as it relates to social prediction. First, to predict an actor's response to a given situation—even an actor whom one knows very well, and whose behavior one has observed in a wide variety of previous situations—one usually must know or correctly infer the *details* of that situation, that is the features of content and context that determine the relative attractiveness of the available response alternatives. Second, beyond knowing the "objective" features of the situation, one must discern or anticipate the meaning of the situation from the private perspective of the actor. Uncertainty about objective features of the situation and/or their subjective construal by the actor increases the difficulty of prediction and the likelihood of error. And failure to recognize and/or make adequate *allowance* for such uncertainty promotes overconfident social prediction, both in the context of our present laboratory research and, more importantly, in everyday social experience as well.

It is worth reemphasizing that construal problems exist in self prediction as well as social prediction. Even when people make personal predictions based on accurate self knowledge, they still are likely to make errors to the extent that details about the specific situations they will face, and/or the way they personally will experience these situations, remain unknown and must be inferred or imagined. And again, failure to make adequate allowance for such uncertainty makes one susceptible to overconfidence and to the various costs of such overconfidence—from social embarrassment to inadequate contingency planning.

Are people really so oblivious to the implications of situational ambiguity and to their own uncertainty and susceptibility to error in resolving such ambiguity? Before attempting to address this issue directly, there is one failing of lay inference and judgment that I feel obliged to mention, especially because it relates so directly to one of the main contributions of social psychology in general, and the Lewinian tradition in particular.

## Lay Dispositionism
## and the Fundamental Attribution Error

Theorists concerned with the attribution process long ago suggested that social perceivers are systematically disposed to favor dispositional attributions over situational ones, even where such attributions are unjustified by the available evidence (cf. Heider, 1944, 1958). It has been argued that people are prone to leap from single acts to broad dispositional inferences, that they tend to ignore or underestimate the "power" of the situation—particularly the power of certain situations to overcome whatever individual "personality" differences may exist among actors. This alleged dispositionalist bias on the part of the layperson, and the "fundamental" attribution error that it disposes the layperson to commit, has been examined extensively in previous discussions (Nisbett & Ross, 1980; Ross, 1977, 1978; Ross & Anderson, 1982). It has even been argued (Nisbett & Ross, 1980) that one of social psychology's most consistent and enduring contributions has been its support for the doctrine of situationism—the demonstration that various situational manipulations can lead to levels of obedience (Milgram, 1965), conformity (Asch, 1955, 1956), compliance (Freedman & Fraser, 1966), bystander intervention (Darley & Batson, 1973; Latané & Darley, 1968, 1970), or delay of gratification (Mischel, 1974; Mischel & Baker, 1975; Mischel & Ebbesen, 1970), that could never have been predicted from any examination of the relevant actors' dispositions.

Previous discussions of dispositionism and the so-called fundamental error generally have emphasized the task of causal attribution, in particular the task of assessing the actor's responsibility for particular outcomes relative to that of certain specific properties of the social objects or situation confronting the actor. Our present discussion of "construal problems" suggests an alternative task, one that invites social perceivers to "construe" the nature of the situation (i.e., its objective features and/or its subjective meaning to the actor) at the same time they form inferences about the actor's personal dispositions. Such cases are common in everyday experience: We are given a capsule description of some action or outcome—for example, Jane yelled at her two year old in the supermarket, or that Joe donated blood last Thursday—and obliged to imagine for ourselves the actual nature of the social context for the actor's response. We may even personally witness the relevant behavior, but be unaware of critical features that determine the meaning of that behavior, and the larger context within which it occurs, to the actor—for example, what Jane's two year old might have done in the preceding hour to help precipitate the rebuke; whether Joe spontaneously volunteered to given blood or was urged to do so by Sue.

Lay dispositionism in such cases, I contend, would not be reflected in the perceivers' choice of causal attributions—indeed, speculations or judgments about causality would likely occur only if someone explicitly posed a question in causal terms. Rather, it would be reflected in the perceivers' readiness to make inferences about the dispositions of the actor (cf. Jones & Davis, 1965), without adjusting their construal of the situation facing that actor. The implications of this hypothesized variant of the fundamental attribution error is perhaps clearest in cases where one's expectations about "normal" or "appropriate" behavior are disconfirmed; that is, one learns, either through firsthand observation or through secondhand report, that an actor of unknown and presumably unexceptional character has behaved in a way that seems "exceptional"— exceptional, at least, given the observed or inferred nature of the "situation." In such cases, I contend, social perceivers are overly disposed to abandon the "null hypothesis" that the actor is "unexceptional" and insufficiently disposed to adjust, recompute, or reconstrue the nature of the situation in a way that would make the relevant behavior relatively unsurprising and unrevealing (or at least *less* surprising and revealing than it would be if their prior situational construal had been correct). Perhaps most important, lay dispositionism is reflected in the perceivers' failure to simply withhold judgment about the actor (i.e., to assume both that their prior construal of the situation had somehow been inaccurate and that a more accurate construal would make the actor's behavior seem less exceptional).

What is hypothesized, in essence, is a lack of attributional *conservatism*—and, where the dispositional inferences made on the basis of one's initial construal of the action and situation would be negative, a lack of attributional *charity*. In accepting seemingly exceptional actions and outcomes at "face value," and in failing to entertain the strong possibility that they reflect the influence of exceptional pressures and constraints (including ones that are not presently apparent and/or ones that arise from the particular subjective meaning of the situation to the actor), the intuitive psychologist resembles the intuitive statistician who is insufficiently "regressive." Both fail to recognize that relatively "exceptional" observations generally reflect relatively less exceptional truths.

It is difficult to imagine an experiment or even program of experiments sufficient to test a hypothesis that is so abstract, and unencumbered by specification of domain or boundary conditions. We can, however, begin to undertake relatively narrow domain-specific tests of the proposed *bias* and/or the processes assumed to underlie it. One such test was provided in a recent series of rather crude pilot studies (Ross & Penning, 1985) that looked at social perceivers' responses to one particular failed prediction. Subjects in each study were asked to predict whether each of two peers (one of whom they judged, on the basis of a photograph, to be a "highly typical" Stanfordite; and one of whom they judged to be an atypical Stanfordite) would prove willing to donate a small sum of money to help sponsor a "Gay Rights are Human Rights" advertisement in a campus newspaper. The amount of information provided about the specific situation confronting the actors at the point when they encountered the opportunity to make their donation varied across studies (e.g., in study one they were told virtually nothing about any appeal for funds, in study two they were told that the actors encountered a booth at a campus thoroughfare) but in each of these pilot studies two criteria were satisfied. First, the descriptions of the situation all left lots of room for construal (e.g., Were the relevant actors alone or accompanied? Was any explicit appeal directed at the person; and if so what was the content and manner of the appeal?) and second, the initial consensus of our subjects was that *neither* of the actors would contribute to the gay rights ad.

At that point, the experimenter first required all subjects to describe their own particular, detailed construal of the situation facing the two actors. Then he informed the subjects that *both* their behavioral predictions were *wrong* — for example (in the modal case where the prediction was two refusals) that both actors had, in fact, made the small contribution sought for the advertisement. Our subjects were then asked, in a series first of open-ended, and then forced-choice questions, to comment on their failed predictions. In particular, they were asked to tell us what could be inferred from the actors' responses. Overwhelmingly, the subjects in our three pilot studies favored dispositional explanations and inferences to situational ones. Far more subjects spontaneously offered exclusively dispositional interpretations (they're both "gay," or "liberals," or "easy marks," etc.) than exclusively situational ones ("someone they knew must have confronted them directly and asked them to contribute" or "somehow the setting must have made it very difficult to refuse"). When both types of factors were cited, dispositional factors were more likely to be cited first and, when forced-choice measures were employed, they were more likely to be rated as highly probable or important.

Obviously, more research is required to probe the domain of applicability and robustness of such findings. But the suggestion that people fail to recognize that situational construals made under conditions of uncertainty are apt to be inaccurate—even when evidence of "exceptional" or at least unanticipated behavior occurring in those situations gives a strong hint of such inaccuracy—is a provocative one in terms of the general arguments offered in this chapter. In fact, the results of this pilot study, coupled with our extensive overconfidence findings, soon prompted a more direct attempt to address those arguments. It is to this new research effort that we now turn our attention.

## Prediction Based On Certain
## Versus Uncertain Situational Construal

One seemingly obvious, and direct, way to determine whether subjects do or do not make adequate inferential allowance for the uncertainties associated with situational construal is to compare their responses under conditions where the certainty of their construals is *manipulated*. If subjects' predictions and social inferences are identical, or more specifically if they are made with equal subjective certainty under conditions where they know their situational construals to be correct and under conditions where they have no particular reason to believe them correct, this finding would suggest that subjects in the latter conditions failed to make adequate allowance for the possibility of error.

Such was the underlying reasoning for a simple pilot study (Dunning, Griffin, & Ross, 1986) conducted using a self prediction paradigm. Subjects in four different experimental conditions were called upon to make predictions about the amount of time or the amount of money they would spend in a specified set of circumstances (e.g., the amount of time they personally would talk during a sixty-minute roundtable discussion with four peers on the issue of abortion, or the amount of money they would spend during an end-of-the-quarter celebration in San Francisco). In each condition details about context or situation were described in very modest detail—that is, leaving lots of room for variable interpretation or construal—and in each condition subjects were asked not only to make specific "best guess" estimates but also to furnish appropriate confidence intervals (specifically, "50%" confidence intervals, such that actual outcome measures would be as likely to lie inside the interval as outside it). After completing their best guesses and confidence intervals for the various situations, subjects were asked to *reconsider* and, if they wished, to adjust their responses in light of such reconsideration.

In one condition, the control condition, subjects were given no relevant instructions during the interval between their original and their reconsidered estimates. In a second condition, which we termed the *uncertain construal condition*, subjects were asked simply to specify their particular construal of contextual or situational details and then, with no guidance about the potential accuracy or inaccuracy of their construals, they were invited to reconsider each estimate and confidence interval. In a third condition, termed the "certain construal" condition, the subjects were similarly asked to specify each situational construal; however, in contrast to the two former conditions, they were told to assume that their situational construals were "exactly correct." In other words, they were invited to make their reconsidered predictions and confidence intervals *conditional* on the accuracy of their prior situational construals.

The results for these three self-prediction conditions can be summarized very succinctly. In all three conditions the size of the confidence intervals offered after the reconsideration period (and construal manipulation) were, on average, identical to the size of the intervals they had offered initially. (In fact, the net change was 3% or less in each of the three conditions.) Thus, simply making it explicit to subjects that their predictions were predicated upon personal construals of the situation (that might or might not be accurate) did not increase the size of the confidence intervals they offered. More importantly, stipulating to subjects that their construals should be assumed *completely accurate* (i.e., that no allowance had to be made for the inherent uncertainty in the process by which they filled in gaps in information, resolved ambiguity, or otherwise went "beyond the information given") did not *decrease* their confidence intervals. Our interpretation for this result, of course, is that subjects in *both* "uncertain" and "certain" construal conditions (as well as those in the control condition) made predictions and offered confidence estimates that made virtually no allowance for the possibility of inaccurate construal.

Our fourth experimental condition becomes important in the light of these findings and the interpretation we have offered for them. It showed that subjects can and will make allowance for the possibility of incorrect construal if that possibility is demonstrated forcefully enough. In this fourth condition, subjects were again invited to specify their situational construals; but, before offering any new predictions and confidence intervals, they were told explicitly to suggest respects in which their initial construals might be *incorrect* (i.e., to furnish *alternative* construals). In this condition, at last, the subjects seemed to recognize the implications of uncertain situational construal. Even though the degree of their actual information (or lack of information) about the situations in question was identical to that of subjects in the "control" and "uncertain construal" conditions, their mean confidence intervals were the only ones to show a significant and consistent increase (averaging over 30% in contrast to the net changes of no more than 3% in the other three conditions).

In follow-up research we are employing essentially the same reasoning and experimental paradigm to explore social prediction and interpersonal inference. Our working hypothesis again is that subjects who are called upon to make predictions and dispositional inferences about their peers will exhibit just as much subjective certainty when they do so under conditions where their situational construals (and/or their guesses about the relevant *actors'* construals) are of indeterminate accuracy as they do under conditions where the complete accuracy of such construals has been stipulated. Only extreme measures, such as the explicit invitation to furnish alternative, highly divergent construals, will induce subjects to make adequate inferential allowance for the uncertainty of these construals. In these follow-up studies, we plan not only to expand the range of situations (real, as well as hypothetical) and range of inference tasks examined, but also, wherever possible, to examine the *accuracy* of our subjects' predictions and judgments about each other. In this way, we hope to demonstrate more clearly that predictions and judgments predicated on uncertain situational construals are, as we hypothesized earlier, made with inappropriately high subjective confidence precisely because the actors or observers in question have failed to make adequate inferential allowance for that uncertainty.

## SUBJECTIVE CONSTRUAL AND THE QUEST FOR SUCCESSFUL SOCIAL INTERVENTIONS AND MORE POWERFUL THEORIES

Stanley Schachter taught his students to value sharply focussed ideas and artfully constructed experiments—and he was rarely patient with or impressed by discussions of paradigm limitations, discipline-wide crises, or other topics similarly far removed from the specifics of research. In my own case, I'm afraid his teaching was not completely successful. With trepidation about the response of my mentor, I shall conclude this chapter with some observations about the relevance of "construal considerations" to problems of application and to the task of theory construction and validation.

For the applied researcher, the point to be emphasized is fairly obvious. Successful real world interventions are likely to require *more*, not less, concern with the "meaning" of content and context than successful laboratory experiments. This is not to deny that the failures of well-intentioned social intervention to end prejudice, overcome educational disadvantages, improve health habits, or resolve social conflicts may often be a matter of objective constraints rather than social construal. Frequently, the innovator simply cannot control the most important situational factors that stand in the way of success. My point is that social interventions, as they are conceived "in theory," are often only distant relatives of the actual "manipulations" delivered in the field; and the subjective experiences of the *recipients* of the interventions may bear even less family resemblance to those ideal versions of them conceived in the mind of the researcher. Such problems, I believe, often can be traced to a failure in will or craftsmanship in bringing the social experiment to life. Humanitarian impulses or political exigencies lead the innovator to concentrate on large samples, less than optimal "manipulations" of the variables deemed to be important, and less than adequate measurement of intervening processes. Good laboratory experiments, we learned from our mentor, demand lots of pretesting, and frequent trips "back to the drawing board" when it becomes apparent that we were not manipulating or measuring what we had planned to manipulate or measure. Good social reform experiments demand no less. Indeed, in the hands of a real craftsman, interventions carefully designed to overcome a problem can, at least sometimes, succeed. (The skeptical reader is invited to read Elliot Aronson's (1978) book: *The Jigsaw Classroom*, which describes the successful application of Group Dynamics theory and Festingerian guile to the problem of combating racial animosity in the schools.)

If the social innovator too frequently neglects the methodological traditions and insights of laboratory research, the ambitious theory builder too frequently neglects an important lesson about the value of "mundane" or "experimental realism" (cf. Aronson & Carlsmith, 1969). Good social psychology experiments are often rather complex social dramas, in which subjects have much to construe in the light of their personal goals, experiences, and expectations. As such, good experiments are potentially "noisy" affairs in which the effect of the investigators' manipulations, and the processes they are supposed to manipulate, can easily be "swamped" by a variety of unmanipulated (but occasionally measurable) processes that influence different subjects to different degrees. Such considerations continually tempt us to employ less noisy, more antiseptic procedures, in which extraneous influences of the sort that operate in everyday contexts are held to a minimum—that is, the procedures employed in most conventional "social cognition" research today. The reward for eliminating ecologically-representative levels of background noise and competing influences can be considerable, at least in the short run. Highly significant, highly replicable, and hence highly "publishable" results are perhaps the most obvious of these rewards. But the cost of procedures that simultaneously eliminate both realism and noise are also formidable. One loses the capacity to produce theories and empirical generalizations that are not merely "correct," but also *powerful* relative to competing processes, that is, theories and generalizations likely to be useful in the goal of understanding, predicting, and controlling behavior in the real social contexts. One loses the inspiration to draw ideas from direct social experience and observation, in the Lewinian tradition. Most of all, one loses the opportunity to make one's experiments tell a story that is somehow exciting and nonobvious, yet congruent with intuition (or at least with tutored reflection) about the real world. In short, one loses the opportunity to follow the example of our distinguished mentor, Stan Schachter.

## POSTSCRIPT: REFLECTIONS AND LESSONS

In writing this chapter, I resisted the temptation to wax nostalgic about the "good old days" when we all tried so hard to unravel the mysteries of obesity (or emotion, or smoking, or the stock market), while coping with the particular anxieties and delights of graduate school, Manhattan, and above all working with Stanley Schachter (and with each other!). After reading the early, still uncensored, drafts of chapters by my colleagues, I feel confident that Stan's charisma, and the challenge and excitement of following his lead, will be amply documented. Nevertheless, I would be remiss if I failed to acknowledge the magnitude of my personal and intellectual debt, and to reflect at least briefly about some lessons that were offered to us and to the field.

My debt began the day I attended the first meeting of Stan's group dynamics seminar. He asked us how we would determine the relationship between some particular feature of a group (I forget which feature) and some particular type of individual response. One intrepid student plunged in quickly and brightly and began to describe how she would measure the first of the two variables under consideration; and that was as far as she got. The beginnings of her answer provoked an immediate and thoroughly intemperate outburst from Stan. For two minutes we heard a passionate sermon on the sin of merely *measuring* something that could readily be *manipulated.*

I thought, this man is really going to tell us how to do psychology. I was wrong. He never again uttered so general or didactic a message. We had to "abstract" the lessons for ourselves, in trying to solve specific research questions, and in using his feedback (pointed expressions of boredom, gestures searching the heavens for patience, jocular explosions of mock anger or disbelief, remarkable enthusiasm when we figured out some small detail of an experimental manipulation or behavioral measure, and genuine excitement when we at last had some real data at hand) as guidance.

Some of the lessons were prosaic, for example, that details matter, even *tiny* details. When procedural details had to be worked out, "cost effectiveness" was irrelevant and "satisficing" was forbidden. You worked on a procedural problem until you "got it right" (and if you couldn't get it right, you switched to another experiment or even another research topic). If a fivefold increase in time or effort was required for a barely perceptible improvement in procedural elegance, the benefit was reckoned to be quite commensurate with cost.

Other lessons were less prosaic and less likely to win universal approval. If obsessiveness and compulsiveness in figuring out how to do an experiment was reckoned to be no vice, even a modest degree of diligence in "cleaning up" an area was reckoned to be no virtue. Stan's priority was clear. The next experiment to be done was whichever one seemed most exciting and important in view of the questions and opportunities at hand. Not only did he seem to think that it was appropriate for *him* to leave it for others to "fill in gaps," replicate, extend, explore limitations, and the like; he also seemed to think it was appropriate for *us* to do likewise. Experiments that were primarily "about other experiments," especially experiments that attempted to rule out (or worse still prove the validity of) less interesting alternative interpretations were anathema. Arguments that an experiment, in some absolute sense, "deserved to be done" or would "probably be publishable" were poor ones to justify actually doing it. The best argument for an experiment seemed to be that it convincingly "told a story," that it captured a real world phenomenon in a way that clarified the relevance of that phenomenon to a new theory or the relevance of that theory to other phenomena.

There is obviously a great deal more to be said about the lessons to be learned from an apprenticeship with Stanley Schachter. Lessons about the importance of making graduate students feel that they are special, and that they are working "at the cutting edge." A man whose competitiveness was obvious on a tennis court or in a card game, he never seemed to compete with his students—to prove that he was quicker, or deeper, or more knowledgeable than we were, or to show us that he was the real source of the ideas in which we took so much pleasure and pride. Perhaps that is why he made it so easy, after an apprenticeship in which we so consistently stuck to *his* research agenda, to strike out on our own. I'd like to think that he takes pleasure in the diversity of interests and approaches shown in this volume. I know that I consciously try to emulate Stan in some respects (fondness for an experiment that "tells a story") and that I stray far from his path in others (my "nonobvious" hypotheses never work!). But the most important lesson I learned from working with Stanley Schachter is one that can be learned by anyone who studies his remarkable corpus of research. The lesson is that psychology is most fun when it is done most seriously. We, his apprentices, discovered another that is almost as important: When psychology is most fun—when we sit around plotting the details of a nicely conceived experiment, or trying to make sense of a curious social phenomenon—we are often doing our most serious work. For this lesson, above all the others, he has my gratitude and affection.

## ACKNOWLEDGMENTS

I would like to acknowledge helpful comments received from colleagues who read earlier drafts of this chapter, including David Dunning, Dale Griffin, Neil Grunberg, Al Hastorf, Mark Lepper, Connie Stillinger and Amos Tversky. Special acknowledgement is also owed to my friend and collaborator, Richard Nisbett. Not only did he supply his usual quota of trenchant observations and criticisms, he also encouraged me to borrow heavily from a forthcoming book we are co-authoring (tentatively titled *The Person and the Situation*), which provides more extensive and less parochial coverage of the "social construal" problem featured in this Festschrift chapter.

## REFERENCES

Abbey, A. (1982). Sex differences in attributions for friendly behavior: Do males misperceive females' friendliness? *Journal of Personality and Social Psychology, 42,* 830–838.

Abelson, R. P. (1976). Script processing in attitude formation and decision-making. In J. S. Carroll & J. W. Payne (Eds.), *Cognition and social behavior* (pp. 33–46). Hillsdale, NJ: Lawrence Erlbaum Associates.

Abelson, R. P. (1981). Psychological status of the script concept. *American Psychologist, 36,* 715–729.

Allport, G. W. (1954). *The nature of prejudice.* Reading, MA: Addison-Wesley.

Anderson, C. A., Lepper, M. R., & Ross, L. (1980). Perseverance of social theories: The role of explanation in the persistence of discredited information. *Journal of Personality and Social Psychology, 39,* 1037–1049.

Aronson, E., Blaney, N., Stephan, C., Sikes, J., & Snapp, M. (1978). *The jigsaw classroom.* Beverly Hills, CA: Sage.

Aronson, E. & Carlsmith, J. M. (1969). Experimentation in social psychology. In G. Lindzey & E. Aronson (Eds.), *Handbook of Social Psychology.* Reading, MA: Addison-Wesley.

Asch, S. E. (1946). Forming impressions of personality. *Journal of Abnormal and Social Psychology, 41,* 258–290.

Asch, S. E. (1948). The doctrine of suggestion, prestige, and imitation in social psychology. *Psychological Review, 155.*

Asch, S. E. (1952). *Social psychology.* New York: Prentice-Hall.

Asch, S. E. (November 1955). Opinions and social pressure. *Scientific American*, 31–35.

Asch, S. E. (1956). Studies of independence and conformity: A minority of one against a unanimous majority. *Psychological Monographs, 70.*

Ball, D. W. (1972). The definition of the situation: Some theoretical and methodological consequences of taking W. I. Thomas seriously. *Journal of Theory in Social Behavior, 2,* 61–82.

Bartlett, F. C. (1932). *Remembering: A study in experimental and social psychology.* Cambridge: Cambridge University Press.

Bem, D. J. & Funder, D. C. (1978). Predicting more of the people more of the time: Assessing the personality of situations. *Psychological Review, 85,* 485–501.

Bower, G. H., Black, J. B., & Turner, T. J. (1979). Scripts in text comprehension and memory. *Cognitive Psychology, 11,* 177–220.

Bruner, J. S. (1957). Going beyond the information given. In H. Gruber, K. R. Hammond, & R. Jesser (Eds.), *Contemporary approaches to cognition* (pp. 41–69). Cambridge, MA: Harvard University Press.

Brunswik, E. (1956). *Perception and the representative design of psychological experiments.* Berkeley and Los Angeles: University of California Press.

Carlsmith, J. M., Ellsworth, P. C., & Aronson, E. (1976). *Methods of research in social psychology.* Menlo Park, CA: Addison–Wesley.

Darley, J. M. & Batson, C. D. (1973). From Jerusalem to Jericho: A study of situational and dispositional variables in helping behavior. *Journal of Personality and Social Psychology, 27,* 100–108.

De Soto, C. B. (1961). The predilection for single orderings. *Journal of Abnormal and Social Psychology, 62,* 16–23.

Dunning, D., Griffin, D., & Ross, L. (1986). *The role of situational construal in overconfident personal prediction.* Manuscript in preparation, Stanford University.

Dunning, D., Milojkovic, J., & Ross, L. (1986). *The overconfidence effect in social prediction.* Manuscript in preparation, Stanford University.

Endler, N. S. (1983). Interactionism: A personality model, but not yet a theory. In M. M. Page (Ed.), *Nebraska Symposium on Motivation.* Lincoln, NE: University of Nebraska Press.

Fischhoff, B. (1975). Hindsight ≠ foresight: The effect of outcome knowledge on judgment under uncertainty. *Journal of Experimental Psychology: Human Perception and Performance, 1,* 288–299.

Fischhoff, B. & Beyth, R. (1975). I knew it would happen—Remembered probabilities of once-future things. *Organizational Behavior and Human Performance, 13,* 1–16.

Fiske, S. T. & Taylor, S. E. (1984). *Social cognition.* New York: Random.

Forgas, J. P. (1976). The perception of social episodes: Categorical and dimensional representations in two different social milieus. *Journal of Personality and Social Psychology, 33,* 199–209.

Freedman, J. L. & Fraser, S. C. (1966). Compliance without pressure: The foot-in-the-door technique. *Journal of Personality and Social Psychology, 4,* 195–202.

Goffman, E. (1959). *The presentation of self in everyday life.* New York: Doubleday.

Hamilton, D. L. (1979). A cognitive–attributional analysis of stereotyping. In L. Berkowitz (Ed.), *Advances in experimental social psychology* (pp. 53–84, Vol. 12). New York: Academic Press.

Hastorf, A. & Cantril, H. (1954). They saw a game: A case study. *Journal of Abnormal and Social Psychology, 49,* 129–134.

Heider, F. (1944). Social perception and phenomenal causality. *Psychological Review, 51,* 358–373.

Heider, F. (1958). *The psychology of interpersonal relations.* New York: Wiley.

Holmes, D. S. (1968). Dimensions of projection. *Psychological Bulletin, 69,* 248–268.

Jennings, D. L., Lepper, M. R., & Ross, L. (1981). Persistence of impressions of personal persuasiveness: Perseverance of erroneous self-assessments outside the debriefing paradigm. *Personality and Social Psychology, 7,* 257–262.

Jones, E. E. & Davis, K. E. (1965). From acts to dispositions: The attribution process in person perception. In L. Berkowitz (Ed.), *Advances in experimental social psychology* (pp. 220–266, Vol. 2). New York: Academic press.

Kahneman, D., Slovic, P., & Tversky, A. (Eds.) (1982). *Judgment under uncertainty: Heuristics and biases.* New York: Cambridge University Press.

Katz, D. (1960). The functional approach to the study of attitudes. *Public Opinion Quarterly, 24,* 163–204.

Katz, D. & Allport, F. (1931). *Students' attitudes.* Syracuse: Craftsman Press.

Kelley, H. H. & Stahelski, A. J. (1970). Beliefs about others: Social interaction basis of cooperators' and competitors' beliefs about others. *Journal of Personality and Social Psychology, 16,* 66–91.

Kelly, G. A. (1955). *A theory of personality: The psychology of personal constructs.* New York: Norton.

Koffka, K. (1935). *Principles of gestalt psychology.* New York: Harcourt Brace Jovanovich.

Latané, B. & Darley, J. M. (1968). Group inhibition of bystander intervention in emergencies. *Journal of Personality and Social Psychology, 10,* 215–221.

Latané, B. & Darley, J. M. (1970). *The unresponsive bystander: Why doesn't he help?.* New York: Appleton–Century–Crofts.

Lepper, M. R., Ross, L., & Lau, R. R. (1986). Persistence of inaccurate beliefs about the self: Perseverance effects in the classroom. *Journal of Personality and Social Psychology, 50,* 482–491.

Lewin, K. (1935). *A dynamic theory of personality.* New York: McGraw–Hill.

Lewin, K. (1936). *Principles of topological psychology.* New York: McGraw–Hill.

Lord, C. G., Ross, L., & Lepper, M. R. (1979). Biased assimilation and attitude polarization: The effects of prior theories on subsequently considered evidence. *Journal of Personality and Social Psychology, 37,* 2098–2109.

Magnusson, D. & Endler, N. S. (Eds.) (1977). *Personality at the crossroads:*

*Current issues in interactional psychology.* Hillsdale, NJ: Lawrence Erlbaum Associates.

Mead, G. H. (1934). *Mind, self and society.* Chicago: University of Chicago Press.

Merleau-Ponty, M. (1962). *The phenomenology of perception.* London: Routledge and Kegan Paul.

Milgram, S. (1965). Some conditions of obedience and disobedience to authority. *Human Relations, 18,* 57–76.

Mischel, W. (1973). Toward a cognitive social learning reconceptualization of personality. *Psychological Review, 80,* 252–283.

Mischel, W. (1974). Processes in delay of gratification. In L. Berkowitz (Ed.), *Advances in Experimental Social Psychology* (Vol. 7). New York: Academic press.

Mischel, W. & Baker, N. (1975). Cognitive appraisals and transformations in delay behavior. *Journal of Personality and Social Psychology, 31,* 254–261.

Mischel, W. & Ebbesen, E. (1970). Attention in delay of gratification. *Journal of Personality and Social Psychology, 16,* 329–337.

Murray, H. A. (1938). *Explorations in personality.* New York: Oxford University Press.

Nisbett, R. E. & Ross, L. (1980). *Human inference: Strategies and shortcomings of social judgment.* Englewood Cliffs, NJ: Prentice-Hall.

Pervin, L. A. (1978). Definitions, measurements, and classifications of stimuli, situations, and environments. *Human Ecology, 6,* 71–105.

Piaget, J. (1936). *La naissance de l'intelligence chez l'enfant.* Neuchatel et Paris: Delachau et Niestle.

Ross, L. (1977). The intuitive psychologist and his shortcomings: Distortions in the attribution process. In L. Berkowitz (Ed.), *Advances in experimental social psychology* (Vol. 10). New York: Academic Press.

Ross, L. (1978). Afterthoughts on the intuitive psychologist. In L. Berkowitz (Ed.), *Cognitive theories in social psychology* (pp. 385–400). New York: Academic Press.

Ross, L. & Anderson, C. A. (1982). Shortcomings in the attribution process: On the origins and maintenance of erroneous social assessments. In D. Kahneman, P. Slovic, & A. Tversky (Eds.), *Judgment under uncertainty: Heuristics and biases.* New York: Cambridge University Press.

Ross, L., Bierbrauer, G., & Hoffman, S. (1976). The role of attribution processes in conformity and dissent: Revisiting the Asch situation. *American Psychologist, 31,* 148–157.

Ross, L., Greene, D., & House, P. (1977). The false consensus effect: An egocentric bias in social perception and attribution processes. *Journal of Experimental Social Psychology, 13,* 279–301.

Ross, L. & Lepper, M. R. (1980). The perseverence of beliefs: Empirical and normative considerations. In R. A. Schweder & D. Fiske (Eds.), *New directions for methodology of behavioral science: Fallible judgment in behavioral research* (pp. 17–36). San Francisco: Jossey-Bass.

Ross, L., Lepper, M. R., & Hubbard, M. (1975). Perseverance in self-perception and social perception: Biased attributional processes in the debriefing paradigm. *Journal of Personality and Social Psychology, 32,* 880–892.

Ross, L., Lepper, M. R., Strack, F., & Steinmetz, J. (1977). Social explanation and social expectation: Effects of real and hypothetical explanations on subjective likelihood. *Journal of Personality and Social Psychology, 35,* 817–829.

Ross, L. & Penning, P. (1985). *The dispositionalist bias in accounting for behavioral disconfirmation.* Unpublished manuscript, Stanford University.

Rumelhart, D. E. (1976). Basic processes in reading: Perception and comprehension. In D. LaBerge & S. J. Samuels (Eds.), *Understanding and summarizing brief stories.* Hillsdale, NJ: Lawrence Erlbaum Associates.

Schachter, S. & Singer, J. E. (1962). Cognitive, social and physiological determinants of emotional state. *Psychological Review, 69,* 379–399.

Schank, R. C. & Abelson, R. P. (1977). *Scripts, plans, goals, and understanding.* Hillsdale, NJ: Lawrence Erlbaum Associates.

Schutz, A. (1970). *On phenomenology and social relations.* Chicago: University of Chicago Press.

Sherif, M. (1937). An experimental approach to the study of attitudes. *Sociometry, 1,* 90–98.

Snyder, M. (1981). On the self-perpetuating nature of social stereotypes. In D. L. Hamilton (Ed.), *Cognitive processes in stereotyping and intergroup behavior* (pp. 183–212). Hillsdale, NJ: Lawrence Erlbaum Associates.

Taylor, S. E. & Fiske, S. T. (1981). Getting inside the head: Methodologies for process analysis. In J. Harvey, W. Ickes, & R. Kidd (Eds.), *New directions in attribution research* (Vol. 3). Hillsdale, NJ: Lawrence Erlbaum Associates.

Thomas, W. I. (1928). *Situational analysis: The behavior pattern and the situation.* Chicago: University of Chicago Press.

Triandis, H. C., Vassiliou, V., & Nassiakou, M. (1968). Three cross-cultural studies of subjective culture. *Journal of Personality and Social Psychology Monograph Supplement, 8,* 1–42.

Vallone, R. (1986). *Exploring the hostile media phenomenon.* Unpublished doctoral dissertation, Stanford University.

Vallone, R., Lin, S., & Ross, L. (1986). *Accuracy, confidence, and calibration in predictions about the self.* Manuscript in preparation, Stanford University.

Vallone, R., Ross, L., &.Lepper, M. R. (1985). The hostile media phenomenon: Biased perception and perceptions of media bias in coverage of the Beirut Massacre. *Journal of Personality and Social Psychology, 49,* 577–585.

Waller, W. W. (1961). *The sociology of teaching.* New York: Wiley.

Walster, E., Berscheid, E., Abrahams, D., & Aronson, E. (1967). Effectiveness of debriefing following deception experiments. *Journal of Personality and Social Psychology, 6,* 371–380.

# 8

# Social Psychological Risk
# and Protective Factors
# in Health and Illness

Judith Rodin
*Yale University*

## INTRODUCTION

I applied to graduate school in social psychology because I was sick of testing animals, having already had a long and ambivalent undergraduate career with rats, dogs, and snakes. I set off for Columbia with high hopes for a salvation full of people as subjects and weekends free from changing food dishes and water bottles. With such foolish ambitions it was my just reward that I spent my graduate years feeding and watering people instead of animals, and worrying about the hypothalamus I thought I had left behind at Penn. I owe this perverse turn of fate to Stanley Schachter. What is most remarkable is that he made me believe that I had come to graduate school in social psychology in order to study food intake regulation. With such massive dissonance to reduce, it is no wonder that I am still working in this area today.

Our work in the physiological processes underlying obesity—and the externality hypothesis more specifically—was solidified in one of Stan's annual graduate research seminars. Each student picked a different part of the body in that seminar, pushed by Stan's growing interest in the physiological controls of food intake. Stan is remarkable in getting students to charge unabashed into any new area that seems useful to solving the problem that absorbs him at the time. We all did it. My paper on the ventromedial hypothalamic (VMH) syndrome—obesity produced by VMH lesions—was the impetus for the book that Stan and I did together a few years later. Schachter's research seminars were irreverent and demanding. We learned to be critical of a lot of published work and not to be constrained by traditional boundaries within psychology and even between psychology and other disciplines. Stan's own striking

**151**

desire to work on any problem that caught his interest made him the exemplar multidisciplinary scientist. We went where the questions led us—often into mine fields and certainly not without criticism—but it was one of the most important lessons that I learned from him.

We made long trips to Stan's house in Amagansett each summer to bring him the data we were dishing up in steamy New York City. We all loved those visits. I learned from Stan the value of getting away to write and think, and the importance of having large chunks of time for really creative work.

Stanley's students shared an office next to his in those days. He wanted us there when he had an idea to discuss. It was something none of us wanted to miss. He taught us how to sort the A from the B+ ideas, as he called them, and to value and indulge in the crafting of the perfect operationalization. Schachter has been both faulted and admired for the cleverness of his studies; not to see past the cleverness is to miss the consummate social psychologist—one whose every experiment is a tribute to the importance of the situational variable.

While many psychologists have been absorbed by the mind-body question, it took Schachter's far-reaching inquiries into the nature of emotion, the determinants of food-intake regulation and the psychobiology of smoking to demonstrate how social-environmental factors modulate or fundamentally change a variety of processes thought previously to be biologically pre-wired. Certainly without intending to create a new field, Schachter helped to catalyze increasing awareness of the importance of multidisciplinary approaches to understanding the etiology of maladaptive health behaviors and disease. For this reason, his work stands as one of the cornerstones of the newly emergent field of health psychology and many of his former students now see their primary scientific affiliation in this area. The questions we ask focus on the role of psychosocial variables on health-damaging behavior, morbidity, or mortality. Where relationships are observed, pathophysiological mediators are then sought.

But Schachter also urged us to pursue another question as well: For whom does the postulated relationship not hold true and why? What can we learn from the smokers who quit on their own, despite an apparently strong habit, or the people who successfully maintain normal weight despite the pressures of environmental cues (Schachter, 1982). Often, with the same overt profile of risk factors as those who do fall ill or those who fail to stop engaging in health-damaging behaviors, some people simply do fine. For many years Schachter has been urging us to study what biological or psychological factors might be at work. Only now are we beginning to appreciate the wisdom of this second approach—the investigation of the protective factors. While the search for ways to demonstrate the effects of psychological factors on physical outcomes has led many to consider those for whom effects are not observed as noise, an annoyance that merely decreases the statistical reliability of our findings, Schachter's contention has been that we may learn even more by studying the "noise." I return to this point in the second section of the paper, but I first consider some examples of cases where biological outcomes are affected by social and environmental variables, as Schachter suggested would be true.

## EFFECTS OF ENVIRONMENTAL
## AND BEHAVIORAL VARIABLES
## ON THE ETIOLOGY OF DISEASE-RELEVANT PROCESSES

**Environmental and Cognitive Influences on Insulin Secretion.** The early formulation of the externality hypothesis held that overweight people were more responsive to environmental cues—both food and nonfood-related—than normal weight people and that normals instead were more responsive to internal physiological signals (Schachter, 1968, 1971; Schachter & Rodin, 1974). It turned out that, as usual, the world is never quite that simple. Not all overweight people are external and many normal weight people are. Unraveling these complexities and trying to understand both the etiology of externality and the role that externality played in the etiology and maintenance of overweight kept me and my colleagues busy for the next several years (Rodin, 1981a, 1981b; Rodin & Slochower, 1976; Rodin, Slochower, & Fleming, 1977).

The conceptual schism between internal and external control lost some of its clarity as we learned that external cues may directly trigger internal-physiological processes such as insulin or gastric acid secretion, which are related to the regulation of food intake, and that internal states such as deprivation can modulate responsiveness to external cues (Rodin, 1981a). Thanks to Stan's urging, I had pursued biological training at Irvine and became excited at the prospect of studying this environment/physiology interaction in food intake regulation. The Irvine program was one of several summer training institutes funded by the National Science Foundation and sponsored by a Social Science Research Council committee. At the time the institutes were conceived and designed, Stan was a member of the SSRC committee and Jerry Singer was its professional staff. The program was an innovative forerunner of many current efforts to create multidisciplinary scientists and several of Stan's students participated, including Lynn Kozlowski and Neil Grunberg.

I tried to understand how external cues trigger internal physiological processes by concentrating on the hormone, insulin. Insulin is a small protein, produced by the B cells of the pancreas, that regulates carbohydrate metabolism. By promoting or facilitating the entry of glucose into cells, insulin lowers the amount of glucose in the blood. This effect promotes glucose metabolism and utilization. Other functions of insulin include regulating the metabolism of amino acids, converting the carbon from glucose into glycogen, and storing glucose in the liver and muscles. Most important for present consideration, insulin also influences fatty-acid synthesis and the storage and mobilization of lipid substrates in adipose tissue (Bjorntorp & Sjostrom, 1971; Mann & Crofford, 1970).

Since Pavlov (1927), it has been known that the autonomic and endocrine responses involved in the metabolism of food can occur even before food enters the mouth. These include salivation; increases in gastric motility, gastric acid and exocrine pancreatic secretion; and a number of endocrine secretions, of which insulin is one. We considered what might happen to the anticipatory autonomic and endocrine responses of someone who is especially responsive to external and sensory stimuli. First, heightened responsiveness to food could trigger greater anticipatory digestive responses of all kinds: exaggerated salivation, gastrointestinal (GI) motility, and hormone release. Second, these GI factors could act upon exaggerated postingestional responses. Third, oral and pancreatic responses and consequent hepatic and other adjustments would then shift energy metabolism in an anabolic (energy storage) direction to a greater extent. As a consequence, a higher amount of what is eaten could be diverted toward its sequestration into fat storage. Consequently, someone could literally be "turned on" by food cues, resulting in overresponsiveness of all anabolic factors (Powley, 1977; Rodin, 1978, 1981a). Rather than secreting quantities of hormones and digestive enzymes appropriate for effective utilization of the ingested material, such a person might oversecrete in response to external cues, store ingested calories as fat, and then ingest more calories for immediate energy use.

To examine aspects of this hypothesis using insulin as the endocrine response of interest, we asked subjects to come to the laboratory at lunchtime, after having eaten nothing since the end of dinner on the preceding evening (Rodin, 1978). While we were drawing blood samples, a steak was brought in and cooked in front of them, grilling and crackling in a frying pan to provide rich visual, auditory, and olfactory food cues. I believe that Stan would have enjoyed the staging of that dramatic performance. Those subjects whose eating behavior was most responsive to environmental stimuli associated with food (externals) also showed the greatest insulin response to the sight and smell and sound of the grilling steak. Furthermore, obesity per se enhanced this effect in an additive fashion.

In the next study we asked whether the insulin response could be magnified by presenting highly preferred foods (Rodin, 1978). This time the foods were all carbohydrates. Experimental subjects were tested on two separate days with presentations of food at three different levels of palatability. The insulin response of externally responsive subjects was significantly more affected by palatability than that of the nonexternal subjects.

Although these studies did not examine the effects of the elevated insulin response to the sight of palatable food on food intake, animal studies suggest that such secretions do influence eating and weight gain and thus may have pathophysiological implications. An especially strong piece of evidence for this speculation comes from the work of Berthoud, Trimble, Siegel, Bereiter, and Jeanrenaud (1980) and Berthoud, Bereiter, Trimble, Siegel, and Jeanrenaud (1981) who studied seemingly identical rats of the same breed, sex, and age. When insulin secretion was elicited by saccharin placed on the tongue, this seemingly homogeneous group could be split into two, a high and a low responder group, in terms of the amplitude of their insulin secretion. On a normal, laboratory-chow diet the groups' body weights and basal insulinemia were similar. But on an ad libitum diet of highly palatable food, the so-called cafeteria diet of chocolate chip cookies, salami, and cheese, the high insulin responders gained a great deal more weight than the low responders. Thus we would expect, as this study suggests, that the tendency toward insulin hyperresponsiveness is important but requires plentiful and palatable food in order to lead to weight gain. The availability of sufficiently palatable food is certainly likely for a large part of modernized society at present.

To consider directly whether hyperinsulinemia is causally related to increased food intake in humans, we next turned to an acute, direct manipulation of insulin levels. Exogenous administration of insulin has been shown reliably to increase hunger and food intake in a variety of species (Booth, 1972; Booth & Brookover, 1968; Brandes, 1977; Grossman & Stein, 1948; Kanarek, Marks-Kaufman, & Lipeles, 1980; Lovett & Booth, 1970; McKay, Callaway, & Barnes, 1940; Panksepp, Pollack, & Krost, 1975; Silverstone & Besser, 1971; Smith & Epstein, 1969; Vasselli & Sclafani, 1979). However, there have been studies suggesting that hyperinsulinemia is also associated with decreased food intake in animals (Nicolaidis, 1981; Nicolaidis & Rowland, 1976; Porte & Woods, 1981; Woods, et al., 1979). To begin to understand these apparently contradictory findings, we investigated the effects of hyperinsulinemia while controlling for, and manipulating, levels of blood glucose in order to examine the contribution of insulin, independent of hypoglycemia. Until recently, it was assumed that when insulin-induced hyperphagia occurred, it was due to concomitant hypoglycemia. Also attributed to hypoglycemia was an exaggerated reactivity to the taste of food following injections of regular or protamine-zinc insulin in animals and people (Booth & Brookover, 1968; Geiselman & Novin, 1982; Lotter & Woods, 1977).

I was fortunate to have an active collaboration with a group of endocrinologists at Yale, enabling me to uncouple insulin and glucose using the insulin/glucose clamp technique (Rodin, Wack, Ferrannini, & DeFronzo, 1985). With the clamp, the rate of insulin and glucose infusion is adjusted on the basis of empirically derived formulas, and rapid and repeated measures of plasma glucose permit desired levels of steady-state hyperglycemia, hypoglycemia, or hyperinsulinemia to be obtained. Thus, the influence of increased levels of circulating insulin can be assessed independently from that of alterations in blood-glucose concentration.

Subjects were randomly assigned to one of four conditions: hyperinsulinemia-hyperglycemia; hyperinsulinemia-hypoglycemia; euinsulinemia (basal insulin) -hyperglycemia; saline control. Subjects were maintained in those states for 2½ hours during which, at 30-minute intervals, they rated the intensity and pleasantness of varying concentrations of sucrose, and their hunger, thirst, mood states, and bodily symptoms.

There were no effects of the manipulations on ratings of perceived sweetness intensity, and strong effects on ratings of perceived pleasantness. Hyperinsulinemia (regardless of glucose levels) was associated with increased preference for the sweeter tastes. Subjects in the two hyperinsulinemic conditions also reported significantly increasing hunger over time, relative to their own baseline and to subjects in saline control and euinsulinemic conditions.

At the conclusion of the study, subjects were given lunch consisting of a chocolate-flavored complete liquid diet. They were permitted to drink as much as they wished, and they drank from a container that was hidden from their view. (The last time that procedure was tried, by Stan and Ron Gordon when we were graduate students, the first two subjects drank so much they threw up and Ron stopped the study. The Yalies may be more circumspect in their gluttony, so we had no similar catastrophe.) Subjects in both hyperinsulinemic groups drank significantly more than controls and were not different from one another in the amount they consumed.

All of these data taken together suggest strongly that hyperinsulinemia, at two very different levels of blood glucose, may be associated with increased hunger, heightened perceived pleasantness of sweet taste, and increased intake of chocolate milkshake. Because chronic insulin levels are elevated by overeating and by obesity, a feedback loop is suggested by these findings in which hyperinsulinemia in turn leads to increased consumption which, unless compensated for, could lead to further weight gain. Because acute hyperinsulinemia can also be produced in some individuals by simply looking at or thinking about food, it too can in turn lead to increased consumption and possibly weight gain.

It has been speculated that the effects of insulin on food intake may be specific to carbohydrates. In other words, higher levels of plasma insulin may be associated with increased preference for carbohydrates in particular. For example, Kanarek et al. (1980) showed that rats allowed free access to separate dietary sources of protein, carbohydrate, and fat following exogenous insulin administration increased their intake solely by increasing carbohydrate consumption. We are studying these effects in people and if they are replicable, the chronic and acute types of hyperinsulinemia just discussed may lead to increased preference for carbohydrates in particular. Certainly carbohydrate craving is a common complaint of many people who struggle to control their weight.

**Role of Social/Environmental Variables in Bulimia.**    One of Stan's greatest lessons for me was to feel free enough to tackle new problems, just because they were interesting. He also made it clear that interesting because of personal relevance was surely in the ball game. For him, that was smoking and then money; for me it was women and weight concerns. Most women are preoccupied with their weight to some degree and many feel fat, regardless of what they actually weigh. Elaborating and commenting on the causes and consequences of these concerns has been extraordinarily interesting, in part because as a woman I feel them so strongly myself. Stan always taught us to trust our intuitions—they are data, he argued. For me that has definitely rung true in this work. Three theory and review papers, more fun for me than anything else I have written, have guided the studies we are now beginning in this area (Rodin, Silberstein, & Striegel-Moore, 1985; Striegel-Moore, Silberstein, & Rodin, 1986; Silberstein, Striegel-Moore, & Rodin, 1987). Our analyses have led us to assert that weight concerns and dieting are normative for the largest majority of women in Western society at present, and that eating disorders like bulimia (a syndrome of binging and purging large amounts of food), can be understood best as a likely consequence of this "normative" behavior when taken to greater extremes.

We argued that while beauty ideals have varied considerably in Western cultures over the course of centuries, women have often been willing to alter their bodies to conform to each era's beauty ideal. Indeed, concern with one's appearance and making efforts to enhance and preserve one's beauty are central features of the female sex-role stereotype (Brownmiller, 1984). Several studies have documented that physically attractive women are perceived as more feminine, and unattractive women as more masculine, and that thinness and feminin- ity are linked.

Interestingly, there also appears to be a relationship between certain types of eating behavior and femininity. Women who were described as eating small meals were rated significantly more feminine and more attractive than women who ate large meals, whereas meal size descrip- tions had no effect on ratings of male targets. Women may also restrict their food intake in the service of making a favorable impression on men (Chaiken & Pliner, 1984).

Surely one root of women's fear of overweight lies in the harsh negative views of society toward obesity. Even overweight is met with punishment—psychological, social, and economic—and the sanctions appear more severe for women than men. Attractiveness is highly rewarded, and again more so for women than for men. Furthermore, our own data suggest that the body is far more crucial in determining attractiveness for women. Since self-perceived attractiveness and self- esteem are correlated for women, we have hypothesized that a woman's body weight in particular, and her satisfaction or dissatisfaction with it, would be major variables in her overall satisfaction with herself. Our data from a large scale survey of almost two thousand women support this hypothesis.

A significant number of women face a frustrating paradox: While society prescribes a thin beauty ideal, and thinness strongly influences self-esteem, their own genes predispose them to a considerably heavier body weight. Women are genetically programmed to have a proportion- ately higher body fat composition than men—a sex difference that appears to hold across all races and cultures (Bennett, 1984; Tanner, 1978)—and the differences between sexes in fatness increase dramatically, on the average, across the life span. Current society promotes dieting as the pathway to thinness, and as we would expect, significantly more women than men report dieting at any time (e.g., Nielsen, 1979; Nylander, 1971). Before the age of 13, 80% of American girls report that they have already been on a weight loss diet, as compared to 10% of boys (Hawkins, Turrell, & Jackson, 1983).

On the basis of studies investigating the physiological changes that occur as a result of dieting, we believe that dieting is not only an ineffective way to attain long-term weight loss, but that it may in fact contribute to subsequent weight gain and binge eating. A substantial decrease in daily caloric intake will result in a reduced metabolic rate, which thus impedes weight loss, and the suppression of metabolic rate caused by dieting is most pronounced when basal metabolic rate is low from the outset. Since women have lower metabolic rates than men, women are particularly likely to find that, despite their efforts, they cannot lose as much as they would like. Upon resuming normal caloric intake, a person's metabolic rate does not immediately rebound to its original level (Even & Nicolaidis, 1981). Thus, even normal eating after a period of dieting may promote weight gain. Numerous other physiological changes that are induced by food restriction contribute to increased efficiency in food utilization and an increased proportion of fat in body composition (Bjorntorp & Yang, 1982; Faust, Johnson, Stern, & Hirsch, 1978; Fried, Hill, Nickel, & DiGirolamo, 1983; Gruen & Greenwood, 1981; Miller, Faust, Goldberg, & Hirsch, 1983; Walks, Lavan, Presta, Yang, & Bjorntorp, 1983). Hence, dieting ultimately produces precisely the opposite effects than intended.

We proposed that a prolonged history of repeated dieting, induced by our rigid social norms regarding thinness and attractiveness, constitutes a major risk factor for bulimia. Animal research in which we are collaborating with a group of investigators at Penn suggests that regaining occurs significantly more rapidly after a second dieting cycle than a first. We conjectured that those women who have engaged in the greatest number of repeated dieting attempts will be the least successful at achieving their target weight by dieting. These women may be most vulnerable, then, to attempting other weight loss strategies, including purging. Data from our current studies are supporting this hypothesis.

Perhaps the most compelling way that environmental variables inform our understanding of the development of bulimia is in considering why this disorder is escalating so greatly at the present time. One factor is a shift toward an increasingly thin standard for women. Not only has the beauty ideal for women become increasingly thin, but it is now also more universally similar and more widely distributed, due to the advent of mass media. Changes in measurements toward increasing thinness over time have been documented in Miss America contestants, Playboy centerfolds, and female models in magazine advertisements (Garner, Garfinkel, Schwartz, & Thompson, 1980; Snow & Harris, 1985). During the same time period, however, the average body weight of women under 30 years of age has actually increased (Metropolitan Life Foundation, 1983; Society of Actuaries, 1959, 1979).

Models on television and in magazines are seen as realistic representations of what people look like, as compared with painted figures who are more readily acknowledged to be artistic creations. Even though the magazine model or television actress has undergone hours of make-up preparation as well as time-consuming and rigorous work-out regimens to achieve the "look," her audience thinks that her public persona is what she really looks like. Her "look" is then rapidly and widely disseminated, so that the public receives a uniform picture of beauty.

Current sociocultural influences teach women not only what the ideal body looks like, but also how to try to attain it, including how to diet, purge, and engage in other disregulating behaviors. These rituals are nearly prescribed by the mass-market weight control industry. For example, the 1981 best-seller, the *Beverly Hills Dietbook*, advocated a form of bulimia in which binges are "compensated" by eating massive quantities of raw fruit to induce diarrhea. In addition to the mass media making available what one might call manuals for "how to develop an eating disorder," females more directly teach others how to diet, and how to binge and purge and starve. Schwartz, Thompson, and Johnson (1981) found that most college women who purge almost always know another female student who purges, while women who do not purge rarely know someone who does.

A positive feedback loop is thus established: The more women there are with disordered eating, the more likely there are to be even more women with disordered eating. I certainly do not mean to imply that psychopathology is merely learned behavior—but I suggest that the public's heightened awareness of eating disorders and a young woman's likelihood of personal exposure to the behaviors may be a significant factor in the increased emergence of eating disorders in the last several years.

In the past decade, along with the fitness movement, there has been a redefinition of the ideal female body, which is characterized not merely by thinness but by firm, shapely muscles (while avoiding too much muscularity) as well. Although the possible health benefits from increased exercise are very real, the current emphasis on fitness may itself be contributing to the increased incidence of bulimia. The strong implication is that anyone who "works out" can achieve the lean, healthy-looking ideal, and that such attainment is a direct consequence of personal effort and therefore worthy of pride and admiration. Conversely, the inability to achieve the "aerobics instructor look" may leave women feeling defeated, ashamed, and desperate. The pursuit of fitness becomes another preoccupation and even obsession for many.

**Effects of Social/Environmental Variables on Aging.**   One of the significant lessons in Schachter's work, beginning with the studies on emotionality, has been the notion that processes assumed to be biologically determined are capable of being dramatically altered by environmental stimuli. I remembered this lesson well as I approached the study of aging. So much work in aging has been influenced by a model of genetically determined biological decline. But Schachter taught us to look to the role of the environment before accepting biological determinism as a sole explanation for physiological effects. Stimulated by this lesson, I have been testing the hypothesis that loss of control produced by environmental challenges and stressors might have an especially strong health impact on older people because their homeostatic regulatory mechanisms are less effective. This assumption is based on two kinds of evidence.

First, there are considerable data showing the impact of loss of control, regardless of the age of the person, on the etiology of disease and on the course of recovery from illness or surgical procedures (see Rodin, 1980, 1986 for reviews). Second, there is evidence for increasing physical vulnerability and decline in old age. Despite this greater potential for decline, however, our hypothesis has led us to see biologically determined decline associated with old age as capable of being mitigated by manipulations of the environment that enhance perceived control. Indeed, from our work we assert that the degree of biologically mandated decline with aging has been overestimated because environmental and personal events associated with old age commonly produce a loss of control. This is clearly a Schachterian hypothesis.

As a function of age per se, older people are exposed to various social and personal conditions that challenge their sense of personal control (e.g., retirement, bereavement, reduced physical strength and vigor). In addition, they are undergoing physiological changes as a function of growing old that make them more vulnerable to the effects of uncontrollable stressors or general loss of control (e.g., immune system depression, increase in chronic illness). The relationship between control and health is presumed to hold for all ages but our model assumes that it increases roughly as a function of chronological age.

We devised a number of experiments that tested the effects of control-relevant interventions. We conducted the studies in nursing homes, both because they were tight experimental settings and because they represented such clear control-limiting environments. We showed that manipulations of increased choice and responsibility improved psychological and physical status. Indeed, even death rate was influenced, suggesting possible life-promoting effects of enhanced feelings of control (Langer & Rodin, 1976; Rodin & Langer, 1977).

We also taught elderly nursing home residents coping skills that enhanced their repertoire of control-relevant behaviors (Rodin, 1983). We found that these subjects showed a significant reduction in feelings of stress, significant increases in problem-solving ability, and most strikingly, significant long-term reductions in corticosteroid level. Corticosteroids are elevated in times of stress, especially uncontrollable stress, and elevated levels are implicated in atherosclerosis and immunosuppression. The reduction in corticosteroid level correlated significantly with increased feelings of control. Eighteen months following this intervention, the control/coping skills group showed substantial improvements in health.

Next, as part of a larger study investigating the determinants of course of recovery from hospitalization, we randomly selected a subset of subjects scheduled to enter nursing homes (Bers, Bohm, & Rodin, unpublished data). For half of these subjects, we devised a family interaction task intended to increase perceived control over the entry decision. The other half served as controls. While subjects were still in the hospital, prior to the manipulation, we also measured other aspects of control and coping that we believed might promote more favorable recovery outcome.

Whether or not they perceived that they had control over the decision to enter the nursing home carried the greatest weight in predicting which subjects had gone home by the end of one year after entry, and which still remained in the nursing home. Several other psychological variables, related to coping style and self concept, were also more important in discriminating the two groups than was illness severity at the time of admission to the nursing home.

We also considered illness status after one year. Not surprisingly, those in better health when leaving the hospital and those going home immediately, rather than going to a nursing home, were more likely to be in better health at the end of one year. The next most important measured correlate of health at one year was perceived control regarding the nursing home decision. Perceived control was also significantly correlated with lower levels of urinary free cortisol. The findings strongly suggest that perceived control contributes to whether or not people who enter nursing homes after acute hospitalization leave and, in addition, how well they recover from the illnesses that initially led to hospitalization.

While integrated patterns of various hormones are probably the best predictors of health-relevant outcomes, corticosteroids are particularly interesting in studies of aging because numerous experiments have shown that the metabolism of adrenocortical hormones declines with age, possibly in relation to decrease in weight and alterations in tissue components of the cortex (Grad, Kral, Payne, & Berensen, 1967; Romanoff, Morris, Welch, Grace, & Pincus, 1963; Serio et al., 1969). It has also been reported that cortisol may disappear from the circulation of older subjects at a slower rate than in younger persons (West et al., 1961). Corticosteroids also strongly affect immune function. Because of the recent animal demonstrations of the effects of control relevant processes on immune function (Sklar & Anisman, 1979; Visintainer, Volpicelli, & Seligman, 1982), we also addressed this question with humans. This is an issue of special significance for aging because many deaths in elderly people can be attributed to a loss of immunologic competence (Ader, Rodin, & Carl, 1981). Immunologic competence can be briefly explained as the capacity to identify and reject material foreign to the particular individual, and to accept material furnished with markers of self. This is accomplished by a complex system including many cellular, humoral, and hormonal factors.

Environmental and psychosocial events that affect immunity may be more common among the elderly; bereavement and overcrowding are examples. In addition, many biological changes that are associated with aging, independent of disease, affect immune function and vice versa. For example, decline of thymus function has been demonstrated to occur with aging, which is associated with a decline in T cell-dependent cell-mediated immunity.

Our studies of the effects of control on immune function in aging have been based on a longitudinal cohort of 300 men and women, between the ages of 62 and 91, selected at random from census tracts in South Central Connecticut, whom we have been studying for five years. The work is still in progress so the data must be considered preliminary, but we have found striking effects of predictability and control on immune function thus far. It appears that unpredictability and lack of control suppress the number of helper cells and lower the ability of the T cells to mobilize an effective response to an antigen challenge.

We conclude from the data that we have collected until now that lack of predictability and control in relation to a highly stressful event is related to decreases in the number of available helper T cells and to the body's reduced efficiency in counteracting a foreign histocompatability antigen. These data, if upheld with a larger number of subjects, could help to explain the high variability in studies of immune response to bereavement in humans by suggesting it is not the occurrence of stress per se, but the predictability of the stressor and its effects on perceived control, in interaction with health and nutritional status, that determine effects on the immune system. We are seeking further data to determine whether this relationship is stronger as a function of age per se, whether older people rebound from these effects more slowly, and whether the course of disease is affected by immunosuppression differentially as a function of age. Although we expect detrimental effects on health, it is also possible that stress may affect intervening mechanisms such as the immune system but not manifest itself in an alteration in overall health. But Schachter taught us to go after the biggest payoff questions first and then retreat to the more conservative questions if the initial question proved wrong. This is the strategy we are following in the immunology work.

## PROTECTIVE FACTORS THAT MODIFY EFFECTS OF SOCIAL/ENVIRONMENTAL FACTORS ON HEALTH-RELEVANT OUTCOMES

**Externality–Insulin Relationships.**    One interesting observation that we made, regarding insulin release in response to environmental food cues, is the extraordinary between-subject variability of the phenomenon (Rodin, 1978, 1985). By contrast, this response appears to be highly reliable within a single subject from measurement to measurement. Certainly the animal data of Berthoud et al. (1980, 1981) suggest that this between-subject variability has important pathophysiological consequences. With their animals, no differences in prior weight history, current weight or basal insulinemia seemed to account for the differences in insulin responsiveness. If this were also true for humans, we would be forced to look beyond the most obvious explanations for possible protective factors that distinguish among individuals. Genetic variables, in interaction with early experience factors, seem a likely candidate. This investigation, which we have not yet begun, is crucial to our understanding of the mediators between biological responsiveness and the impact of environmental variables.

**Sociocultural Variables and Bulimia.**    One area where we have already begun to apply conceptually the protective factors analysis is in our studies of bulimia. For example, since women at greatest risk for bulimia should be those who have accepted and internalized the sociocultural mores about thinness and attractiveness most fully, women who hold these views less strongly should be more protected. To explore this hypothesis, we developed a series of attitude statements based on these sociocultural values (e.g., "attractiveness increases the likelihood of professional success"), and asked women the extent to which they held those values and the extent to which they saw American society in general as holding those values. Those women with the greatest disparity between self and society were least likely to show any evidence of eating disorders (Striegel-Moore et al., 1986).

But how do women come to internalize these attitudes differently? One source of influence is the subculture within which they live. While attitudes about thinness and obesity pervade our entire society, they also are intensified within certain strata. Women of higher socioeconomic status are most likely to emulate closely the trend setters of beauty and fashion and therefore, not surprisingly, they exhibit greater weight preoccupation. Obesity traditionally has been least punished (and of greatest prevalence) in the lower socioeconomic classes. While epidemiological studies drawing representative samples across social classes are still missing, we would expect that differential emphasis on weight and appearance constitutes an important mediating variable in a relationship between social class and bulimia.

Certain subcultures appear to amplify sociocultural pressures and hence place their members at greater risk for bulimia. Prime examples are those subcultures where optimal weight is specified, explicitly or implicitly, for the performance of one's vocation or avocation. Members of professions that dictate a certain body weight—dancers, models, actresses, athletes—have significantly greater incidence of eating disorders than individuals whose job performance is unrelated to their appearance and weight.

We conjecture that certain family characteristics may also amplify or reduce the sociocultural imperatives toward thinness. For example, we hypothesize that a daughter's risk for bulimia is relatively increased if the family places heavy emphasis on appearance and thinness; if the family believes and promotes the myth that weight is under volitional control and thus holds the daughter responsible for regulating it; if family members, particularly females, model weight preoccupation and dieting; if the daughter is evaluated critically with regard to her weight by members of the family; if the daughter is reinforced for her efforts to lose weight; and if family members compete regarding the achievement of the thin ideal. Low levels of these factors in the family should, by contrast, serve as protective factors.

**Aging and External Influences.**    One of the most striking findings in our studies of aging has been the extraordinary resilience displayed by many individuals in the face of substantial environmental variables thought to be causally related to biological decline, such as stress and loss of control. Indeed it is in the study of aging that evidence for variability in response, both physiological and psychological, is the greatest. Moreover, the outcome of the aging process in general is not always decline. Not only are some diseases less likely to occur in old age, such as autoimmune disease, but the impact of many life events such as the death of a spouse is sometimes less in old age. It has been suggested that this occurs because loss of a spouse is both more expected and more normative for one's age in an older person than a younger person (Neugarten, 1972). Only by studying those whose health is unaffected by objectively great stressors and other environmental challenges as they age will we understand fully the psychobiological determinants of adaptation and maladaptation. Again, genetic factors in interaction with certain life experiences should prove significant.


## CONCLUSIONS

Reviewing some of our current work and the enormous intellectual debt it owes to Schachter's work and teaching, I am struck by the type of analysis of individual differences that Stan initiated. His thinking created the new biopsychosocial approach that permeates the field of health and behavior, although I suspect that he will hate the word "biopsychosocial." Allow me the poetic license because it does graphically convey the interaction of individual variables with environment and biology that Schachter taught us to wonder about. Indeed, he taught us to obsess and worry about the wisdom of the body and the processes that can make it go awry, with such enormous success that huge numbers of people—not only his fortunate students—owe much of their scientific work to him.

But ultimately the most important lesson I learned from Stan was how to do the work and not which problems to study. He was adamant when we were students about thinking clearly and systematically, and about finding the most interesting way to test ideas. He taught us to think in terms of interactions, arguing that if you could not both increase and decrease experimentally the effect, you did not understand the phenomenon. He also taught us the excitement of looking at data. His fun with data was contagious. He made me see that the work should be excellent, but if it is not also fun, it is not worth doing. When I sit in my office thinking, as I often do, how amazing it is that I get paid for having such fun, I also think how much of that I owe to Stanley.


## REFERENCES

Ader, R., Rodin, J., & Carl, J.C. (1981). Immunology and behavior in aging. In Parron, D.L., Solomon, F., & Rodin, J. (Eds.) *Health, behavior and aging.* Washington, D.C.: National Academy Press.

Bennett, W.I. (1984). Dieting: Ideology versus physiology. *Psychiatric Clinics of North America, 7,* 321–334.

Berthoud, H.R., Trimble, E.R., Siegel, E.G., Bereiter, D.A., & Jeanrenaud, B. (1980). Cephalic-phase insulin secretion in normal and pancreatic islet-transplanted rats. *American Journal of Physiology, 238,* E336–E340.

Berthoud, H.R., Bereiter, D.A., Trimble, E.R., Siegel, E.G., & Jeanrenaud, B. (1981). Cephalic-phase, reflex insulin secretion. *Diabetologia, 20,* 393–401.

Bjorntorp, P. & Sjostrom, L. (1971). Number and size of adipose tissue fat cells in relation to metabolism in human obesity. *Metabolism, 20,* 703–713.

Bjorntorp, P. & Yang, M.U. (1982). Refeeding after tasting in the rat: Effects on body composition and food efficiency. *American Journal of Clinical Nutrition, 36,* 444–449.

Booth, D.A. (1972). Modulation of the feeding response to peripheral insulin, 2-deoxyglucose or 3-O-methyl glucose injection. *Physiology and Behavior 8,* 1069–1076.

Booth, D.A. & Brookover, T. (1968). Hunger elicited in the rat by a single injection of bovine crystalline insulin. *Physiology and Behavior, 3,* 439–446.

Brandes J. (1977). Insulin induced overeating in the rat. *Physiology and Behavior, 18,* 1095–1102.

Brownmiller, S. (1984). *Femininity.* New York: Simon & Schuster.

Chaiken, S. & Pliner, P. (1984). *Women, but not men, are what they eat: The effect of meal size and gender on perceived femininity and masculinity.* Unpublished manuscript, Vanderbilt University, Nashville, TN.

Even, P. & Nicolaidis, S. (1981). Changes in efficiency of ingestants are a major factor of regulation of energy balance. In L.A. Cioffi, W.P.T. James, & T.B. Van Itallie (Eds.), *The body weight regulatory system: Normal and disturbed mechanisms.* New York: Raven Press.

Faust, I.M., Johnson, P.R., Stern, J.S., & Hirsch, J. (1978). Diet-induced adipocyte number increase in adult rats: A new model of obesity. *American Journal of Physiology, 235,* E279–E286.

Fried, S.K., Hill, J.O., Nickel, M., & DiGirolamo, M. (1983). Prolonged effects of fasting-refeeding on rat adipose tissue lipoprotein lipase activity. Influence of caloric restriction during refeeding. *Journal of Nutrition, 113,* 1861–1869.

Garner, D.M., Garfinkel, P.E., Schwartz, D., & Thompson, M. (1980). Cultural expectations of thinness in women. *Psychological Reports, 47,* 483–491.

Geiselman, P.J. & Novin, D. (1982). The role of carbohydrates in appetite, hunger and obesity. *Appetite, 3,* 203–223.

Grad, B., Kral, V.A., Payne, R.C., & Berensen, J. (1967). Plasma and urinary corticoids in young and old persons. *Journal of Gerontology, 12,* 1447.

Grossman M. & Stein, I.F. (1948). Vagotomy and hunger-producing action of insulin in man. *Journal of Applied Physiology, 1,* 263–269.

Gruen, R.K. & Greenwood, M.R.C. (1981) Adipose tissue lipoprotein lipase and glycerol release in fasted Zucker (fa/fa) rats. *American Journal of Physiology, 241,* E76–E83.

Hawkins, R.C., Jr., Turell, S., & Jackson, L.J. (1983). Desirable and undesirable masculine and feminine traits in relation to students' dietary tendencies and body image dissatisfaction. *Sex Roles, 9,* 705–724.

Kanarek, R.B., Marks-Kaufman, R., & Lipeles, B.J. (1980). Increased carbohydrate consumption as a function of insulin administration in rats. *Physiology and Behavior, 25,* 779–782.

Langer, E. & Rodin, J. (1976). The effects of choice and enhanced personal responsibility for the aged: A field experiment in an institutional setting. *Journal of Personality and Social Psychology, 34,* 191–198.

Lotter, E.C. & Woods, S.C. (1977). Injections of insulin and changes of body weight. *Physiology and Behavior, 18(2)*, 293–297.

Lovett, D. & Booth, D. (1970). Four effects of exogenous insulin on food intake. *Quarterly Journal of Experimental Psychology, 22*, 406–419.

Mann, G.U. & Crofford, O.B. (1970). Insulin levels in primates by immunoassay. *Science, 8*, 1343–1349.

McKay, E., Calaway, J., & Barnes, R. (1940). Hyperalimentation in normal animals produced by protamine insulin. *Journal of Clinical Nutrition, 20*, 59–66.

Metropolitan Life Foundation. (1983). *Statistical Bulletin, 64*, 2–9.

Miller, W.H., Faust, I.M., Goldberg, A.C., & Hirsch, J. (1983). Effects of severe long-term food deprivation and refeeding on adipose tissue cells in the rat. *American Journal of Physiology, 245*, E74–E80.

Neugarten, B. (1972). Personality and aging process. *Gerontologist, 12*, 9–14.

Nicolaidis, A. (1981). Lateral hypothalamic control of metabolic factors related to feeding. *Diabetologia, 20 (S)*, 426–434.

Nicolaidis, S. & Rowland, N. (1976). Regulatory drinking in rats with permanent access to a bitter fluid source. *Physiology and Behavior, 14 (6)*, 819–824.

Nielsen, A.C. (1979). *Who is dieting and why?* Chicago, IL: Nielsen Company, Research Department.

Nylander, J. (1971). The feeling of being fat and dieting in a school population: Epidemiologic interview investigation. *Acta Sociomedica Scandinavica, 3*, 17–26.

Panksepp, J., Pollack, A., & Krost, K. (1975). Feeding in response to repeated protamine zinc insulin injections. *Physiology and Behavior, 14*, 487–493.

Pavlov, I. (1927). *Conditioned reflexes.* Oxford, England: Oxford University Press.

Porte, D. & Woods, S.C. (1981). Regulation of food-intake and bodyweight by insulin. *Diabetologia, 20*, 274–280.

Powley, T. (1977). The ventromedial hypothalamic syndrome, satiety and a cephalic phase hypothesis. *Psychological Review, 84*, 89–102.

Rodin, J. (1978). Has the distinction between internal versus external control of feeding outlived its usefulness? In G.A. Bray (Ed.), *Recent advances in obesity research* (Vol. 2, pp. 75–85). London: Newman.

Rodin, J. (1980). Managing the stress of aging: The role of control and coping. In H. Ursin & S. Levine (Eds.), *Coping and health.* New York: Plenum Publishing Corporation.

Rodin, J. (1981a). Current status of the internal-external hypothesis for obesity: What went wrong? *American Psychologist, 36*, 361–372.

Rodin, J. (1981b). Social and environmental determinants of eating behavior. In L. Cioffi, W.P.T. James, & T.B. Van Itallie (Eds.), *The body weight regulatory system: Normal and disturbed mechanisms.* New York: Raven Press.

Rodin, J. (1983). Behavioral medicine: Beneficial effects of self control training in aging. *Revue International, 32*, 153–181.

Rodin, J. (1985). Insulin levels, hunger, and food intake: An example of feedback loops in body weight regulation. *Health Psychology, 4*, 1–18.

Rodin, J. (1986). Aging and health: Effects of the sense of control. *Science. 233,* 1271–1276.

Rodin, J. & Langer, E. (1977). Long-term effect of a control-relevant intervention. *Journal of Personality and Social Psychology, 35,* 897–902.

Rodin, J., Silberstein, L.R., & Striegel-Moore, R.H. (1985). Women and weight: A normative discontent. In T.B. Sonderegger (Ed.), *Nebraska symposium on motivation: Vol. 32. Psychology and gender* (pp. 267–307). Lincoln: University of Nebraska Press.

Rodin, J. & Slochower, J. (1976). Externality in nonobese: The effects of environmental responsiveness on weight. *Journal of Personality and Social Psychology, 33,* 338–344.

Rodin, J., Slochower, J., & Fleming, B. (1977). The effects of degree of obesity, age of onset, and energy deficit on external responsiveness. *Journal of Comparative and Physiological Psychology, 91,* 586–597.

Rodin, J., Wack, J., Ferrannini, E., & DeFronzo, R. (1985). Effects of insulin and glucose on feeding behavior. *Metabolism, 34,* 826–831.

Romanoff, L.P., Morris, C.W., Welch, P., Grace, M.P., & Pincus, G. (1963). Metabolism of progesterone-4-C$^{14}$ in young and elderly men. *Journal of Clinical Endocrine Metabolism, 23,* 286–291.

Schachter, S. (1968). Obesity and eating. *Science, 161,* 751–756.

Schachter, S. (1971). *Emotion, obesity, and crime.* NY: Academic Press.

Schachter, S. (1982). Recidivism and self-cure of smoking and obesity. *American Psychologist, 37,* 436–444.

Schachter, S. & Rodin, J. (1974). *Obese humans and rats.* Potomac, MD: Lawrence Erlbaum Associates.

Schwartz, D.M., Thompson, M.G., & Johnson, C.L. (1981). Anorexia nervosa and bulimia: The socio-cultural context. *International Journal of Eating Disorders, 1,* 20–36.

Serio, M., Piolanti, P., Capelli, G., Magistris, L., Ricci, F., Anzalone, M., & Guisti, G. (1969). The miscible pool and turnover rate of cortisol in the aged, and variations in relation to time of day. *Experimental Gerontology, 4,* 95–99.

Silberstein, L.R., Striegel-Moore, R.H., & Rodin, J. (1987). Feeling fat: A woman's shame. In H.B. Lewis (Ed.), *The role of shame in symptom formation.* Hillsdale, N.J.: Lawrence Erlbaum Associates.

Silverstone, T. & Besser, M. (1971). Insulin, blood sugar and hunger. *Postgraduate Medical Journal, 47,* 427–429.

Sklar, L.S. & Anisman, H. (1979). Stress and coping factors influence tumor growth. *Science, 205,* 513–515.

Smith, G.P. & Epstein, A.N. (1969). Increased feeding in response to decreased glucose utilization in the rat and monkey. *American Journal of Physiology, 217,* 1083–1087.

Snow, J.T. & Harris, M.B. (1985). *An analysis of weight and diet content in five women's interest magazines.* Unpublished manuscript, University of New Mexico, Albuquerque.

Society of Actuaries. (1959). *Build and blood pressure study.* Washington, DC.

Society of Actuaries and Association of Life Insurance Medical Directors of America. (1979). *Build and blood pressure study.* Chicago, IL.

Striegel-Moore, R.H., Silberstein, L.R., & Rodin, J. (1986). Toward an understanding of risk factors for bulimia. *American Psychologist, 41,* 246–263.

Tanner, J.M. (1978). *Foetus into man: Physical growth from conception to maturity.* Cambridge, MA: Harvard University Press.

Vasselli, J.R., & Sclafani, A. (1979). Hyperreactivity to aversive diets in rats produced by injections of insulin or tolbutamide but not by food deprivation. *Physiology and Behavior, 23,* 557–567.

Visintainer, M.A., Volpicelli, J.R., & Seligman, M.E.P. (1982). Tumor rejection in rats after inescapable or escapable shock. *Science, 216,* 437–439.

Walks, D., Lavan, M., Presta, E., Yang, M.U., & Bjorntorp, P. (1983). Refeeding after fasting in the rat: Effects of dietary-induced obesity on energy balance regulation. *American Journal of Clinical Nutrition, 37,* 387–395.

West, C.D., Brown, H., Simons, E.L., Carter, D.B., Kumagai, L.F., & Englert, E. (1961). Adrenocortical function and cortisol metabolism in old age. *Journal of Clinical Endocrine Metabolism, 21,* 1197–2002.

Woods, S.C., McKay, L.D., & Porte, D. (1979). Intracerebroventricular infusion of insulin reduces food-intake and body-weight of baboons. *Nature, 282,* 503–505.

# 9
## Internal and External
## Control of Behavior

C. Peter Herman
*University of Toronto*

Assessing Schachter's influence on my career seems to require imagining how my career might have proceeded without Schachter's influence. This task is beyond me. Schachter's influence on me has been so enormous that all I can realistically do is attempt to describe the ways in which my work, in substance and style, is patterned on his. And to begin with, maybe I can try to explain why his particular influence on me has been so disproportionate.

## MY ADOPTION

My own psychological make-up—including a nontrivial tendency toward authoritarian submissiveness—made me an especially devoted student. Schachter, who graduated from Yale precisely 25 years before I did, was a generation ahead of me. (An academic generation may be less than 25 years, but for me this was more than an academic relationship.) When I came to Columbia, I did so without the blessings of my own father, who, as a "practical" man, regarded academics as a second-rate career choice. (While I was in graduate school, my father was temporarily an inmate of the Duke Rice Clinic, and happened somehow to play a round of golf with Darwyn Linder, then at Duke, who had actually heard of—and spoke highly of—Schachter. The influence of this endorsement of my career choice, however, was short-lived; even after I received my doctorate, my father would remind me that "psychology makes a good background for law.") Thus, in working with Schachter, I was explicitly rejecting the career trajectory (law–medicine) my family had in mind for me. Although becoming a professor was an estimable ambition for many of my cohort, for me it was a "step down." One need not be an expert in the area of cognitive dissonance or attribution to deduce the heightened intensity of my devotion to the choice I had freely made, at the expense of various anticipated rewards of status and wealth. In effect, I rejected my father's path in order to pursue Schachter's, with predictable consequences for my identity. (Schachter's tendency to refer to me, as I suppose he must have referred to others, as "my boy," did nothing to reduce the power of my filial allegiance. In 1968, when I arrived at Columbia, Schachter did not have a son of his own, let alone a son who shared his research interests.)

Other factors intensified the bond. I had to work my way into Schachter's esteem, as did we all—and many, of course, failed—so that earning and retaining that esteem became at times a goal that superseded all others. And it took me what seemed like quite a while to earn that esteem; I felt that I was slower than some of the other students of my era to "catch on" to thinking in the way that Schachter approved of. Finally, I was never very appreciative of New York, or even the somewhat more welcoming environs of Columbia itself. It was clear to me—and I heard myself saying it frequently—that it was only working with Schachter that made it all worthwhile.

In retrospect, maybe Schachter held out higher hopes for me than he let on. (His reaction to my first in-class comment was a rueful "Herman, you've got a long way to go.") I came to Columbia with a good recommendation from Dick Nisbett and a high quantitative GRE score, which is what Schachter looked for; and I naively failed to apply for financial aid, it never having occurred to me that someone would pay me to go to graduate school, especially when I didn't need assistance. This latter "credential" may have endeared me further to Schachter, who at least nowadays reminisces about the former "Golden Age" when students were all bright and well-prepared and highly motivated and—just to make everything consistent—independently wealthy. (Schachter would become upset with me if I stayed in New York over Christmas break rather than going to Palm Beach; and he was sorely disappointed when I refused to buy a huge lock from the gate of a castle at a Sotheby's auction he dragged me to.) The "special treatment" I received seemed at the time to consist mainly of disparagement of every suggestion I made; the other side of this treatment—his unwillingness to have me do less than best—was less salient at the time.

Now that I have made a name for myself—he warned me that the day would come when I and my unworthy generation would be regarded as bigshots, thereby putting academic fame into a new and less flattering light—he is more openly accepting and appreciative. Partially, this may be due to my association with Janet Polivy, with whom he gets along famously. She may be the closest thing to a Schachter student who never worked with Schachter; and she is able to convivially argue with, and occasionally convince, him about the merits of some preferably outrageous viewpoint. Her first book was dedicated to him. As the world of academics unfolds for me, with all its shortcomings, his acceptance and appreciation remain for me the single most powerful index of personal success.

It is thus fairly easy to reconstruct the preconditions for a powerful cathexis: I was, characterologically, an ideal Schachter student. This readiness-for-imprinting, however, does not really describe the specific ways in which Schachter has influenced me. It explains to some extent why Schachter had such a strong influence on me, but not what that influence was.

## INTERNAL/EXTERNAL

A thought experiment: To determine Schachter's influence, try to describe what he's really like. Because he is perceived in different ways by different people—I remember being startled once by hearing Dick Nisbett describe him as "Mr. Main Effect," because I've always thought of him as "Mr. Interaction"—perhaps my view of him will reveal his most salient characteristics *for me*, and thus his distinctive influence on me.

It is difficult to decide whether his main contribution—or in my case, influence—is methodological or substantive. He has his distinctive way of doing things; and he does distinctive things. Let's consider content.

I have an unshakeable belief that Schachter's major substantive contribution can be summed up in the overused (but not very well understood) distinction between internal and external determinants of behavior, and the proposal that consummatory behavior is jointly determined by both internal and external factors. I use the word "unshakeable" because Schachter himself seems determined at times to prove me wrong, usually by championing an exclusively physiological ("internal") explanation for what had heretofore been seen as the resultant of both internal and external influences.

The "urinalysis" of smoking is a good example of the periodic allure for Schachter of physiological reductionism: For the addicted smoker, all "psychological" influences, it seemed, were to be reduced to their influence on urinary pH, which determined nicotine reuptake, which in turn determined smoking, which was merely behavior in the service of maintaining a regulated level of nicotine in the bloodstream. Schachter's proposal that "the mind is in the bladder" and that stress affects smoking rate only because it affects urinary pH seems on the surface to exemplify reductionism to the point of making fun of "normal" psychology. (And this from the man who convinced me that the group was a legitimate unit of analysis for psychologists!)

The attempt to reduce "mental" determinants (e.g., stress) to their internal/physiological substrate certainly departs from Schachter's more characteristic emphasis on joint internal and external control; but it does not necessarily require a full rejection of the external control of smoking. First, one must not confuse "psychological" or "mental" with "external," even though neither class of variable is "internal." In the original eating studies (viz. Schachter, Goldman, & Gordon, 1968), Schachter manipulated anxiety/stress because it was expected to affect the internal state of the gut through strictly physiological means (i.e., the temporary elevation of blood sugar in response to sympathetic activation); here, as in the later smoking work, we see that a so-called mental state "masks" a physiological state, but stress was never conceived as an "external" influence on the order of cue salience.

It is important to remember that while he was busy demonstrating the "internal" substrate of mental events in the pH studies, Schachter did not manipulate external cues. Not in the series of pH studies, but elsewhere (cf. my dissertation: Herman, 1974), we have noted the control of smoking by explicitly manipulated external cues—visual salience manipulations with no evident effect on pH—in light (i.e., unaddicted) smokers and even in heavy smokers who are not at the moment in a state of nicotine deficit. The pH studies, in my view, overextend Schachter's reductionistic tendency—by giving the impression that external cues, like vague psychological states, are unimportant in the control of behavior. Of course, these studies were designed to combat vague "psychologizing"—a malodorous term for Schachter—and so they emphasized the reduction of psychological states to physiological states (internal cues) without taking external cues into account. Schachter's own conclusion that "the mind is in the bladder" thus is attributable partly to his (legitimate) attack on "psychologizing" and partly to his neglect of the external cue dimension in this instance. His infatuation with the hidden power of urinary pH, I believe, blinded him to the fact that it's not the only power at work.

Although Schachter conducted some smoking studies before my dissertation, it's fair to argue that my study provided the bridge from the eating research to smoking. Light (unaddicted) smokers were to be construed as "obese" (i.e., under external control) while heavy smokers—those who smoked, not weighed, a lot—were to be the "normals," responsive to internal cues. Despite the fact that my dissertation experiment worked out quite nicely, though, the power of external cues—unmediated by physiologically-based cravings—was neglected over the next few years. Why did this happen? Why does Schachter periodically decide that the "real" cause of behavior lies at the molecular level or at the level of macronumerology? I don't know. Maybe it has something to do with his liver or his birth sign. Whatever the cause, it has produced some violent swings, with the "secret cause" of behavior located at one moment in our cells and at another moment in our demographic characteristics. Schachter falls in love with these secret causes; and he loves falling in love with them. But unromantic as he affects to be, he should know that love is single minded whereas behavior is rarely controlled by a single variable.

## FROM INTERACTION TO BOUNDED ZONES

Another continuing problem throughout the 1970's was the absence of an adequate framework for discussing the relative influences of internal and external cues—even once we've dismissed mental states as a legitimate causal influence (but see below). The interplay of internal and external cues—in the control of emotion, eating, smoking, or whatever— remains at the heart of Schachterian theorizing, at least as I see it. But Schachter's discussion of internal and external cues went slightly astray in the transition from the work on emotion to the work on eating, probably because the way these two sorts of factors "interact" is radically different when one attempts to account for the labelling of a phenomenological state (emotion) from when one attempts to account for the control of overt, consummatory behavior (eating or smoking). In the emotion theory, internal (physiological) and external (environmental label) effects fully *interacted*, in the sense that an authentic emotional experience required the simultaneous presence of both internal arousal and an appropriate emotional label supplied by the environment and mediated cognitively. The relation of internal to external cues was very explicit in this work, and the requirement that they interact was explicit (see Fig. 9.1); a great deal of attention was paid to the anomalous situations in which either the internal or the external cue was absent, suppressed, or inordinately heightened.

When we arrived at the research on eating, however, we moved from a general theory of (emotional) behavior to a theory of individual (obese/normal) differences, and the truly interactive theory of internal and external cues was exchanged for a theory in which the behavior of one sort of individual (obese) was controlled by one sort of cue, whereas the behavior of the other sort (normal) was controlled by both, in an indeterminate way. The early discussions of the labelling of hunger seemed a reasonable extension of the emotion work: The obese are

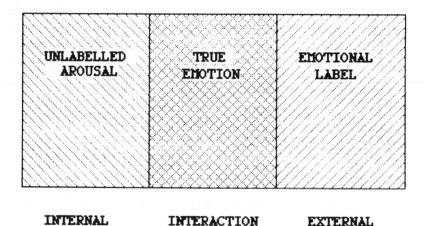

FIGURE 9.1.    Depiction of fully interactive model of emotion.

aberrant in that they use only one sort of cue (external) to determine whether or not they are hungry. The obese, who for whatever reason do not respond to the internal component, are thus not experiencing true hunger—much as an individual who does not respond to his own adrenalin might not have a true emotion, but merely act in accordance with environmental prompts regarding appropriate emotional behavior. The obese are an anomalous case, lacking internal cues, or more pre-cisely the ability/willingness to respond on the basis of such cues. But the parallel here is between emotion and hunger. Eating, which is at least one step removed from hunger, requires a different analysis, one that departs from the fully interactive models of emotion and hunger labelling.

The problem becomes clearer when we consider the normals. In the case of emotion, emotional state was jointly determined by internal and external cues. But what determined the hunger state of the normal individual? In Schachter's formulation, hunger was simply a matter of internal state, and probably a direct function of caloric deprivation. External cues do not enter into the determination of hunger—even though they may affect eating. (If external cues do affect eating in normals, they do so independently of hunger, and sometimes in opposi-tion to hunger.) The necessary interaction has disappeared in the transi-tion from emotion to normals' hunger, probably because whereas there are many emotions, hunger is unitary. The external label was necessary to decide which emotion one was feeling, given a state of internal arousal. With hunger, it is not clear that we need help from the environ-ment in identifying our internal state. Perhaps external cues might indicate to us what we are hungry *for*, but as yet there has been virtually no discussion of this possibility; and even if it were true, we would still not need external labels to tell us that we were hungry per se.

Much of the work that I have been engaged in recently has concerned the place of internal and external controls for normals. (My foregoing analysis of Schachter's "errors" obviously reflects my own current concerns.) In the late 1970's, Lynn Kozlowski (see Herman & Kozlowski, 1979; Herman & Polivy, 1984; Kozlowski & Herman, 1984) brought to me a "model" of regulatory behavior based on the pharmacological "window of effectiveness." This "window" represents the range of drug dosages that are effective but not toxic. A dose less than the lower boundary of the window has no appreciable effect, while a dose above the window's upper boundary has too much of an effect for the patient's well-being. Within the window, however, there was a range of dosages that were effective but nontoxic. What good is this window model? Well, if there is a range of effective but nontoxic dosages, it shouldn't matter too much (to the patient) which value within the range is chosen or maintained; all values within the window fulfill the crucial criteria of effectiveness and nontoxicity. Lynn, of course, was interested in smoking, and had little difficulty applying this model to nicotine, the most important implication being that smokers—even heavy, fully regulating smokers— might have a "window" of acceptable nicotine dosages that would keep them from experiencing either withdrawal or overdose. The window model, then, departed radically from some traditional regulatory models in that it proposed that regulation occurred not at a single value, but rather "within the window." The fully regulating smoker could be satisfied with a range of blood nicotine values. This proposal may explain why studies of nicotine titration often fail to show precise regulation at a "point."

The second implication of the "window model"—or as we came to call it, the "boundary model"—was that if there was a *range* of acceptable values for the regulated substance, then the individual should be under no biological (internal) pressure to increase or decrease the dosage as long as he was "in the window." And if internal pressures (read, internal cues) were weakened or absent altogether when the smoker was within the window, then suddenly we had an opportunity to insinuate external cues back into the control of behavior. Within the window (our "range of biological indifference"), external cues ought to be relatively powerful, inasmuch as internal cues are in abeyance and behavior is no longer constrained by the aversive consequences of withdrawal or overdose (see Fig. 9.2).

Schachter had assumed, along with many others, that nicotine was

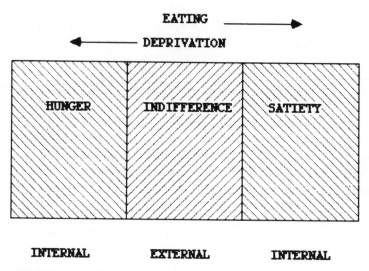

FIGURE 9.2.   Schematic boundary model of eating, emphasizing zones of exclusive internal or external control.

regulated at a point; likewise, implicitly, blood sugar, or whatever it is that is regulated by the normal eater, was assumed to be regulated with respect to a single value. This assumption is the simplest one you can make about regulation, so until its problematic implications were made explicit, it was probably worth holding onto.

The boundary model suggested that instead of a point, we had an acceptable range, all of whose values satisfied regulatory requirements; and if variation within this range were physiologically permissible, then external cues might account for such variation while at the same time leaving the individual within a regulatory framework. This is a powerful idea, I believe. And its power over me stems directly from my continuing ambition to model eating within a comprehensive framework that takes full account of internal and external cues. And my continuing ambition obviously says a lot about Schachter's abiding influence on my reading of what the important questions are.

Explicit tests of this idea involve the manipulation of internal state along with the orthogonal manipulation of external cues. The prediction is generally that when the person is in a state of intense hunger/ withdrawal or satiation/overdose, external cues will have a negligible effect, because the demand to restore a benign physiological state will take precedence. When the subject is "indifferent," however (i.e., within the window), external cues may exert strong control over eating or smoking, up to the point where physiological equilibrium is threatened.

Reanalysis of some of the old smoking and eating data—examining the effects of external cues in subjects who are deprived or not—indicates general support for the idea. My own current research is premised on it.

Comparison of Figs. 9.1 and 9.2 indicates that the boundary model is not fully interactive in the sense that characterized the Schachter and Singer model of emotion. It involves internal and external cues, but they do not act simultaneously; at least, either one or the other is relatively predominant at any given time. (For Schachter, a truly interactive model was one in which, if you set the value of either component at zero, you got nothing; with no arousal, or with no label, you got no true emotion.) The boundary model is perhaps better thought of as additive or hydraulic, although neither of these terms conveys much of the essence of the model either. Clearly, though, the normal eater is governed by both internal and external cues—as Schachter maintained all along—but we are now attempting to specify the manner in which such cues operate; or to put it another way, we are trying to demonstrate when internal cues are likely to exert control, and when people are likely to be responsive to external cues. This is, in effect, a *state* model, not a trait model of internality/externality, as the original Schachter obese/normal distinction has usually been read.

## MOVING FORWARD AND CIRCLING BACK

By focussing on this question—how exactly do internal and external cues control eating—I have remained squarely within the tradition established by Schachter back in the 1960's. Clearly, I am working on problems that he, and everyone else it seems, has long abandoned. Schachter has commented repeatedly on my unusual staying power; less charitably, he remarks on his own lower threshold for boredom, implying that any normal person would have become bored with my research by now. (My twentieth year of research on eating will be 1988.) Although I'll grant that eating research has lost much of its excitement over the course of the past fifteen years—largely because of Schachter's withdrawal from the field, but probably also because of the nature of the research popularity cycle, which naturally looks for the new and different—I remain enchanted (a Schachterian word) with the issues surrounding the control of eating. My guess is that almost any problem can be made interesting, if the researcher brings to it some enthusiasm and fresh ideas. Schachter himself has demonstrated this repeatedly. In the case of eating, the problems were not solved; nor were the original ideas or data discredited—as is sometimes claimed. For some reason, I have been able to generate enough new ideas about eating to keep me interested in my research without needing a new topic to induce enthusiasm. Perhaps I am unique in that I have had Janet and Lynn around to make suggestions or observations that—sufficiently brooded upon—lead to new insights.

Ironically, as of this writing, Schachter is giving indications of returning to the area of eating, or at least weight. The *American Psychologist* (1982) "recidivism" paper—a wonderfully iconoclastic effort—elicited a variety of stimulating responses. Many, perhaps most, of these responses were negative, but Schachter seems to be fueled by controversy. In any case, he is intent on defending the argument of that paper, and I welcome his return (from Wall Street) to the battlefields that he knows so well.

## WILLPOWER: DOWN BUT NOT OUT

Schachter's proposal in the recidivism paper that efforts to lose weight eventually pay off for many overweight adults suggests what is perhaps a belated recognition of another term in the equation of eating and weight regulation—an element long overlooked in the discussion of internal and external cues. Effort is neither an internal/physiological nor an external/environmental variable; accordingly, there was really no room for it in Schachter's theorizing. Indeed, discussions of effort as a causal variable smack of the sort of psychologizing that Schachter has customarily disdained. Alas, it seems that we are being forced to recognize the validity of willful intent as an important influence on behavior. (Willful intent, of course, comes from somewhere; and perhaps our descendants will be able to account for it in terms of passive physiological and environmental inputs.)

Schachter knew, of course, that some people tried to behave in ways that were dictated by neither internal nor external cues. Both smokers and eaters occasionally attempt to resist the push of internal demand and the pull of external enticements, especially because there seems to be ample motivation for smokers not to smoke and for all of us not to overeat. The first study I did after leaving Columbia—the study that was eventually published as Herman and Mack (1975)—seemed (and still seems) to require the invocation of a "restraint" mechanism in dieters. Indeed, we continue to define dieters in terms of their self-reported efforts to restrain their intake (despite hunger and attractive food cues). Although Schachter acknowledged that many people were dieters and tried with varying success to restrict their intake, he never provided a conceptual niche for this sort of "mental" mechanism in his models of eating or smoking. (We provide a niche for "restraint" by including it as a "cognitive boundary" within the zone of indifference separating hunger from satiety. Our analysis of the counter-regulation phenomenon that we have explored depends on the presumptive effect on the diet boundary of our independent variable manipulations [i.e., whether the diet boundary has been breached or not by our manipulations].)

The recidivism paper represents a swing in the direction of recognizing the importance of "self-willed" restraint; I'd like to think that our work through the second half of the 1970's opened him up to considering dieting as a major component of eating behavior and a major contributor to weight change. It is with no little pride that I discover that I have had an effect on Schachter's thinking, and that restraint is a construct that appears in his graduate courses. A close look at my dissertation reveals, however, that the notion of restraint was evident way back then; and insofar as I can reconstruct the thinking and writing that went into that dissertation, I am forced to give Schachter the credit for suggesting the restraint notion in the first place. All I did was, as he would put it, "take it seriously."

## A DEFENSE OF REVISIONISM

My intention was to describe Schachter's influence on me, but it seems that I have described (1) my own thinking and (2) the ways in which Schachter erred. The astute reader, however, will recognize that my own thinking is premised almost entirely on Schachter's. I have adopted his questions as my own. I have adopted his terminology and research techniques as my own. And to the extent that I have criticized him, I feel as if I am not attacking him but defending him by "adjusting" his thinking to take account of some difficulties that the original theorizing couldn't quite handle. I remain amazed—though I guess I shouldn't be—that my work is often taken to be an attack on Schachter. I am seen by some as a follower of Nisbett, whose 1972 paper on hunger and obesity was widely viewed as an attack, but which for me was a provocative extension of Schachter's previous work. I am seen (e.g., by Stanton Peele, in his *Science of Experience,* 1983) as a critic of the entire Schachter–Nisbett–Rodin school, by virtue of my focus on restraint, which does not fit easily into the internal/external framework. (Peele was astounded to learn, too late, that I was a Schachter student, and indeed a Schachter loyalist.)

Does revision of someone's work constitute an attack on that work? Or is it in some respects a way of paying homage? My best guess is that whether one is to be thought of as attacking or extending someone else's contribution depends less on what changes one recommends than on the attitude that one brings to the enterprise. One could have done what I have done in an antagonistic way; God knows that Schachter-bashing has long been a popular sport. But it was always evident to those who know me well that I have tried to do the sort of work that he would want me to do. Schachter himself seems pleased with what we have done, which is what counts. He knows that I am still working for him.

I despair of making any clearer the debt I owe to Schachter with respect to the nature of my work. It perhaps remains to be explained why I have persisted with eating/obesity/dieting research. I personally have never had a "weight problem." My father and grandfather were both graduates of the Duke Rice Clinic—although neither of them was particularly fat—so perhaps I come by my interest in these issues honestly. Also, my favorite uncle died (at the age of 47) from a heart-attack brought on, I am convinced, by strenuous dieting. So dieting, and the narcissism that it betrays, has always been a major irritant for me. Other reasons for staying in this area include the fact that this area overlaps with virtually every other area of psychology—physiological, perception, cognition, social, personality, and abnormal—allowing one tremendous freedom and range in one's research. And Kozlowski's "window" has breathed fresh life into a research program that might have gone stale. Mainly, though, I'm doing it because that's what Schachter taught me, and the ways of playing with ideas that he taught me have kept me from losing my enthusiasm.

## THE SCHACHTER STYLE

I have tried to indicate the sorts of problems that Schachter articulated for me, and that have preoccupied me since I fell under his influence. What remains is to indicate the "stylistic" legacy—the form of the research, leaving aside for the moment its content. What are the distinctive methodological features of Schachterian research that I have adopted?

First, experimentation. In the area of eating, it is easy to ask questions, directly. People are more than willing to tell you why they eat the way they do. This won't wash. Schachter has emphasized the extent to which people are effectively unaware of the actual determinants of their behavior; people, in short, indulge in facile "psychologizing" when it comes to explaining their own behavior. Interviews are often revealing—but not of the truth; rather, they indicate how easily satisfied people are with the "consensual" explanations for behavior. Schachter's mistrust of people's explanations of their own behavior reached its peak, of course, in Nisbett & Wilson (1977). So we use the "obvious" explanations as a foil against which we may display more acutely analytical explanations. It should be emphasized, perhaps, that we do not necessarily mistrust people's rendition of facts (e.g., whether they diet, or have lost weight, or even how much they eat); what we discount is their rendition of *why* they behave that way. Causality is to be inferred from the observed effects of independent variable manipulations on behavior.

The requirement that we actually observe the effect of independent variable manipulations on actual (overt) consummatory behavior dictates that our studies be labor intensive. Although our equipment needs are minimal—Schachter made us proud that our productivity was achieved despite the pitiful resources we had available to us in the "lab" at Columbia—the costs in terms of repetitive experimenter person hours is high, especially considering that after an hour or two of subject running, we are usually left with what amounts to one or two data points of value. The effort invested in data collection is so great, in fact, that we naturally treat these data with extreme care. We analyze these data every which way, looking for a pattern—even if not the one we initially expected—because they are so costly to us. The inclination to "throw the data into the computer and see what emerges" is anathema to us, because the computer usually ends up giving us a single ANOVA table, which doesn't begin to satisfy our craving for a more fine-grained analysis and search of the data. It appears that some of the newer statistical programs for personal computers will permit the sort of intensive combing of the data that we have come to demand; so it seems likely that we will be able to once again "take our data to bed with us," as we were taught, but now electronically.

That our questions often concern interactions (or patterns of predominance) of internal and external cues requires that our research designs reflect the orthogonal manipulation of such variables; and because we more often than not make differential predictions for different types of individuals (obese/normal, dieter/nondieter, heavy/light smoker), our designs tend toward the $2 \times 2 \times 2$. We prefer predictions that emphasize statistical interactions, for the simple reason that it is more difficult to come up with a convincing alternative explanation for an interaction—ideally, a cross-over interaction—than for a main effect. The emphasis is on not simply demonstrating something, but demonstrating something that (1) goes beyond conventional wisdom and (2) is defensible in the face of conventional wisdom. We are usually making an argument for a slightly offbeat proposition, and that means that we are very much aware of the requirements of successful advocacy; we operate under a virtual adversary system.

Schachter and his students are not known for the disinterested collection of facts, nor for the impartial presentation of competing interpretations; this more "passive" scientific role is a valid one, in my view, but it's not a role I have been trained for or especially enjoy. I am a strong believer, though, in the need for both sorts of science—fact collecting with an eye to eventual theoretical integration, and theoretical aggressiveness combined with empirical demonstration—even though I am personally in the latter camp. I also believe that it is possible to allow the unexpected results of these "demonstrations" to alter one's theorizing. Where do good ideas come from? I don't know; but I do know that they seem most likely to emerge when one is trying to make sense of a pattern of data that does not conform to one's original expectation.

What else has Schachter taught me? One thing that is often taken for granted, but shouldn't be: Stay with research. The temptations to get involved in other pursuits is often strong. I myself have succumbed to the extent of giving nine years to the *Journal of Personality;* this time was not wasted—I enjoy reviewing, and I learned a few things—but it was too much of an intrusion on research. Another Greek gift is an invitation to write a chapter. If you have a major theoretical advance to promote, then a chapter can be a useful vehicle; but of all the chapters I have written, I think that only two were really worth writing; and chapter writing, with its deadlines, tends to cut into research. In academia, there are all sorts of opportunities to get involved in things—professional associations, administration, and so on—and as one's research reputation grows, so grows the volume of these opportunities. There is prestige and sometimes some other rewards associated with these positions. I for one, however, am learning, slowly, that the *excitement* lies in pure research. This is not necessarily true for everyone, obviously; but I now see that it is true for me, as it has always been for Schachter; and I now understand why he snorts at my nonresearch involvements. You have to pay your dues; but you don't have to pay more than your dues to remain in good standing in the academy.

Another thing: communication. Schachter is an elegant stylist, for an academic psychologist. Occasionally he has been charged with being too cute, or slippery. Well, cute, maybe. But slipperiness is more often the concomitant of dull, complex prose that substitutes technical jargon for clarity of thought. If you cannot communicate crisply with your audience, then you are probably not communicating with yourself (i.e., thinking) very clearly in the first place. Scientific writing need not be boring, or ponderous. We are not in a morgue, but in a marketplace of ideas, where attractiveness counts. I myself have often been accused of glibness and a dangerous tendency toward humor, even of the self-deprecatory kind. A light touch, though, need not reflect conceptual weakness; and you can take ideas seriously without taking yourself (and your colleagues) too seriously.

This chapter, as it happens, has turned out to be more serious than I had anticipated. The fact is that my relationship to Schachter, along with my relationship to Polivy, is what I really care about professionally. It is not as easy to make light of it as I would have imagined, even though the reader might have appreciated more lightness.

## INTERNAL/EXTERNAL: A REPRISE

When I went to work for Schachter, I was under his control; I was entirely external, looking for direction. Now I feel more internally controlled. But when I look inside, I recognize that my own internal sense of direction is provided not by some spontaneous guide, but by my internalization of Schachter, the image of him that I carried away with me when I left Columbia. He remains with me, and I defer to his wisdom when I am faced with confusion or with a difficult choice. It's only fitting, I suppose, that his real and imagined expectations for me fully reflect the ambiguities of internal and external control. One could do worse than to try to live up to those expectations.

## REFERENCES

Herman, C.P. (1974). External and internal cues as determinants of the smoking behavior of light and heavy smokers. *Journal of Personality and Social Psychology, 30*, 664–672.

Herman, C.P. & Kozlowski, L.T. (Spring, 1979). Indulgence, excess, and restraint: Perspectives on consummatory control in everyday life. In N. Zinberg (Ed.), Special issue of *Journal of Drug Issues*, 185–196.

Herman, C.P. & Mack, D. (1975). Restrained and unrestrained eating. *Journal of Personality, 43*, 647–660.

Herman, C.P. & Polivy, J. (1984). A boundary model for the regulation of eating. In A.J. Stunkard & E. Stellar (Eds.), *Eating and its Disorders* (pp. 141–156). New York: Raven.

Kozlowski, L.T. & Herman, C.P. (1984). The interaction of psychosocial and biological determinants of tobacco use: More on the boundary model. *Journal of Applied Social Psychology, 14*, 244–256.

Nisbett, R.E. (1972). Hunger, obesity, and the ventromedial hypothalamus. *Psychological Review, 79*, 433–453.

Nisbett, R.E. & Wilson, T.D. (1977). Telling more than we can know: Verbal reports on mental processes. *Psychological Review, 84*, 231–259.

Peele, S. (1983). *The science of experience.* Lexington, MA: D.C. Heath.

Schachter, S. (1982). Recidivism and self-cure of smoking and obesity. *American Psychologist, 37,* 436–444.

Schachter, S., Goldman, R., & Gordon, A. (1968). Effect of fear, food deprivation and obesity on eating. *Journal of Personality and Social Psychology, 10* 91–97.

# Observations, Demonstrations, and Applications: Research on Cigarettes, Coffee, Walking, and Sense-of-Direction

Lynn T. Kozlowski
*University of Toronto* and *Addiction Research Foundation*

About five years out of Columbia, I was lunching with Stanley Schachter at a conference in Toronto. He was chatting with a noted psychologist and they fell to comparing their experiences with graduate students. Schachter, I think, had contrived to give me a brief postdoctoral lesson: "I find that students start by doing your work and you take credit for it; then they leave, continue to do your work, and give you no credit for it (and they should); finally, they do their own work and give you no credit for it (and they shouldn't)." I didn't comment, but I did feel that my head (and those of many other Schachter students) had been resting under the nail that had just been so squarely hit.

I doubt that Schachter has had a successful student who did not benefit from the opportunity to do his work. And, I suspect that many of us have had disengagement periods, during which we were still following through on notions that were born in our stays in Schachter's lab, yet the work was now appearing often exclusively under our own by-line. The final element in Schachter's account was from my point of view the most important: It was another indication of his desire that his students come to do good work of their own and on their own. I have long respected him as a master who knows how to make good use of his apprentices; and this means in part that he promotes and savors their transformation into masters.

I have traded enough anecdotes with colleagues and friends to know that not all of us who worked with him dealt with exactly the same man. I take it as my task to show my own view of Schachter. I have tried to avoid turning this tribute to Schachter into mainly an advertisement for myself, but I realize that some readers will need an introduction to the brand of applied experimental psychology that I have been pursuing.

## BACKGROUND

When I was an undergraduate at Wesleyan University, I took two courses in psychology in 1966–67: first, the year long introductory course and second, a seminar in physiological psychology taught by Russell Leaf. This was during my sophomore year, and I was trying to decide between a psychology and an English major. Although I did well in the physiological seminar, Leaf noticed that I was not cut out for a career as a physiological psychologist (perhaps because I was the only one of the six students to decline the opportunity of elective surgery on a white rat). Leaf took me aside. I told him I was leaning toward English rather than psychology. He countered with, "You should take a look at the work of Stanley Schachter; you might find a model there for a type of psychology that would be more to your liking."

I went to the library and read everything of Schachter's that I could find. I was charmed by a man who at one turn was quoting Walt Whitman's poetry and at another was needling college students with a question, "With how many men other than your father has your mother had extramarital relations?", allowing as the most flattering option the answer "4 and under." Despite the attractions to the work, I followed my interest in poetry and writing into the English department. But I remembered Schachter.

Months after I graduated from Wesleyan, I was teaching English in a public high school (I have never known more tiring and difficult work), and I was dreaming of going to graduate school in psychology. I was planning on only giving it a try. If I didn't like graduate study in psychology, I reasoned that I could stop after a year and try some other profession. I applied to Columbia because of Schachter, and I intended to go there only if Schachter agreed to take me as a student. I was drawn by his mix of psychological and physiological interests. And I was drawn by the fine jobs attained by his earlier students; after all, the object of going to graduate school was to get a better job.

When I was accepted in the spring of 1970, I went for an interview to meet him. Engagingly, he outlined the results of some of his current research on eating and body weight. (I was expecting to do work on emotion; the eating work came as a surprise.) I was entertained by his presentation. We then talked of my studies in Dublin. (I had spent a term at Trinity College in 1968.) He had friends in Dublin and we talked about the city. As the interview was closing, I became eager, almost insistent, to know if he would accept me as a student. He seemed hesitant to make a decision before September. At last, as I was leaving, he relented: "Okay, how can I resist a student who has read poetry in a

Dublin pub." The acceptance, offered playfully, was taken seriously. I would be back in this office in September.

## THE FIRST YEAR

Schachter's research seminar was designed to get some research done on topics of interest to Schachter. This one was devoted mainly to filling in the most troublesome gaps in previous eating and smoking research conducted in Schachter's lab. I was assigned to review the literature on water drinking in rats with lesions of the ventromedial hypothalamus and encouraged to design a study on the effects of water palatability on intake in obese and normally-weighted humans. Schachter was interested in testing the generality of the "externality" findings by seeing if the eating effects could be found with water drinking.

I argued that the best way to manipulate the palatability of water was by changing its temperature. Quinine adulteration of water made water into a different substance altogether (flat tonic water?). Ice water was generally viewed as more palatable than room temperature or tepid water. Schachter seemed pleased with this analysis and a study was designed.

At about midsemester, I was practicing scholarly, cocktail-party poses while standing next to Schachter and a visiting colloquium speaker; they were talking about the pleasures and perils of graduate students in general. (Could this be the academic analogue of talking about the weather?) Schachter decided to turn from the general and put his arm on my particular shoulder: "Take him; he will be absolutely useless to me in his first year; by the third year, I might get something worthwhile from him; but then by the following year he'll be working on his doctoral dissertation." I think I smiled insipidly. I know I said nothing. However, I did resolve to prove him wrong and demonstrate my usefulness before the year was over.

I did complete my first psychology experiment before the end of the year (Kozlowski & Schachter, 1975). This study owes its publication in part to the use of a somewhat embarrassing nonparametric test for interaction. This interaction test helped us recover from cruel and unusual punishment by a single subject who drank water as if he were a camel at the last oasis. Our study showed that obese subjects drank more water than did normal subjects when the water cue was prominent, but did not do so when the water cue was remote. The water palatability manipulation had no differential effect on obese and normals.

My formal training spilled over into the summer of the first year. Schachter had been instrumental in the creation of a "Social Science

Research Council/National Science Foundation Summer Training Institute in Psychobiology" at the University of California, Irvine. He described the program as "medical school in six weeks." This hyperbolic bit of salesmanship was not needed. Schachter wanted me to go; I wanted to go; and my wife was dying to spend the summer on a California beach. The program was excellent and crucial to my own education in matters biological. And it allowed me, at last, to go Schachter one better: I have seen hypothalami as well as eaten them.

The most explicit lessons of my early graduate training concerned the execution of laboratory experiments and the analysis of the data. I consider this Schachter's core curriculum. One could survive a number of stupid remarks in class (and avoid the attribution of idiocy), but a single substandard performance of research put one in danger of being washed out of Schachter's lab as well as out of his good graces. I hasten to add that substandard performance was not judged on the basis of disappointing results.

### The Need to "Perform" Studies

Early in the preparations for the water-drinking study, I was impressed by the attention that was being paid to detail. I remember the time we spent considering the shape of the water pitcher and the shape and size of the water glass. I spent days looking for just the right kind of glass pitcher, one that would look appealing with ice in it. I finally located the perfect pitcher in a shop near my apartment in the Bronx. Schachter and I were both pleased about it. (Looking back, it seems decidedly foolhardy to have begun a study with a one-of-a-kind glass pitcher that was intended for use by at least 80 ham-handed Columbia and Barnard undergraduates. Last I knew this pitcher was still pouring years after I graduated and doing duty as the water pitcher for colloquium speakers.)

I was getting a kick out of preparing the props and stage. And Schachter encouraged my interest in the details of the experimental setting. He gave his blessing to an idea I had for reducing the suspicion of subjects that they were being watched through an observation mirror. (They needed to be watched, to measure sip-by-sip drinking during an unaccompanied stay in the lab with the prized pitcher and the old fashioned glass.) Brown wrapping paper (sometimes with face-sized tears in the middle or a vertical gap between two pieces) was being used to give the appearance of blocking off an unneeded mirror. I developed a way of covering the entire mirror but for a 1 to 2 inch irregular space along the bottom edge. It looked as if the paper had been torn with a slightly irregular edge, and it proved to be a convincing bit of subterfuge. The subjects were mostly unaware that they were being watched by a bent-over graduate student peering through the small gap.

I learned much of what I know about psychology from the talented students who were alongside me or just ahead of me in the Columbia program. Sometimes, however, I was led astray. As I prepared for my first psychology experiment, I was told the story of an enterprising college graduate who had spent a post-B.S. year at his alma mater cranking out experiments, so that his publication list would have a head start on others in graduate school. This entrepreneur put all of his experimental instructions on audio tape. He could, then, deal with almost as many subjects per hour as there were rooms per floor.

When I was told to draft a 'spiel' for the water-drinking study, I imagined it would be put on cassette tape, and the experiment would soon thereafter be off and running, gobbling up all the chubby 'subject' cells in the Columbia student body. When I read the draft to Schachter, he made a few suggestions and said: "Memorize it and we'll run through it in the lab." I soon realized that, not only was taping out of the question, I was also not to be allowed to read from a script. I was expected to act it out. I was to be judged, not just on the script, but on my performance of it. And it wouldn't do to woodenly greet subjects, sit them in their chair, and read them stiff lines scrolling past my mind's eye. I would need to emulate Schachter's social style: seem friendly (but not ingratiating), frank (but not earnest), articulate (but not highfalutin), and relaxed (but not bored).

I rewrote the script to give myself additional casual lines. I practiced as if it were a Broadway debut. When the appointed hour of the "dry-run" arrived, I had arranged a practice subject from among the other graduate students. I had expected Schachter to watch my performance from the observation room. Instead, he followed us into the small lab and sat off to the side. I think his presence in the room served at least two purposes. First, and most important, he wanted to try to get a feel for what was happening from the subject's point of view. Getting beyond what a study is alleged to involve by putting oneself as completely as possible in the place of the subject is one of the keys to good laboratory research. Second, he was making the test a bit more challenging for me. (I make no apologies for this obviously sadistic streak: cats have duties to their mice.) Besides, if I could perform as if he weren't there, when he was clearly next to me in a small room, I could probably be a persuasive performer in front of real subjects. The audition went well enough: I got the job.

## A Primer on Data Analysis

After 10 or so subjects had been run, Schachter asked to take a look at the data. He said to put it on data sheets and we would meet to look them over. From looking over Peter Herman's shoulder, I knew that a data sheet was one of those wide, ruled and columned sheets on which subjects were rows and your questionnaire responses and behavioral measures were columns. I dedicated one sheet for each of the 8 cells of the experiment.

Schachter put the data sheets on his lap and rocked back in his chair to study them. He explained that it was too early to tell much and instructed that the organization of the data on the page was crucial for *seeing* patterns in the data. He insisted that *all* the data for each subject be arrayed in data sheets, so that they could be looked at. This meant that I had to add such things as "time the subject had been run," "birth order" and "average daily intake of cigarettes" (even though the study had nothing to do with cigarettes or birth order). If I left a question off the sheets, he argued that it would likely be forgotten and, therefore, some relationship that might smile up at you from the page would be doomed to oblivion in a file cabinet. He explained in addition that, if I organized the page so that variables of interest were bunched together, then I was providing myself with even more opportunity to see relationships that might otherwise be missed.

During the management of the data from this first experiment, I learned also that statistical trees (descriptive or inferential) could sometimes obscure the subject-by-subject forest of results. The only solution to this problem was to sit for hours pondering the data sheets. Statistics, it seemed, were best used (when dealing with smallish datasets) to confirm what a subject-by-subject inspection of the results has already shown you.

Modern computer spreadsheets (sorting, grouping, printing out results so that interesting columns can be arranged and rearranged next to each other *ad infinitum* and easily) do what we did then by means of organization, *ad hoc* origami (bending a column of interest to the side of a column of importance), recopying, photocopying, and cutting and pasting. Now, when I explore data on my computer spreadsheet, I employ the same principles I was taught with my first hand-written data sheets.

The researcher who has only one idea about his study (usually the one that carried him into the study) and feeds the results to an analysis of variance program on the computer is engaging in an extremely conservative statistical procedure. To be revealed in such a procedure, patterns have to be expected. On the other hand, given enough cleverness and diligence, we in this Schachter school can find ourselves doing hundreds of statistical or quasistatistical analyses and suffering excess risk of being tricked by chance. An appreciation of this methodological problem of multiple significance tests has made me less concerned about the sanctity of the .05 level of statistical significance and more impressed by replication as the truest indication of reliability. I should add that living with one's data this intimately does not invariably lead to published articles. I can guarantee you that both Schachter and I have files crammed with "failed" studies.

The main lesson again. Look at your results case by case and in various arrangements. Ruminate. Take walks through the data. Sit with the data sheets. Look for patterns. Look for funny, anomalous cases. Try to understand them. Try to develop an understanding and an account of what happened and why. Ponder. I do not like to think of this as "massaging" the data. It is more like figuring out the results or mapping them onto reasonable ideas. From then to now, such inspection of data has been a special pleasure for me. I love it. It is one of the main things I love about my work. For this style of researcher, being without data on data sheets is as incapacitating as an absence of wood to a carpenter.

As I have shown, the data on the sheets do not necessarily have to have been collected by you; useful data can be found in a number of accessible archives (Kozlowski, 1981; Kozlowski, 1986; Kozlowski, Frecker, & Lei, 1982; Kozlowski, Rickert, Robinson, & Grunberg, 1980). In honor of this occasion, I have prepared a brief demonstration on the use of preexisting data sources. Most of us are aware, though no one talks about it publicly, that Stanley Schachter has one of the most misspelled surnames in modern psychology. (This issue brings to mind the classic Nisbett/Nesbitt confusion: Are they one or two psychologists? Which one is real?) The Social Science Citation Index can be used to turn idle speculation about the damage done to name and fame into a publishable report. Table 10.1 shows the results of an analysis of the Citation Index. A 5% error rate is not high for undergraduate essays, but society should expect more from the scientific literature. As an offering to Schachter, I have developed a mnemonic for his name: Just think of a child's name for a train—a choo-choo—and you'll get by the tough spots—Schachter.

## GETTING FROM THERE
## TO HERE AND OTHER LESSONS

I am confident that Schachter would acknowledge the lessons described so far as lessons he had set out to teach. Next I discuss lessons I *took*

TABLE 10.1
Percentage of Misspelled Citations from the Social Sciences Citation Index
(1976 to 1980 Cumulation) For Two, Not Four, Noted Psychologists

|  | % Misspelled | Total Number |
| --- | --- | --- |
| L. Festinger | 0 | 1,000 |
| S. Schachter | 5.9 | 941 |
| S. Schacter[a] | — | 55 |
| S. Shachter[a] | — | 4 |

Note: Citations were measured in inches and transformed by use of the formula 1 inch = 5 cites. Data are approximate, but in the right ballpark.
[a]Incorrect spelling.

from my time with Schachter, whether or not he intended to *give* them as lessons. At the same time, I try to account for what has become of me since I left Columbia. Although I have remained a psychologist, I have often published articles in journals concerned with public health, behavioral pharmacology, epidemiology, and general science, to place my work before the most relevant audience of researchers.

## Why So Much On Cigarettes?

My first studies of cigarette smoking did not arise out of a preoccupation with or even an appreciation of the public health consequences of smoking. During my time at Columbia and before, Schachter was a devoted and dependent cigarette smoker. I think he wondered why he smoked. I think he saw cigarettes affording a clear link to his work on emotionality and arousal. He at first considered a self-inflicted jolt of nicotine as equivalent to an "epinephrine informed" manipulation: The smoker should be less emotional because of the opportunity to attribute most emotional arousal to this nonemotional source. This model eventually fell to the floridly reductionistic "pH-model" which proposed that (1) all smokers were addicted to nicotine, (2) under stress, nicotine left the body more rapidly (because of increased urinary acidity), and hence (3) smokers needed to smoke more under stress just to keep themselves out of nicotine withdrawal (Schachter et al., 1977).

My own view of the pH work was that the extremely reductionistic model was offered as a thoughtful provocation—a useful, but playful, scientific strategem. It was not as if the world of smoking could really be reduced to the bladder; it was as if we could ultimately learn important things about what controls smoking by pushing this simple model as far as it could go. I am surprised at the umbrage apparent in some of the reactions to Schachter's reductionism (e.g., Peele, 1983).

My graduate training in experimental social psychology and attribution theory left me with the overwhelming belief that many of the phenomena for which social psychologists had been spilling ink were to be found mainly in the carefully tended, rarefied atmosphere of the laboratory; and, when they were found outside the laboratory, they were more likely to be concerned with hair splitting than important matters. I longed to study phenomena that would replicate, be robust, be of some practical importance, and be of interest to more than other social psychologists. In effect, I responded to my own crisis over the value of experimental social psychology by focusing on a topic that had a clear and significant ecological niche in our society and that, at the same time, was amenable to a variety of ways of being studied, including some of the experimental ways I had been learning. (Mine was of course not the only available growth path out of the problems of the social psychology of the day, as evidenced by my colleagues in this volume.)

Cigarette smoking is of practical and scientific interest in several respects. Tobacco peddling is big business. Tobacco taxes are of great consequence to most governments. Cigarette smoking (tobacco use) is one of the most dangerous "drug" habits world wide. It has the advantage of being probably as addictive as heroin, while at the same time being as available and as legal as soap. Tobacco use has a rich economic and social history. Aspects of tobacco use are the stuff of anthropology, social psychology, sociology, public health, behavioral pharmacology, medicine, clinical psychology, neurosciences, health psychology, biopsychology, consumer psychology, and muckraking. Cigarette smoking is an observable behavior that occurs at a high operant rate (e.g., often 3 puffs per minute, 5 cigarettes per hour) in a multitude of settings: This is a great help in doing behavioral studies. And reasonably good records on cigarette smoking have been archived for years, permitting data-based studies that are impossible on many black-market drugs. In short, this domesticated drug of widespread and poorly understood abuse had a lot to offer the advanced as well as the beginning researcher.

### The Examined Life Often Leads To Publications

Goethe (Auden & Kronenberger, 1966) said:

> The mere observing of a thing is no use whatsoever. Observing turns into beholding, beholding into thinking, thinking into establishing connections,

so that one may say that every attentive glance we cast on the world is an act of theorizing. However, this ought to be done consciously, with self-criticism, with freedom, and, to use a daring word, with irony (p. 350).

Schachter was often finding research ideas from his own attentive glance at his own life and the lives of his friends. I learned to listen to my own hunches and to things I "theorized" about the behavior of others. Other social scientists get ideas from observations of their life. Schachter's example encouraged (1) conscious work at it, (2) self-criticism, (3) freedom and novelty, and (4) a joy in irony. (Irony can be defined here as incongruity between what might be expected and what actually occurs.) The last point is crucial to the esthetic of a Schachterian idea.

Not all useful ideas from the examined life are ironic. I think the unironic realities of his own addiction to nicotine directed us during the research on nicotine regulation and urinary pH. In my own case, my work on smoking has been greatly influenced as well by my own unrelenting sensitivity to cigarette smoke. Smoking always made me sick. From my early adolescence, I had made several attempts to take up cigarette smoking, but was always unsuccessful, mainly because I started out with a low tolerance for cigarette smoke and was not very good at developing an increased tolerance for it.

This lucky fact led me first to an analysis of how direct, unpleasant physical reactions to smoking could influence recruitment to smoking (Kozlowski & Harford, 1976). True "never smokers," we argued, provided the purest opportunity for studying psychosocial determinants of smoking and "triers" should be studied in terms of both psychosocial and biological determinants of use. In turn this work led Brett Silverstein and me to study how low-yield cigarettes could offer child-sized doses of tar and nicotine to young smokers, thereby easing the recruitment of more sensitive individuals to cigarette smoking (Silverstein, Feld, & Kozlowski, 1980). Similarly, Brett and I looked at the effects of manipulations of urinary pH on the willingness of male and female "nonsmokers" to smoke additional cigarettes (Silverstein, Kelly, Swan, & Kozlowski, 1982). In both of these projects with Brett, we found that females were more sensitive than males to the aversiveness of cigarettes. Next my delicate constitution led me to stress the importance of biologically-based "upper boundary" effects (acute toxic effects) on the regulation of tobacco intake in both novice and practiced smokers (Kozlowski & Herman, 1984). (This model is discussed later.)

One of my most important and most applied research findings on smoking originated in an ironical Schachterian flash of recognition. While spending a sabbatical from Wesleyan at the University of

Pennsylvania, I was having dinner with a small group of graduate students. One of them was smoking. She commented: "These low-yield cigarettes are hard to smoke." I asked what she meant. She said: "It's hard to keep your fingers over the little holes." I knew at that moment that this bright woman could not be alone in her misperception of the fundamental nature of the tar and nicotine yields of cigarettes. She had no inkling that blocking the air-dilution vents on her cigarette filter was defeating the crucial design element that made her cigarettes the "lowest tar cigarettes on the market." Low-yield cigarettes are not produced by the use of special low-tar tobaccos: Unblocked air vents dilute each puff of smoke by as much as 85% with ambient air and produce the lower yields in standard smoking machine tests.

The simple behavioral maneuvers of pushing the cigarette farther in the mouth or covering the vents with fingers turn these cigarettes into medium to high yield cigarettes. To add to the interest of the hole-blocking problem, it was apparent that some smokers were simply not aware that they were blocking the vents, while others were aware but ignorant of the consequences of their behavior (for example, those smokers we found who carried rolls of tape with them to tape over the vents). Our research on this topic revealed not only that this behavioral subversion of low-yield cigarettes occurred with alarming frequency (about 40% of long-term low-yield smokers), it also had dramatic effects on the actual tar, nicotine, and carbon monoxide yields of cigarettes (yields easily jumping from 1 mg tar to 15 mg tar) (e.g., Kozlowski, Rickert, Pope, Robinson, & Frecker, 1982; Kozlowski, 1983).

In the course of my Schachter-like puttering about the lab while conducting this research, I discovered (saw) a simple method for detecting the hole-blocking of filter cigarettes, without having to either watch or talk to the smokers. Hole-blocking had a systematic effect on the tar-stain patterns left in spent filters. If the vents were blocked, the tar stain spread uniformly across the smoker end of the filter; if the vents were unblocked, a discrete, bull's-eye stain was ringed by unstained filter. This unobtrusive evidence of compensatory smoking provides a handy tool for studying smoking and for giving feedback to smokers in smoking modification programs. The stain-pattern test has proven especially useful to those smokers who were unaware that they were blocking the filter vents.

### Tar And Nicotine Ratings
### May Be Hazardous To Your Health

The promotion of lower yield cigarettes has been the core of the cigarette industry's response to the antismoking movement. Switching to a lower-yield cigarette helps smokers justify continued smoking, despite the publicized health risks. (This is not to deny public-health benefits from low-yield cigarettes, Kozlowski, 1984.) In Schachter's lab at Columbia, we took tar and nicotine yields at face value. When wanting to come up with a low nicotine–high nicotine cigarette manipulation, we simply consulted the Federal Trade Commission's published tables of tar and nicotine yields and picked brands, as if they were tables in a chemical dictionary. When one popular brand changed in a year from a 1.3 mg nicotine cigarette to a 1.2 mg nicotine cigarette, we fretted about the difference in strength. I came to learn that we had primitive and mistaken notions of tar and nicotine yields. We treated the nicotine numbers as if they told us the nicotine content of the cigarette, much the way the label on a vitamin bottle tells the vitamin content of each pill.

I discovered in 1983 that the standard smoking-machine procedure was born in the chemical laboratory of the world's largest cigarette manufacturer in the 1930s (Kozlowski, 1983). These chemists were not interested in smoking behavior; they wanted a standard procedure for comparing tobacco types when made into cigarettes. On the basis of the judgment of these experts, rather than empirical data on actual human smoking, a two-second long, 35 ml puff, once a minute was called the standard. I learned that the 1.3 to 1.2 drop in nicotine yield that had concerned us at Columbia could be achieved by altering a cigarette's burn rate, so that just half of the last puff would be lost to the smoking machine (Kozlowski, Rickert, Robinson, & Grunberg, 1980). Given the intrinsic variability in human smoking behavior, it was obvious that we, along with other smoking researchers and smokers, had been over-valuing standard tar and nicotine yields as indicators of actual tar and nicotine yields to smokers.

As a result of further staring at spent cigarette butts, it occurred to us that an effective and practical indicator of actual tar and nicotine yields might be found in the intensity of the tar stains (Kozlowski, Rickert, Pope, & Robinson, 1982). This study introduced a completely new way of giving tar and nicotine information to cigarette smokers. We showed that the appearance of the tar stain on the spent filter could be used by smokers to measure how much smoke (tar and nicotine) had been drawn through a cigarette. Tar stains were rated by means of comparison to a scale of colored papers that were selected to match the results of heavy, standard, and light smoking on a filter cigarette. This color-matching technique can provide smokers with personalized information on tar and nicotine yields and can do so as well as (and at a fraction of the cost of) chemical assays of residual nicotine in the cigarette filter.

## The Best Studies In Life May Be Nearly Free

One of the reviewers of the urinary pH/smoking studies (Schachter et al., 1977) charged that we should have done plasma nicotine assays, noting that Schachter "must have enough money" to pay for these expensive assays. (I trust that this reviewer was raising a question of professional rather than personal finances.) During my days at Columbia, whatever the true state of research funding, I never had any reason to doubt that Schachter ran a low-budget, penny-pinching operation. He would hook up the cardiotachometer only after being convinced a simple pulse would not do.

Working on a tight budget forces an extra measure of ingenuity from the designer of experiments. One must create interesting studies that are also within the resources at hand. If one comes in under-budget on one or two studies, one may reap the dividend of doing a third or fourth study without having to go hat-in-hand and rhetoric-in-tongue to some supercilious funding agency.

Schachter and I never discussed research funding. He never took me aside and gave me a lesson in how to get grants. My guess is that he took it as something of a personal challenge to produce important studies for peanuts. And I suppose that he thought that, if his operation was lean, it would be toward the bottom of the list of projects to be cut from the roles of funding agencies when times got tough. If the Columbia subject pool had been more heavily stocked with smokers and fats, it might have taken longer to get around to studies in synagogues or airlines (e.g., Goldman, Jaffa, & Schachter, 1968). Schachter, of course, has a long history of doing studies in natural settings. I learned that interesting studies were to be found everywhere and at low cost.

I think this background gave me the courage to treat communal coffee pots as subjects in my research on the effect of caffeine on coffee drinking (Kozlowski, 1976a). This project was, as far as I know, the first study in humans on the effects of caffeine content of coffee on coffee intake. I took some limited access coffee pots (in faculty lounges at schools) and got permission to supply them with decaffeinated coffee that had varying levels of caffeine added. I simply measured how much coffee was drunk from these pots as a function of the caffeine content of the coffee. A crude regulation of caffeine intake was found, and this crude regulation was to provide clues that aided in the development of the boundary model.

Because of my experience in Schachter's lab and because of my own temperament, I have a long standing suspicion of expensive, large-scale studies. Simply put, they are not my style. (I don't think they are Schachter's style either.) I prefer short, cheap, interlocking studies. The key color-matching study (described earlier) took a few days to run and cost under $100 for materials and subjects (Kozlowski et al., 1982); yet it demonstrated a technique that can be very useful and practical for educating smokers about their exposure to cigarette smoke. The color-matching technique offers only approximate information about actual tar and nicotine yields, but it is fair to note that, in the land of the almost totally blind standard tar and nicotine yield, a one-eyed color-matching technique would be King.

## Telling Me What I Am Doing

One of Schachter's handiest gifts to me was a simple, easy-to-grasp conception of the brand of psychology I was inclined to do. He was fond of advising his students to write scientific papers so a third-grader could understand them, then one's colleagues would understand them. I mention this because it was as if Schachter used the same "third-grade clarity principle" in telling me what I was doing.

He said that my doctoral thesis was a "what is the phenomenon" thesis (Kozlowski, 1976b). I was proposing to study the effects of caffeine manipulations (in coffee) on the nicotine intake of cigarette smokers. He said some students went in for theoretical, hypothesis-driven research, but I seemed to want to take inherently interesting (and practical) phenomena and measure them. He construed rightly that I cared little about predicting what would happen to the cigarette smoking of a coffee-drinking cigarette smoker if one manipulated caffeine content of coffee (Kozlowski, 1976a). I wanted to see what happened. (He gave Stanley Milgram as an example of a "what is the phenomenon" researcher.)

This label has proven very useful to me in defending some of my research interests (e.g., Kozlowski & Bryant, 1977; Kozlowski & Cutting, 1977). In both of these studies, I found myself asking basic "what is the phenomenon" questions.

While teaching seminars on environmental psychology at Wesleyan, I became interested in the research literature on cognitive maps. I was struck that, although almost everyone cared about the quality of their own cognitive maps, almost no one used the phrase "cognitive map" outside of the scientific study of way finding and environmental perception. The person finding a new way home or exploring in a new neighborhood seemed to be thinking and talking about having a good or bad "sense of direction." We found that people were so attached to their own estimation of their "sense of direction" that most individuals readily offered either prideful, self-congratulatory tales of feats of successful locomotion through their concrete life-space or baleful tales of getting hopelessly and embarrassingly lost. Kendall Bryant and I wondered if self-reports of "sense of direction" (i.e., spatial orientation ability) related to actual differences in spatial orientation ability. We found that self-reports of "sense of direction" were as good as an individual's cognitive map of a familiar territory (the Wesleyan campus) (Kozlowski & Bryant, 1977).

Jim Cutting and I (Cutting & Kozlowski, 1977; Kozlowski & Cutting, 1977) wondered what information was present in a person's walk. Some people claimed that they could identify their friends by "the way they walked" and that they could also identify the gender of unfamiliar walkers from the way they walked. While considering Gunnar Johansson's work on point-light displays of human movement (Johansson, 1975), we realized that such displays would provide ideal stimuli for testing these beliefs. Johansson had shown that lights mounted on key joints gave the viewer little sense of the human form if no movement was taking place, but a compelling sense of seeing a human moving, once the human started to move with these point-lights on the joints. Here we had a stimulus that carried movement information, but little "form" and no "familiarity" cues—a nearly ideal opportunity to test if people could identify individual walkers or gender from the walk. Our studies demonstrated the phenomena in question and eventually led to an explanation of how information about the center of gravity was responsible for the accurate gender judgments (Cutting, Proffitt, & Kozlowski, 1978).

The main significance of this labelling of myself as a particular breed of researcher may have been that it seemed to me Schachter was giving his blessing to this activity. I felt as if this province of research was being recognized and given approval by my mentor. I realized, too, that Schachter was not trying to talk me out of it and bend me in a direction closer to his own, more hypothesis-driven, style of research.

### The Boundary Model

I know Peter Herman has a lot to say in this volume about our Boundary Model (e.g., Kozlowski & Herman, 1984). One might suppose that I can hardly argue that I have remained a phenomenon-based researcher, given my involvement with this model of psychosocial and biological influences on drug-taking and eating. I see the model as being in the tradition of Schachter and Singer's work on the psychosocial and physiological determinants of emotion. Drug researchers have tended to emphasize either psychosocial or biological determinants of drug taking. One researcher's pet variable has been another's nuisance variable. We argued that drug-taking was biologically regulated mainly when intake was "too little" (and lower boundary, withdrawal effects were at issue) or "too much" (and upper boundary, acute toxicity effects were at issue); in between these boundaries, psychosocial factors had the opportunity to determine drug taking. For example, 10 cigarettes per day might be the result of needing to avoid deficit effects, but an increase to 20 per day might be the result of social pressure (others smoking around you). The boundary model insists upon the simultaneous consideration of both kinds of variable and argues that interpretations of behavior can be misleading, if generated from only one heuristic point of view. (Is light smoker X a light smoker because of social pressures to smoke as little as possible or because of relatively low tolerance to the acute toxic effects of smoking?)

My initial contribution to the boundary model arose clearly out of my work as a "what is the phenomenon" researcher. As noted earlier, I was interested in whether caffeine manipulations influenced coffee consumption (Kozlowski, 1976a); and I found that the regulation of caffeine intake was imprecise within a wide range of caffeine intake, despite important regions of "too little" or "too much" use. Many of the details of the model, then, derive in my mind from these "facts" of caffeine use.

### An Irreverence for Expertise

Eugene Galanter in his section of a seminar for first-year students had argued that Ph.D. degrees should not be considered discipline specific. His favorite example was that any Ph.D. in anything should be able to take a book on how to build a house and build one. (I agree in principle, but would not want to live in a house of my construction.) Schachter's *modus operandi* was in ways more extreme: For Schachter, prior ignorance of an area seemed more often an asset than a liability. I saw this most clearly in the work on urinary pH and cigarette smoking. The effects of pH on nicotine excretion had been well characterized, but no one had thought to explore their behavioral implications. Experts in the pharmacology of nicotine seemed readier to discourage than encourage what appeared to be a far-fetched study. In a recent review of the effects of urinary pH on cigarette smoking and smoking cessation, Neil Grunberg and I (Grunberg & Kozlowski, 1986) have continued to be concerned about deficiencies in expert opinions on this topic.

In my own case, experts on the machine testing of cigarettes were in general doubtful that simple changes in puff number were responsible for a substantial chunk of the reductions in tar and nicotine yield. As discussed earlier, the experts were wrong to ignore this issue (Kozlowski et al., 1980; Kozlowski, 1981). The expert opinion on the significance of smokers' blocking vent holes on ventilated-filter cigarettes was less uniform, but none of it encouraged the study of the matter. Some experts argued that "everybody knows this already," others said, "nobody does this," and others said "if they do it, it doesn't make much difference." The experts were wrong on all counts.

## SCHACHTER AS AVUNCULAR HOMUNCULUS

Whenever I have a favorite research child, I hold it up to Schachter in my mind and trust he would get a kick out of it. I don't mean just that he would think well of it, I mean he would enjoy it, smile about it. (I imagine these reactions; I can't guarantee them; I am not good about keeping in touch.) I find that the results I am readiest to show off involve not so much the counter-intuitive as the ignored and simple explanation. (One of the joys of the urinary pH/smoking work was the demonstration that the "mind" could be seconded to the bladder, when it came to accounting for stress-related variation in cigarette smoking.) Having my work guided by this avuncular homunculus, has helped keep the work fresh and enjoyable to me. Although Schachter has a cynical streak as broad as the Mississippi River, I found working under his direction invigorating and engaging: He could always suspend his disbelief and press ahead with the puzzle of data on his lap.

## CLOSING

I need to thank Stanley Schachter, not only for the opportunity to work for and with him, but also for the opportunity to work with a number of stimulating siblings. I have enjoyed and benefited from collaborations with Peter Herman, Brett Silverstein, and Neil Grunberg. Stanley Schachter is my professional father. I owe him the start of a career that has pleased me greatly; I owe him his support, advice, and kindness. I can imagine the ambivalence with which he will receive this collection of essays. He will understand why, in closing, I must also add a small dash of apology to this somewhat unseemly public cup of gratitude.

## ACKNOWLEDGMENTS

Thanks go to Peter Herman and NSERC grant No. A1036. The opinions expressed here are my own and not necessarily those of the Addiction Research Foundation.

# REFERENCES

Auden, W.H. & Kronenberger, L. (1966). *The viking book of aphorisms.* New York: Viking Press.

Cutting, J. E. & Kozlowski, L. T. (1977). Recognizing friends by their walk: Gait perception without familiarity cues. *Bulletin of the Psychonomic Society, 9,* 353–356.

Cutting, J.E., Proffitt, D., & Kozlowski, L. T. (1978). A biomechanical invariant for gait perception. *Journal of Experimental Psychology: Human Perception and Performance, 4,* 357–372.

Goldman, R., Jaffa, M., & Schachter, S. (1968). Yom Kippur, Air France, dormitory food, and the eating behavior of obese and normal persons. *Journal of Personality and Social Psychology, 10,* 117–123.

Grunberg, N.E. & Kozlowski, L. T. (1986). Alkaline therapy as an adjunct to smoking cessation programs. *International Journal of Biosocial Research, 8,* 43–52.

Johansson, G. (1975). Visual motion perception. *Scientific American, 232,* 76–89.

Kozlowski, L. T. (1976a). Effect of caffeine on coffee drinking. *Nature, 264,* 354–355.

Kozlowski, L. T. (1976b). Effects of caffeine consumption on nicotine consumption. *Psychopharmacology, 47,* 165–168.

Kozlowski, L. T. (1981). Tar and nicotine delivery of cigarettes: What a difference a puff makes. *Journal of the American Medical Association, 245,* 158–159.

Kozlowski, L. T. (1983). Physical indicators of actual tar and nicotine yields of cigarettes. In J. Grabowski & C. L. Bell (Eds.), *Measurement in the analysis and treatment of smoking behavior* (pp. 50–61). (NIDA Research Monograph 48, DHHS publication number (ADM) 83-1285). Washington, D.C.: U.S. Government Printing Office.

Kozlowski, L. T. (1984). Less hazardous tobacco use as a treatment for the smoking and health problem. In R. J. Smart, H. D. Cappell, F. Glaser, Y. Israel, H. Kalant, W. Schmitt, & E. M. Sellers (Eds.), *Research advances in alcohol and drug problems* (Vol. 8, pp. 309–328). New York: Plenum.

Kozlowski, L. T. (1986). Pack size, reported cigarette smoking rates, and public health. *American Journal of Public Health 76,* 1337–1338.

Kozlowski, L. T. & Bryant, K. (1977). Sense of direction, spatial orientation, and cognitive maps. *Journal of Experimental Psychology: Human Perception and Performance, 3,* 590–598.

Kozlowski, L. T. & Cutting, J. E. (1977). Recognizing the sex of a walker from a dynamic point–light display. *Perception & Psychophysics, 21,* 575–580.

Kozlowski, L. T., Frecker, R. C., & Lei, H. (1982). Nicotine yields of cigarettes, plasma nicotine in smokers, and public health. *Preventive Medicine, 11,* 240–244.

Kozlowski, L. T. & Harford, M.A. (1976). On the significance of never using a drug: An example from cigarette smoking. *Journal of Abnormal Psychology, 85,* 433–434.

Kozlowski, L. T. & Herman, C. P. (1984). The interaction of psychosocial and biological determinants of tobacco use: More on the boundary model. *Journal of Applied Social Psychology, 14,* 244–256.

Kozlowski, L. T., Rickert, W. S., Robinson, J. C., & Grunberg, N. E. (1980). Have tar and nicotine yields of cigarettes changed? *Science, 209,* 1550–1551.

Kozlowski, L. T., Rickert, W. S., Pope, M. A., & Robinson, J. C. (1982). A color-matching technique for monitoring tar–nicotine yields to smokers. *American Journal of Public Health, 72,* 597–599.

Kozlowski, L. T., Rickert, W. S., Pope, M. A., Robinson, J. C., & Frecker, R. C. (1982). Estimating the yield to smokers of tar, nicotine, and carbon monoxide from the "lowest-yield" ventilated-filter cigarettes. *British Journal of Addiction, 77,* 159–165.

Kozlowski, L. T. & Schachter, S. (1975). Effects of cue prominence and palatability on the drinking of obese and normal humans. *Journal of Personality and Social Psychology, 32,* 1055–1059.

Peele, S. (1983). *The science of experience: A direction for psychology.* Lexington, MA: Lexington.

Schachter, S., Silverstein, B., Kozlowski, L. T., Perlick, D., Herman, C. P., & Liebling, B. (1977). Studies on the interaction of psychological and pharmacological determinants of smoking. *Journal of Experimental Psychology: General, 106,* 3–40.

Silverstein, B., Feld, S., & Kozlowski, L. T. (1980). The availability of low-tar cigarettes as a cause of cigarette smoking among teenage females. *Journal of Health and Social Behavior, 21,* 383–388.

Silverstein, B., Kelly, E., Swan, J., & Kozlowski, L. T. (1982). Physiological predisposition to becoming a cigarette smoker: Experimental evidence for a sex difference. *Addictive Behaviors, 7,* 83–86.

# 11

## Cigarette Smoking and Money: Developing New Research Lines[1]

Neil E. Grunberg
*Uniformed Services University of the Health Sciences*

## A MEMORABLE INTRODUCTION

I slept fitfully in our miserable two room apartment on Broadway and 107th Street. The heat and humidity of late August, 1975, were oppressive; the bright orange glow of the night sky cut through our cheap, plastic curtains; and sounds of breaking bottles, sirens, and human screams startled me awake if I dared to rest in this new environment. But my heart pounded mostly in anticipation of the morning and my first day in graduate school.

I arose early, hurried out of the apartment, and walked up Broadway. In less than 10 blocks I passed donut shops, garbage, fresh fruit and vegetable stands, garbage, Chinese restaurants, Cuban restaurants, pizzerias, coffee shops, bars, grocery stores, garbage, clothing stores, drug stores, banks, apartment houses, and people, hundreds or perhaps thousands of people. It certainly did not look like the Stanford campus where I had spent the previous four years. Finally, I entered the majestic Columbia University gates and found my way to Schermerhorn Hall and the appointed room below ground level.

I was early so I had a chance to sit, relax as best I could, and watch people filter into the dreary and poorly lit room. One fellow wore a crisp white shirt, black well-ironed pants, and oxford shoes. Another fellow

[1]The opinions or assertions contained herein are the private ones of the author and are not to be construed as official or reflecting the views of the Department of Defense or the Uniformed Services University of the Health Sciences.

sauntered into the room, pipe in hand, and collapsed comfortably in a chair so that his well-worn tweed jacket crumpled casually around him. A woman, dressed like my mother, quietly entered the room and carefully placed her pad and pen on the table in front of her. Another woman, wearing 3 inch high heels, flashed her long red fingernails as she gestured while speaking with a woman who wore ballet shoes. Others filtered in carrying briefcases or bookbags. I wondered if they sold Levis, Adidas, or backpacks in New York.

A few minutes after the appointed meeting time two men came into the room. Actually, the first man exploded into the room; the second man entered the room as if he was standing on a slow-moving conveyor belt. The first man had a tousled head of blonde hair on top of boyish good looks, a wide grin, and a tall, athletic frame. Although he wore a tie (a rather ugly brightly-colored tie), he looked like the college students whom I had recently left. He introduced himself as the chairman and laughed infectiously. I was stunned. The other man stared into space and barely moved a muscle beneath his black suit jacket and matching shirt. His long peppered grey beard, wild hair, and thick glasses made it difficult to interpret his seemingly stone-faced expression. He silently wrote his name on the blackboard as a means of introduction. I thought about volleyball and football games in the California sun.

After introductory remarks welcoming us to the Psychology Department, the chairman instructed us to meet individually with the department's director of graduate studies. I went on to that meeting clutching my brand new graduate school handbook. The office was bright and the professor was friendly. He explained that he would make a list of faculty members who were compatible with my research interests and background and that I should see each person for a brief interview. Then, I should turn in a list of my choices for major advisors. Later, I would be informed of my assignment. When asked about my interests, I explained that I chose Columbia largely to work in neurophysiology. The graduate director told me that work was being done at the medical school, miles away, and therefore I should not consider neurophysiology as a viable alternative. He wrote down names of four physiological psychologists for me to see.

While we were talking, a slim man, deeply tanned, wearing a conservative white shirt, black knit tie, brown slacks, and Clark Trek shoes, quietly but confidently, politely but firmly, interrupted us. He held a pencil in his right hand and a cigarette in his left. Both implements looked so comfortable in each hand that they appeared to be part of each hand, as if they had become additional digits. He wasn't tall but he moved as if he thought he was. The graduate director stopped talking to me in mid-sentence and spoke with his visitor as if I were not there.

Then, the intruder pardoned himself and left. I thought it was strange that his entry and parting words were gracious, yet he wasted no time having his conversation begin or end.

"That was Schachter," the graduate advisor said with admiration. I nodded knowingly but actually thought, "Schachter? . . . Schachter? . . . Schachter and Singer? . . . familiar."

"He should be on your list. His current work is physiological," the graduate advisor said almost to himself. He handed me my list of people to see. I thanked him and exited.

I looked at my list and searched out offices. One by one I saw the professors. Each office was distinctly different, the topics discussed were clearly different, but the first four interviews were similar. Basically, I introduced myself and was greeted rather warmly. Each of the four professors seemed to be familiar with my background in microbiology and, in many cases, had my file in plain view. Each of the four asked me about my research experience and interests. Then, each professor spent about 15 minutes telling me about his or her current research. I was told that if I had any questions to come back at any time.

I reached the fifth name on my list: Stanley Schachter. When I found that this professor's office was in the social psychology area of the department, I had second thoughts. I had taken one college class in social psychology and, because of that course, I had sworn off psychology—a moratorium that lasted almost two years when I finally broke down, took a psychobiology course, and decided to go on in psychology. But my concern about failing to comply with instructions drove me to find the fifth door.

The door was ajar so I knocked gently and meekly asked, "Dr. Schachter?" He sat behind an enormous desk, yet the desk was dwarfed by a randomly arranged mountain of papers. This corner office was larger than all the others I had visited. Books and journals lined the 15 foot walls, a crumpled Oriental rug covered the floor, boxes of manila envelopes sat near file cabinets, leather furniture was arranged sloppily around the room, an old wool sweater hung on a hatrack, slippers rested nearby.

"Yes?" he responded as he took his feet off the desk.

"My name is Neil Grunberg and I was told to see you. I'm a new graduate student."

He motioned to a large chair and peered at me over the small pull-out side shelf of his desk. Except for the presence of a dirty Columbia coffee cup and a pile of cigarette ashes, this small extension of his desk was the only clear spot within sight. He was dressed identically to our first meeting except that he now wore a tired corduroy jacket. He looked irritated. Unlike the other professors he did not seem to know anything about me. He asked me a few, very few, questions about my background. Then, he began to talk about his research.

He said something about cigarette smoking and urinary pH. I listened but mostly tried to look alert. I had learned from the other interviews that the professors loved to talk about their work and once they started, I just had to hang on for 15 minutes until they said, "Any questions? Thanks for coming by." This time was different.

After less than 5 minutes, this professor said, "O.K., I've told you about my work. What did I find?"

"Pardon me?" I stammered.

"I'll help you get started," he replied.

Without taking his eyes off me, he reached to the top of that paper mountain and grabbed a manila envelope. He pulled it over to the side shelf, flipped it over, and casually drew x and y axes. He labeled the abscissa "pH" and the ordinate "smoking."

"What did I find?" he asked impatiently and thrust his pencil into my hand.

Dazed, I drew something. He looked at it, didn't say anything, but continued: "What study did I do next?" I offered an idea.

"Why?" he snapped. I answered again.

"Then what?" . . . "Why?" . . . "Then what?" . . . "Why?"

This inquisition lasted 45 minutes. I went home, talked with my wife, and decided to work for Schachter. Perhaps it is more accurate to write that Schachter decided that I would work for him.

## CIGARETTE SMOKING AND URINARY pH

At our first research group meeting, he gave me two assignments: "I want you to do a study on the effects of exercise on urinary pH and cigarette smoking. Also, teach me everything there is to know about the liver."

During the next few months, I learned about the art of writing experimental scripts, the headaches of subject recruitment, and the importance of piloting procedures. Everything centered on designing studies that addressed simply stated questions. Do people smoke cigarettes for nicotine? Why do people smoke more under stress? Is the habitual smoker a machine that simply replenishes nicotine? I learned about urinary pH, cigarette smoking, and drug metabolism in the liver. I went in and out of Schachter's office with revised scripts, pilot data, and new facts about the liver.

I was struck by Schachter's insatiable hunger for data. Other things could wait for later in the day or the next day. But when a pilot procedure or full study was completed, he dropped everything to look at data. If the data were not presented in clear tables, he was disgusted. But if the presentation was clear, he became a schoolboy examining a new gadget. The data absorbed his attention and he scribbled analyses all over the summary sheets. Based on these data sessions, we would redesign and refine studies. Ideas generated studies and data generated new ideas.

The urinary pH/smoking story was winding down in the Schachter laboratory, and he was trying to tie up loose ends. While I was working on my exercise and smoking study, Schachter, students senior to me, and former students wrote up studies on smoking and urinary pH (Schachter et al., 1977). The exercise study was a classic Schachter attempt to push a theory to a logical, but counterintuitive, limit. Physical exercise results in acidification of the urine. Therefore, based on the previous work, smoking should increase after exercise. Instead, smokers gasped for air after they ran up and down flights of stairs and the last thing they wanted was a cigarette. There were limits to the pH/smoking model. The results of this study were not too informative or surprising, but I learned how to take a theoretical position derived from previous studies and push it as far as possible under critical empirical examination.

The results of the smoking/pH studies took Schachter deeper into completely reductionist explanations and his new research ideas about smoking reflected this movement away from his cognitive/physiological trademark. For example, I learned cardiovascular psychophysiology in order to help run a study examining the effects of smoking on blood pressure and heart rate when urinary pH was manipulated. Because acidification of the urine increased smoking and increased the percentage of unmetabolized nicotine excreted from the body, then perhaps consumption of an acidifying agent would attenuate the normal increase in heart rate and blood pressure after smoking. Unfortunately, our results were equivocal and difficult to interpret.

In addition to the time in the laboratory, I quickly learned that Schachter's approach was to think constantly about the research question under investigation and to draw from daily experiences to deal with the annoying stumbling blocks that tend to slow down or interfere with the ongoing research. For example, one problem that plagued the work was how to get habitual smokers as subjects for studies in which any suspicion of the purpose would result in a modulation of the behavior (smoking) under investigation. General subject recruitment advertisements brought hundreds of phone calls, but the vast majority of volunteers were nonsmokers. Schachter brought up this problem frequently and it obviously irritated him. One day, walking home from school, I stopped to buy groceries. The customer in front of me bought a pack of cigarettes and was given a free matchbook. The next day I suggested to Schachter that we print matchbooks advertising general psychology experiments. He went wild. I was on top of the world. Debbie Perlick, Del Paulhus, and I distributed 20,000 matchbooks to head shops on Broadway between 72nd and 119th streets. We got our cigarette smoking subjects for the rest of the year and I learned to think about research problems constantly.

As another example of Schachter's integration of research into everyday life, he had me take a pH meter home to examine changes in urinary pH during the course of the day and in response to common foods. He wanted data on variables that affected urinary pH. I measured my urine, my wife's urine, and samples from anybody else I could convince.[2] My wife and I drank orange juice, tomato juice, water, coke, grapefruit juice,[3] and cranberry juice. I measured urinary pH at all times of day, after studying, relaxing, and eating. A pH meter became a permanent fixture in our bathroom. A notebook sat next to it to record time, day, activities, pH values. I showed Schachter tables and graphs of the effects of just about everything on urinary pH. I learned how Schachter looked at data, carefully and in detail.

Around Memorial Day, 1976, I helped pack Schachter's car with some of his boxes of manila folders. He was moving to his summer home. One folder in those now familiar boxes contained the exercise study and other data that I had collected. As Schachter left for the summer he said, "Send me the blood pressure and heart rate data. Also, look into the effects of smoking on free fatty acids (FFA) and figure out whether that may be involved in the urinary pH effect." I understood how to prepare the data before sending it to Amagansett. I also knew what a massive job it would be to answer his FFA question.

## READY FOR SECOND YEAR . . . I THOUGHT

It was the first week of September, 1976, and we had received word that Schachter was returning. I was excited. We had finished the blood pressure and heart rate study, I had taken a medical school course in physiology, and I had some information about FFA. Most importantly, I had expanded the reductionistic explanation for the urinary pH/smoking

[2]The only other samples that I could get regularly were from my parents in New Jersey. Actually, my father took their samples daily to his own laboratory and sent me their data.
[3]To test the effects of each juice on urinary pH, I drank different volumes. Usually, I drank as much as I could stand but, in the case of grapefruit juice, I stopped at a half gallon because I broke out in hives.

phenomenon. My idea involved the liver's microsomal ethanol oxidizing system (MEOS) and the interaction of hydrogen ions with coenzymes. I couldn't wait to tell him.

After looking through some mail, Schachter meandered into the graduate student office and said, "Why's my kid a miser?" I looked at my prepared page on H+, NADP+, NADPH, MEOS, FFA, and nicotine and laughed half-heartedly.

The next day Schachter came into our office and said, "Well? Why's my kid a miser? I asked you yesterday. Don't you have any ideas?" He sat on my desk, talked about his 6 year old's fascination with money, and asked each graduate student to relate any childhood stories about money. After exhausting those present, he got up and said smugly, "That's what we're going to study: The psychology of money."

## THE PSYCHOLOGY OF MONEY

Schachter was serious. Although he was still interested in smoking and particularly smoking cessation (Schachter's 1982 paper on recidivism and self-cure caused quite a stir), the psychology of money became our central focus. As an example of Schachter's insight regarding substantive knowledge necessary to pursue the smoking line further, it is noteworthy that he encouraged me to take pharmacology courses at the medical school; to quote him, "as long as it doesn't interfere with your research."

In some of our discussions during the past 7 years, Schachter has referred to 1976–1978 as "an unusually dry period." He was excited when we began this new topic and he became frustrated with the number of studies that led nowhere interesting. (I can still hear him ask, "So what?" as the acid test for the value of a finding.) For me, this period was an oasis because I learned how he begins a new topic from ground zero. Initially, he had no theories to direct us and he allowed no preconceived notions to constrain us. I learned Schachter's willingness to draw from everyday experiences, discussions, and observations. I learned Schachter's openness to any source of information. I learned Schachter's pragmatic consideration of any field and any methodological approach that could help provide insights about the topic under investigation. I learned how Schachter took a question that interested him, designed studies to examine it, used data to develop broad theories, and then tested the theories with new studies.

## Choosing A General Question

Schachter's problem-oriented approach is evident in much of his work and in the work of many of his students. The research questions are clearly stated and are appealingly interesting: Why do people affiliate? What is the basis for emotions? Why are some people overweight? However, because much of the work on affiliation (Schachter, 1959), emotions (Schachter, 1971), and obesity (Schachter, 1971; Schachter & Rodin, 1974) also involved the examination of a well-developed theoretical position (e.g., social comparison theory), it is sometimes difficult for a reader of Schachter's finely crafted writing to see how he first approaches a new question.

The money research began with a single question that piqued Schachter's curiosity. As we discussed our experiences with money and feelings about money, we generated more questions. Based on library research and discussions with other people, it rapidly became obvious that we could go in many different directions. Schachter decided that it was time to be more directed.

## Developing Specific Questions

After a few months of general reading and discussions, Schachter organized a graduate seminar on the psychology of money. This seminar allowed him to draw outstanding students from other laboratories and specialties including social psychology, personality, psychophysiology, abnormal psychology, developmental psychology, and learning. Permission of the instructor was, of course, required for admission into the new "class."

He explained to the group that he, John Anthony, and I had been kicking around some questions to study regarding the psychology of money. He emphasized that we needed help to develop our ideas and that we particularly wanted insights and perspectives from this group who represented the best that other specialties in psychology had to offer. They all glowed. Everyone was excited to help Schachter come up with ideas. We discussed subsistence, power, depression, greed, philanthropy, insecurity, and dynasties. We drew, as best we could, from anthropology, sociology, philosophy, economics, marketing, business, law, religion, as well as from every aspect of psychology. As our list of ideas took form and became more concrete, we volunteered to work on specific projects, with Schachter's subtle yet masterful coercion driving us.

## Gathering Data

To explore each idea more fully, we continued to do library research and we began empirical studies. Schachter clearly was anxious to have some data. It was on the bases of these first studies that we decided whether to pursue a question or to let it die. To provide a flavor of our approach, a few specific projects are described.

**Money Questionnaire.**   In our seminar discussions it became obvious that even within our small and seemingly homogeneous subsample of graduate students, there were wide differences in economic background and attitudes towards money. Therefore, we all worked to develop a general money questionnaire. It included basic demographic questions, questions about experience with money, and questions such as: "Do you give money to street musicians? Do you give money to beggars? Without looking, how much money do you have in your pockets? Now look and write down the exact amount. How much money would it take for you to consider yourself poor? comfortable? rich?"

We worked hard to clean up each question. We had every member of the department complete it. We coded it, developed indices, and tried to make something out of it. Nothing jumped out at us but Schachter dug through the data with brio (as Bill Apple was fond of saying).

**Gains Versus Losses.**   One of our ideas was based on human psychophysics studies that had been conducted at Columbia (Galanter & Pliner, 1974). This work used cross-modality matching procedures to estimate affective reactions to hypothetical monetary gains and losses. After reading this work and discussing it with Gene Galanter, we postulated that people would work harder to avoid a loss of money than they would to gain that same amount of money. To test this prediction, we brought subjects into the laboratory and told them that they would be left alone and should press the button in front of them as many times as they could until the experimenter returned. If the number of button-pushes exceeded the number in a sealed envelope (which was possible), they would (in one condition) be given three dollars. In the other condition subjects were told that if their number of button-pushes did not exceed the number in the envelope, they would have to pay three dollars out of their own pockets. Most subjects seemed to believe the experimenter. In fact, one stormed out of the loss condition. Every subject participated in both conditions. The order of conditions was counterbalanced after a warm-up trial.

The results were frustrating. Comparing the first experimental trials between subjects, subjects in the loss condition pushed more than those in the gain condition. However, the differences were not significant. During the debriefing, several subjects said that they did not really believe the loss condition. Dropping these subjects, the between subjects comparison was significant but the sample sizes were small.

Within subjects, those who were first in the gain condition and won, pushed significantly harder in the subsequent loss condition. With three unexpected dollars sitting in front of them, they apparently believed that we might take the money back. There were no significant differences between conditions for the subjects who were in the loss condition first.

**Mood and Money.**    Another idea that we wanted to test was whether mood affected spending. We had heard anecdotal reports from psychiatrists and clinical psychologists that some manic–depressives give money away or gleefully throw it out windows when in a manic phase. We speculated that spending was positively related to mood. We also considered some curvilinear functions. We decided that we needed data comparing spending with daily mood.

We briefly considered laboratory studies but rejected this approach to examine spending. We believed that spending had to be studied in the real world. Schachter came up with a solution. He arranged to get years of daily sales data from a major New York department store. The only catch was that we had to copy the data by hand.

As we gathered the sales data, we considered the problem of how to assess the mood of the customers retrospectively. We decided that major news events can affect the general mood of a population. Moreover, we reasoned that well-publicized news events would have been known to the customers who patronized our department store. Therefore, we read hundreds of *New York Times* and *Daily News* cover stories searching for major news events that might have affected mood significantly. We used multidimensional scaling (MDS) techniques to try to determine underlying dimensions of emotional reactions to news events. We then used a semantic differential approach to validate the dimensions that we had tentatively identified. We used two different samples of subjects to determine the dimensional values of each rated news event. Bill Apple and I were pleased with our progress, but Schachter mostly wanted us to compare our data to the sales data.

The MDS portion of this research worked and we developed a technique for rating emotional reactions to news events (Apple & Grunberg, 1982). But the sales data showed no simple relationship to the mood ratings. Schachter felt that the sales data were a source of valuable information and this project mutated into Schachter's stock market analyses that he continued to work on with subsequent students.

**Children and Money.**     The inspiration for the money research was, of course, Schachter's observation about his son. Therefore, children and money was one of our primary interests. To gather information, Bruno Anthony and I interviewed 3–8 year olds and their parents about the children's attitudes toward money and understanding of the concept of money. We were rather startled to discover that parents opened up to us like floodgates on this subject. Brief interviews became long therapy-like sessions as we heard about concerns regarding how to teach children about money without encouraging them to be overly materialistic. When we compared notes, we discovered that parents of 6–7 year olds (the same age as Schachter's son when this all began) seemed particularly concerned with what they described as "sudden interests in money," "fascination with money," or "obsession with money." We designed a study that used memory games and choices to examine these issues empirically. We found that around $6^{1}/2$ years of age children show a marked increase in interest in and understanding of money (Grunberg & Anthony, 1980).

By this time, Schachter's son had passed the miser stage and the stock market work was absorbing Schachter's time. However, he encouraged us to continue this work. As the initial findings stood up, we made predictions about children and altruism. We reasoned that if kids become suddenly fascinated by money at 6–7 years old, they should not be willing to part with it. Therefore, monetary altruism should be a U-shaped function with its trough at 6–7. This prediction was in marked contrast to the commonly cited generalization that altruism increases with age (a generalization based on studies that never examined children under age 6). We also pushed the point further and predicted that material altruism with nonmonetary goods should show a similar, curvilinear pattern. Both predictions were substantiated (Grunberg, Maycock, & Anthony, 1985).

**A Miser Rat.**     One of Schachter's dreams was for us to develop an animal model of miserly behavior. Rick Straub brought his expertise in operant psychology to the "class," and Schachter decided that a miser rat would be useful. I learned shaping techniques from Rick and worked with him building chambers, designing procedures to develop an animal miser, and running rats. We had rats push a bar to receive a ballbearing, carry this token across the chamber, and deposit the token to receive food. We had a chamber with an "investment" hole (i.e., animals received several tokens for each token that they deposited), we tried different schedules of reinforcement, and we tried two deposit hole chambers (one for food, the other for tokens). Schachter impatiently waited for a miser rat and I learned about animal models. The complexity of the procedures and our own dissertations finally ended this line of research.

### Following A Research Line

Our money research taught me how Schachter developed a question into a line of research. Schachter considered a range of disciplines and followed the question wherever it led. He was not restricted to a given paradigm and was not constrained by allegiance to any single theoretical orientation. In addition to the studies already mentioned, we examined the exact dates of wills written in the 1920's (before the establishment of income taxes) to determine whether thoughts of death were related to time of year; we watched rats hoard food pellets to try to learn about saving; we read about Andrew Carnegie to learn about philanthropy. When Schachter suggested that we follow bag ladies around New York and interview them, we said no.

## CIGARETTE SMOKING AND BODY WEIGHT

My interests in appetitive and addictive behaviors continued throughout the "money period." Therefore, I decided to return to a study of cigarette smoking for my dissertation research. I had read with interest Schachter and students' work on obesity and believed that there were commonalities between eating and drug abuse. Because of these interests and because Schachter was cutting down on his three pack a day habit and was gaining weight, we decided that I would examine the relationship between smoking and body weight.

I read everything that I could find on smoking and body weight, smoking and eating, nicotine and body weight, nicotine and eating. Also, Schachter gave me one of those manila envelopes of his with data from an unpublished study that he had done on smoking and eating in obese and normal weight smokers (Schachter & Nesbitt, personal communication).

It became clear that the literature suggested three major explanations for the inverse relationship between smoking and body weight: (1) changes in general food consumption; (2) changes in energy utilization; (3) changes in specific food consumption (Grunberg, 1982, 1986a). There was no convincing research to support any of these three hypotheses. My reanalyses of the Schachter and Nesbitt data suggested that specific food consumption was the best bet but it, too, was not clear. Therefore, I designed human and animal studies to examine the general and specific food consumption hypotheses.

## Smoking And Taste Preferences

The methods for the human laboratory work were based largely on the eating studies that Schachter had done with Nisbett, Rodin, and Herman. Smokers and nonsmokers were recruited for a taste judgment study. Half of the smokers were allowed to smoke immediately before the taste test. Subjects were asked to taste sweet, salty, and bland foods. I found that smokers ate significantly less sweet food than did nonsmokers or smokers not smoking. All groups ate similar amounts of salty and bland foods (Grunberg, 1982).

## Nicotine, Body Weight, And Food Consumption

The human laboratory study did not allow me to examine changes in body weight. It was by necessity an acute study; and it did not address what component of cigarettes might be involved in effects on body weight or eating. To examine the role of nicotine and to assess daily body weight and eating behavior changes for weeks before, during, and after cessation of drug administration, I developed an animal model. My desire to develop an animal model to complement the human study resulted from reading Singer (1963) and Latané and Schachter (1962). I was impressed with these clever studies and their value to examine theories of emotions derived from Schachter and Singer (1962) and Schachter and Wheeler (1962).

I decided to administer nicotine (in different dosages) or saline to Sprague–Dawley rats via Alzet osmotic minipumps. These small cylindrical devices (less than 2.5 cm in length) are implanted subcutaneously between the head and back of each subject. Osmotic pressure of the surrounding aqueous medium forces the minipump to release its contents slowly (at a rate of roughly 0.5 $\mu$l/hour) and continuously for weeks. A wide range of nicotine dosages can be administered in this way without the trauma of daily injections and without injecting large amounts of this toxic drug. In my animal model, body weight and eating behavior were measured for weeks before, during, and after drug administration. This paradigm allowed both between and within subject analyses.

There was an inverse dose–response relationship between nicotine and body weight in rats during drug administration. After cessation of the drug administration period, rats that had received nicotine gained body weight at a greater rate than did controls. These changes in body weight were paralleled by changes in consumption of sweet foods. There were no changes in consumption of nonsweet foods (Grunberg,

1982). The results were completely consistent with the human laboratory findings.

## Do The Laboratory Results
## Generalize To The Real World?

Thinking how Stan might proceed,[4] I thought: "O.K., smoking by humans and nicotine given to rats affects sweet food consumption in the laboratory. What's this have to do with smoking and specific food consumption in the real world?" To determine whether changes in specific food consumption accompany changes in smoking behavior outside the laboratory, we compared United States *per capita* cigarette consumption to United States *per capita* consumption of all major food groups during a 14 year period (Grunberg & Morse, 1984). Consistent with the human and animal laboratory studies, there was a significant inverse relationship between cigarette and sugar consumption. My confidence in the value of the human laboratory paradigm and animal model increased.

## What If Sweet Foods Are Not Available?

Taken together, the laboratory and archival studies suggested that if only bland food was available, there would be no changes in caloric intake during or after nicotine administration and there would be no body weight changes. To test these predictions, we returned to the laboratory and to our animal model.

We found that when only bland food was available, male animals showed no changes in eating behavior during or after cessation of nicotine administration; the body weight effects of nicotine during drug administration were attenuated; and there were no postnicotine excessive body weight gains (Grunberg, Bowen, & Morse, 1984). In contrast, female rats given bland food still showed decreases in eating behavior and body weights during nicotine administration, and excessive body weight gains and increased eating behavior after cessation of nicotine (Grunberg, Bowen, & Winders, 1986). These results suggest that there is a biologically-based sex difference in the effects of nicotine on body weight and food consumption. We are continuing to examine this possibility.

---

[4]After earning my Ph.D. and leaving Columbia, I shifted from "Dr. Schachter" to "Stan."

## The Role Of Taste, Nutrient Content, And Physical Activity

In other studies we determined that the effects of nicotine on sweet food consumption primarily involve the sweet taste, but also involve the carbohydrate content (Grunberg, Bowen, Maycock, & Nespor, 1985). In addition, we have found that for male animals, the excessive body weight gains after cessation of nicotine result partially from decreases in physical activity (Grunberg & Bowen, 1985). In contrast, physical activity is not as important in excessive body weight gains after cessation of nicotine for female animals (Bowen, Eury, & Grunberg, 1986).

## Following A Research Line

We have continued to pursue this line of research in the way that Stan taught me. The data have led us to new answers and to new questions. Currently, we are examining possible biochemical bases of the effects of nicotine on specific food consumption; we are measuring changes in fat depots and body composition; and we are examining the effects of nicotine on consumption of a variety of foods in males and females, animals and humans. We also are considering whether the role of sweet food consumption in the nicotine/body-weight relationship may provide insights into other situations and conditions, including cancer cachexia (Grunberg, 1985), the effects of specific nutrients on mood (Grunberg, 1986b), and commonalities among stress and substance abuse (Grunberg & Baum, 1985).

## SCHACHTER'S LESSONS

The lessons seem so obvious now because, as Stan would say, they are child simple. Choose a problem of interest; identify specific questions to investigate; critically examine data that are gathered; use the empirical findings to guide the research; perform the research programmatically but with an open mind for methods and theories; develop general theories; push those theories to the limit; and, finally, write up the work clearly and in a style that readers will enjoy. For example, there's the classic Schachter line: "Though I am pretty sure that I've eaten a hypothalamus, I doubt that I've ever seen one." (Schachter, 1971, p. 132). How many scientific papers or monographs do people reread for fun?

Stan influenced the way I think, the way I teach, the topics I study, how I study them, and how I write. The government requires me to include in my papers a disclaimer indicating that my opinions and assertions are my own. My disclaimers also should read: "Any opinions or assertions contained herein that are valuable, creative, clever, or glib are the result of exposure to Stanley Schachter and are not to be construed as official or reflecting the views solely of the author."

## REFERENCES

Apple, W. & Grunberg, N. E. (1982). Emotional reactions to news events. *Journal of Applied Social Psychology, 12,* 493–502.

Bowen, D. J., Eury, S. E., & Grunberg, N. E. (1986). Nicotine's effects on female rats' body weight: Caloric intake and physical activity. *Pharmacology Biochemistry and Behavior, 25.*

Galanter, E. & Pliner, P. (1974). Cross-modality matching of money against other continua. In Moskowitz, H. R. et al. (Eds.), *Sensation and measurement* (pp. 65–76). Dordrecht-Holland: D. Reidel Publishing.

Grunberg, N. E. (1982). The effects of nicotine and cigarette smoking on food consumption and taste preferences. *Addictive Behaviors, 7,* 317–331.

Grunberg, N. E. (1985). Specific taste preferences: An alternative explanation for eating changes in cancer patients. In T. G. Burish, S. M. Levy, & B. E. Meyerowitz (Eds.), *Cancer, nutrition, and eating behavior: A biobehavioral perspective* (pp. 43–61). Hillsdale, NJ: Lawrence Erlbaum Associates.

Grunberg, N. E. (1986a). Behavior and biological factors in the relationship between tobacco use and body weight. In E. S. Katkin & S. B. Manuck (Eds.), *Advances in behavioral medicine, Volume 2,* Greenwich, CT: JAI Press.

Grunberg, N. E. (1986b). Nicotine as a psychoactive drug: Appetite regulation. *Psychopharmacology Bulletin, 22,* 875–881.

Grunberg, N. E. & Anthony, B. J. (1980). Monetary awareness in children. *Basic and Applied Social Psychology, 1,* 343–350.

Grunberg, N. E. & Baum, A. (1985). Biological commonalities of stress and substance abuse. In S. Shiffman & T. A. Wills (Eds.), *Coping and substance use* (pp. 25–62). Orlando, FL: Academic Press.

Grunberg, N. E., & Bowen, D. J. (1985). The role of physical activity in nicotine's effects on body weight. *Pharmacology Biochemistry and Behavior, 23,* 851–854.

Grunberg, N. E., Bowen, D. J., & Maycock, V. A., & Nespor, S. M. (1985). The importance of sweet taste and caloric content in the effects of nicotine on specific food consumption. *Psychopharmacology, 87,* 198–203.

Grunberg, N. E., Bowen, D. J., & Morse, D. E. (1984). Effects of nicotine on body weight and food consumption in rats. *Psychopharmacology, 83,* 92–98.

Grunberg, N. E., Bowen, D. J., & Winders, S. E. (1986). Effects of nicotine on body weight and food consumption in female rats. *Psychopharmacology, 90,* 101–105.

Grunberg, N. E., Maycock, V. A., & Anthony, B. J. (1985). Material altruism in children. *Basic and Applied Social Psychology, 6,* 1–11.

Grunberg, N. E. & Morse, D. E. (1984). Cigarette smoking and food consumption in the United States. *Journal of Applied Social Psychology, 14,* 310–317.

Latané, B. & Schachter, S. (1962). Adrenalin and avoidance learning. *Journal of Comparative and Physiological Psychology, 65,* 369–372.

Schachter, S. (1959). *The psychology of affiliation.* Stanford, CA: Stanford University Press.

Schachter, S. (1971). *Emotion, obesity, and crime.* New York: Academic Press.

Schachter, S. (1982). Recidivism and self-cure of smoking and obesity. *American Psychologist, 37,* 436–444.

Schachter, S. (1971). Some extraordinary facts about obese humans and rats. *American Psychologist, 26,* 129–144.

Schachter, S. & Rodin, J. (1974). *Obese humans and rats.* Potomac, MD: Lawrence Erlbaum Associates.

Schachter, S. & Singer, J. E. (1962). Cognitive, social, and physiological determinants of emotional state. *Psychological Review, 69,* 379–399.

Schachter, S. & Wheeler, L. (1962). Epinephrine, chlorpromazine, and amusement. *Journal of Abnormal and Social Psychology, 65,* 121–128.

Schachter, S., Silverstein, B., Kozlowski, L. T., Perlick, D., Herman, C. P., & Liebling, B. (1977). Studies of the interaction of psychological and pharmacological determinants of smoking. *Journal of Experimental Psychology: General, 106,* 3–40.

Singer, J. E. (1963). Sympathetic activation, drugs and fright. *Journal of Comparative and Physiological Psychology, 56,* 612–615.

# Afterword

The preparation of a festschrift produces ambivalence in almost everyone connected with it. The authors want to write the chapters but are
concerned how their mentor will react. The publisher wants to publish
the volume but is unsure about the general audience for the book. And,
most interesting of all, the honoree is taken a little aback, flattered, but
not pleased with all the implications of a tribute to a successful career.
Some festschrifts are written in consultation with the honoree, even to
the point of the one being honored contributing an introduction. Such
collaboration by Stan Schachter on a book written to honor him would
be out of the question. He would dismiss the suggestion that he be
involved out of hand, and would regard the idea of the entire enterprise
as "the stupidest thing I ever heard." This book was planned as a
surprise not because the authors wished to recreate the birthday parties of their youth, but because we knew of the deep impediments and
outright rejection Stan would have presented had he but known of its
planning and existence.

How then will he react when faced with a fait accompli? Stan's actual
reactions to a volume obviously can not be recorded in the volume itself,
but a reasonable approximation can be made because Schachter's behavior and attitudes are nothing if not consistent. Consequently, we have
no trouble imagining his reaction to this festschrift. First he will grumble
and grouse. He will denigrate the concept of the book, the surprise, and
the integrity and ancestry of whatever contributors are in his presence.
However, in some deeper sense, he will be pleased with the book as a
gesture of affection and esteem from a group of people whose lives he
has changed for the better.

When he is alone, Stan will read the book with a good deal of amusement and pride. He probably will read it while lying on the couch in his office. We hope that he won't drift off to sleep too often. His reactions to the individual chapters will resemble the reactions that he had as he reviewed first drafts of dissertations from the same people. For some chapters, he may snort, "Banal." For others, he may mutter, "Unreadable!" Yet he will read all of the chapters and will take great delight in one of his favorite parlor games: seeing how his opinion of each of the authors is thoroughly confirmed by the substance and style of his or her contribution. Because none of the chapters is co-authored, he will not be able to play one of his usual forms of academic solitaire, "Who wrote what part?" But the riches to be found in mining the contents of the chapters for the character of the authors will compensate him for that.

What will be Stan's ultimate reaction to the book? We clearly would not have created it unless we all believed that he would be pleased. Of course, even if he were, he would not let us know, at least not right away. How then, will we ever know? In a library alcove off his living room, in his luxurious Riverside Drive apartment, there is a well-worn maroon leather chair that is one of his favorites. When sitting in that chair, one cannot help but notice that on a nearby bookshelf, at eye level, is a specially bound set of the monographs that Stan has written and co-authored. If this volume finally comes to rest on that shelf, we will get the message.

# Index

Page numbers followed by n indicate footnotes.